An American Family
in the Mexican Revolution

An American Family
in the Mexican Revolution

ROBERT

WOODMANSEE

HERR

in collaboration with

RICHARD HERR

A Scholarly Resources Inc. Imprint
Wilmington, Delaware

© 1999 by Scholarly Resources Inc.
All rights reserved
First published 1999
Printed and bound in the
United States of America

Scholarly Resources Inc.
104 Greenhill Avenue
Wilmington, DE 19805-1897

Photographs courtesy of Robert Woodmansee Herr and Richard Herr

Library of Congress Cataloging-in-Publication Data

Herr, Robert Woodmansee, 1906–
    An American family in the Mexican Revolution / Robert Woodmansee
Herr : in collaboration with Richard Herr.
        p.   cm.
    Includes bibliographical references and index.
    ISBN 0-8420-2724-6
    1. Herr, Irving, 1877–1959 – Correspondence.   2. Herr, Luella,
1880–1966 – Correspondence.   3. Americans – Mexico – Guanajuato –
Correspondence.   4. Mexico – History – 1910–1946.   5. Mexico –
History – Revolution, 1910–1920.   6. Guanajuato (Mexico) – Social
life and customs.   7. Herr, Robert Woodmansee, 1906–   .   8. Herr,
Richard, 1922–   .   I. Herr, Richard, 1922–   .   II. Title.
F1234.H68   1999
972'.4100413 – dc21   98-41058
                                                                                CIP

♾ The paper used in this publication meets the minimum requirements
of the American National Standard for permanence of paper for printed
library materials, z39.48, 1984.

Foreword

This account of the turbulent years of 1910 to 1932 in Mexico is largely a record of the experiences of the Herr family — my parents (Irving and Luella) and their three sons — during those years as documented in voluminous family correspondence and in my mother's "line-a-day" diaries. For clarification and to preserve continuity, in some instances the original language has been slightly modified without changing the tone or import of the writing.

Although this narrative is not intended to be a history of the Mexican Revolution, the course of the revolution is sketched as background for the experiences and commentaries of the Herr family. In a few places the author has added his personal reflections. Details of historical events during these years will no doubt vary according to the source. In those violent times, with reputations at stake, "facts" were notoriously unreliable and perhaps altered to favor the proponent. Accordingly, the firsthand accounts of Irving and Luella Herr are of particular interest. In *The Mexican Revolution* (Cambridge: Cambridge University Press, 1986), Alan Knight tends to confirm evaluations of revolutionary activities given by the Herrs.

I wish to add that without the help and encouragement of my brother Richard Herr, this book would not have happened. As the younger son in the family, he shared in our experiences and has had a major hand in bringing them together and adding perspective. Thank you, Dick.

Robert Woodmansee Herr

Contents

Preface

This is the story of Irving Herr, an American mining engineer, and his family during the first three decades of the twentieth century. My father's profession took him to the mines and mills of California, Nevada, and Alabama as well as Costa Rica and Nicaragua. But his life centered on the silver mine of El Cubo near Guanajuato, Mexico, where he spent over twenty years as engineer, superintendent, and general manager for the Chicago owners of the mine, and where he and my mother, Luella, raised three sons. John and Robert were born shortly after my parents were married in 1904, and I, the latecomer, was only ten when we left Mexico forever in 1932. The years spent there in Mexico coincided with the revolution and its aftermath in the twenties. Thus, our story involves the encounter of two generations of an American family with revolutionary Mexico.

My brother Robert is the author of this narrative, and his recollections from his childhood and youth provide the view of his generation. Our parents wrote extensive and revealing letters — a literary form that the telephone has well-nigh killed — to each other and to my mother's family. My father carried on correspondence with the owners' manager in Chicago and with business associates, and my mother kept a diary. Their papers have been preserved, and the author has winnowed them, along with interviews and letters that were published in U.S. newspapers, to provide the story as witnessed by their generation.

The Mexican Revolution deserves a place among the great revolutions of the 1910s, along with the

Chinese and the Russian revolutions. Although we are familiar with its political and military history and the lives of its leading figures, the history of the Americans who ran the affairs in Mexico of U.S. companies is little known. Most persons who sympathize with the objectives of the Mexican Revolution — and it is hard not to be such a person — very likely think of these Americans as agents of social and economic injustice, never having been on close terms with any of them. The account of the Herr family challenges this preconception.

As a mining engineer, my father obtained a different view than that of a diplomat or a journalist. His college education developed specialized skills that he honed through his practical work in the mines. He became an unusually adept mine supervisor. The mine superintendent, however, was more than just a skilled professional; he made policy decisions and negotiated with governors and rebels, and the mine employees responded to him. On his judgment and acumen and his gift for human relations depended the successful running of the mine and the ultimate value of the owners' investment. When the Mexican Revolution came along, the burden on Dad's shoulders increased, for he had to meet day-to-day threats and crises and make decisions with little or no guidance from Chicago. His life and work in Mexico brought him into intimate contact with Mexicans at various social and economic levels, and his experiences provide a view of American investment both at home and abroad, if not "from below," at least from the end of the chain of command.

In their world, my parents divided their responsibilities as a matter of course. If mining belonged to the Señor, the Señora's realm was the household. My mother hired the cook and maids and dealt with the men who brought provisions, leavening her instructions with sympathy. Most important, the care and education of their sons was the center of her life. When John and Robert departed for New England preparatory schools, my mother's answer, not entirely accidental, we can surmise, although she was forty-one, was a third son. She followed her husband wherever his job took him — well, most of the time, anyway — and my father made her safety and that of their boys his first priority. They were partners, and their letters and the memories of their sons attest to their mutual attachment and respect. Once when my father was absent from Cubo during the threat of attack, it was my mother who gave orders to send the horses away and hide the cash.

Because they made their living in Mexico, the Americans in my father's position developed their own distinctive understanding of the country and its people. Their response was molded by their U.S. upbringing as well as by their Mexican experience. Readers in tune with today's struggles will find some of their words and acts patronizing and even racist, but this was a different time, and disdain was not involved. If my father judged Mexican peons unready for democracy, he preferred them as workers to the laborers of Alabama. Despite our family's ordeals, he came to see in the Mexican Revolution "an ideal worthy of the respect and admiration of all of us."

The story of the Herr family shows how humane the relations across cultures and social classes could be. When, during the revolution, Americans believed that they were in danger and thus fled the country, not once, but repeatedly, my parents never faced hostility from the Mexicans with whom they worked and who worked for them, and, in return, my mother and father responded with appreciation and caring. The Mexicans of the mine were as eager to defend it against armed raiders as was the manager, and they welcomed our family back in more peaceful times with garlands of flowers.

One comes away from my father's experience impressed by how little the operation of a mine abroad differed from that within the United States. Men of wealth took a flyer on a mine and engaged a consulting engineer in a major U.S. city to exploit the venture for them. The relations between the consulting engineer in the home office and the mine superintendent did not differ when the latter crossed the border. The responsibilities of each party were well established. At the mine, wage levels would differ, but the position of the superintendent toward his laborers remained both contractual and supportive. Different cultures and different lifestyles shaped their contacts, but the underlying relationship between workers and their supervisors was much the same in Mexico as it was in the United States. One cannot find evidence in the Herr story that American investors had special plans to exploit an underdeveloped country such as Mexico. Although my father may have been more enlightened and humane than many Americans in Mexico, more what the Mexicans call *simpático*, his career casts into doubt the view that anti-American feeling was generated by the economic activity of these foreigners.

In a sharply stratified society, hatred of a dominant class and xenophobia are repressed emotions, easy to arouse and exploit, and revolutionary leaders, both idealists and opportunists, could stir up anger at stereotyped opponents.

Mexicans had long watched Americans and other foreigners live among them but above them and on Mexican resources. President Woodrow Wilson's order to land the marines in Veracruz turned the American gringos into easy targets for xenophobia. Yet, when individuals came face to face, even in trying circumstances, recognition of their common humanity overcame ideology. My father would meet armed attackers at the gate of the mine, they would share a drink together in the office, and then negotiate in good faith. Even when our family was leaving the country frightened for their lives, soldiers and officials made efforts to protect their safety. The Santa Isabel massacre, when Pancho Villa's followers executed a group of American miners, was unique. Few Americans were killed during the Mexican Revolution. Many more were killed in these years within the United States during strikes such as that at the McNally Mine in Colorado, which was in progress while Americans were fleeing through Veracruz in April 1914.

Where the relations of my mother and father with the Mexican people broke down was outside the world of the mine. Their social life brought them into little contact with the upper level of Mexican society. My mother writes of invitations to official festivities by the government authorities but not of social events involving Mexicans. A few foreign businessmen mixed with Guanajuato society, but for my parents and most of their friends, living abroad meant existing in a world of their own, where they felt comfortable. The isolation that they chose provided a breeding ground for resentment. I remember Dad years later ruefully recounting a contretemps that he had experienced. The Cubo Company had recently acquired a car for him. One day, while driving in the city, he managed to bring his new vehicle into direct contact with a lady of the Guanajuato upper class. Fortunately, she was not hurt and was able to walk away, but he asked the company lawyer to inquire as to what damages he might be liable for. The lady received Dad's emissary with anger, saying that she did not want any money. "If Señor Herr were a gentleman, he would not have sent a lawyer. He would have come in person to apologize." The outburst of Mexican nationalism during the revolution owed much to the lack of integration between foreign and local well-to-do communities.

Unlike my parents, my brothers and I came to terms with the two worlds as we developed our own personalities, growing up part of both worlds but different from both. I cannot forget, for instance, Bob's prolonged metamorphoses on the enchanted train rides between school in New England and summers in Cubo, changing back and forth from a creature adapted to timetables and competition into one at home among the gentle persons dear to his heart.

My brothers learned that with Mother and Dad they spoke only English, and, with servants and Mexican playmates, they spoke Spanish. John and Bob spoke Spanish between themselves, but they never dreamed of being ashamed of their parents' language. They were not immigrants; they were children of a professional employee of an American company who happened to be posted abroad. The culture and the society that their mother was preparing them to join through her lessons was English speaking, and my brothers took it for granted that it was preferable. When I was born in 1922, my father's first official act was to register me with the local notary as an American child. Without question, the distant, somewhat cavalier, attitude of the American colony — what is now familiarly called their body language — fueled the resentment of the Mexican middle classes, the critical *gente decente*.

My parents' life tells of an age different from today's, not only one that is now past but one that also was unique, and brief as historical periods go. In the second half of the nineteenth century the railroad became universal; in the first half of the twentieth the automobile did. In between were a few decades when a new technology was inserted into an old society. The railroad made it possible to travel rapidly, to receive letters and newspapers from distant cities within a few days, to transport heavy goods cheaply, and to move armies effectively, but as soon as one reached the station, one was back in a world that was dependent on equestrian travel and transport. Both the horse and the train were essential to this period. They were crucial to the armies fighting the revolution, to the operations of the mines, and at one point to the escape of the Americans.

The horse-railroad symbiosis gave the Mexican Revolution its character and dominated its history. On the one hand, mail got through or did not according to whether the railroad was repaired or torn up, or in the hands of those in control of your place or their enemies. Americans had to leave the country by train, which meant that they could do so only when the trains were running to the places they were going. When riding in them they were trapped in more or less comfortably furnished metal boxes (called passenger cars) and were at the mercy of those outside who could stop the boxes and board them. On the other hand, the mine could not operate without its horses. When revolutionary units approached, women and children, rifles, cash, and horses were hidden: the women and children for their safety, the rifles for the protection of the mine, and the cash and horses so that the mine could continue to operate.

My first memories of the 1920s include riding on the saddle in front of my mother, until I got my own horse at the age of four or five. The mining company did not acquire an automobile for my father until the late twenties, a handsome Chrysler touring sedan with a convertible top. We tend to associate horses with knights in armor or, at best, the Wild West. Today, those who own horses do so for diversion, not necessity. When I assigned a chapter of this book to an undergraduate seminar, I asked why the "bandits" were so insistent on taking the horses of the mine. Why didn't they just take the cars? Some students replied that there must have been a shortage of gasoline and gave other explanations of this kind. Finally one student asked, "Were there any cars?" How far we are from the world that existed early in this century! In 1928 my father observed perceptively that "I believe the automobile has done almost as much as the Revolution for Mexico." Robert's final "reprise" of 1960 bears him out; technological and revolutionary change went hand in hand to make over the Mexico of the past into the Mexico of today.

The goal of history is to turn what we can know of the lives of countless individuals into an account that is simple enough to grasp and meaningful enough to be instructive. Can the story of these individuals modify our understanding of the Mexican Revolution? The radius of their influence was limited. Respect and affection for my father, for instance, did not govern the behavior of all his employees. Even in the quiet times of the 1920s, there were miners who stole high-grade ore and found a man of influence to buy it. For such people any foreign-owned mine was fair game. My father and our family were immersed in the social and economic structures that Mexico had developed over centuries. The revolution accelerated changes in the structures. Although our story can add a case study to that history, it does little to modify it. However, by focusing on the noncombatant population of a prosperous mining region, the Herr family's account suggests that the revolution had Mexico headed in a fairly positive direction until the Great Depression interrupted its course.

The account furnished here can serve history also in a less direct way. Our sense of moral outrage predisposes us to accept history couched in terms of good guys and bad guys, and so it is with the Mexican Revolution. In its day its partisans viewed the revolution as a heroic struggle against the privilege and injustice of wealthy landowners and foreign investors. A generation later, for many Mexicans, the country's continued poverty and corruption turned this enthusiasm into a cynical *desengaño*, a disillusion that dismissed the affair as a mindless explosion of violence. Both visions have some basis in fact, but if history is to provide an instructive account of the past, it should teach us not to fall prey to such simplistic interpretations. This is where the story of Luella, Irving, and Robert has a place. Looking at Mexico in these years through their words and actions helps us to replace the various myths of the revolution with a more complex and realistic understanding of it.

Robert has written this account from the letters, diaries, and other papers preserved by our parents. Published works that have been of use are referred to in the text or the notes. I have looked for other unpublished materials that would add to the account, but here the pickings have turned out to be slim. The Potter Palmer Estate of Chicago was the owner of the Cubo mine when my father ran it. The Chicago Historical Society has the Potter Palmer Papers, which make occasional mention of the Cubo company but add no useful information about the mine. The Cubo Mining and Milling Company was a separate legal entity that operated out of the office of its president, Henry Leonard Hollis, a consulting mining engineer in Chicago. The papers of the company, if they had been preserved, would have been invaluable, especially if they had held copies of letters sent from the mine. However, the office of Hollis, located in the Railway Exchange Building, 224 South Michigan Avenue, no longer exists, and I could find no one in the building who had heard of him. Hollis died in 1958, and I have not found any trace of his papers.

The Compañía Minera del Cubo, S.A. de C.V., a Mexican corporation, has recently dedicated a building on the mine site to house company archives. Among the papers it contains are those that have been preserved from the time covered by this book, including many, but not all, account books, ledgers, inventories, and records of the output of the mine and mill, a few as early as the 1890s. Some of these records were kept in Irving Herr's hand in the period before 1916. A review of the ledgers yielded information on the wages and salaries paid by the mine at various times. The correspondence that has been preserved is spotty; several binders labeled as containing letters from these years have been emptied and filled with papers of a later date. Carbon copies of some of the correspondence of the mine superintendents with the Chicago office exist, but we could not find any for the periods when my father was in charge. There are, however, copies of his instructions to his subordinates, and correspondence with applicants for positions at the mine in the 1920s. These materials have been exploited, especially for the working of the mine in 1918–19 when he was absent (Chapter 8) and the organization and personnel of the mine in the early 1920s (Chapter 14), sections for which I am responsible. Chapter 9 and part of Chapter 2 are also mine.

I am indebted to Don Rafael Villagómez for the authorization to use the archive of the Cubo Company. At the mine, Ingeniero Oscar Manuel Pérez Rosales provided me with useful documents not located in the archive, and Licenciado Juan Colunga Ibarra opened the archive, unearthed the materials from the early part of the century, and provided me with copies of the documents that I requested. My wife Valerie reviewed the many volumes of this period, sorting out those that contained documents of interest and helping record the information. Moreover, in conversations in person and by telephone, Don Rafael Villagómez has provided me with additional valuable information on the past history of the mine, as has Ingeniero Ricardo Chico Villaseñor. Jean DeVotie Dean and Jack Cunningham, who grew up in Guanajuato with John and Bob, have been other informants on the background of the story told here. The historians David Brading, Tulio Halperin, Alan Knight, and Alex Saragoza gave us encouragement and comments that inspired us to pursue publication, while William Beezley and Richard Hopper have made this possible. We appreciate the valuable introduction that William French has provided. Gail Phillips deserves thanks for typing the manuscript and Michelle Slavin for seeing the book through production. Robert and I are grateful to all these individuals for their interest and willingness to help, and we hope that the result will be to their liking.

Richard Herr

Note about
the Sources

Luella's letters that have been saved, in her unique flowing hand, were those to various members of her family, although most were addressed "Dear Mother." Almost none of her letters written to her husband have survived. Irving's were written to his wife during the time that the two were separated. He also kept carbon copies of correspondence to friends, business associates, and his employer H. L. Hollis. Irving and Luella wrote with a sense of style and a feeling for the right word and expression. Nevertheless, their letters were mailed without revision or, in the case of typewritten letters, without correction of typographical errors. In quoting from their letters, obvious mistakes have been corrected. To avoid overloading the text with unimportant information, personal and place names that have no bearing on the story have been replaced by phrases such as "a nearby mine," "another mine superintendent," or "four friends." When the frequent use of ellipses to mark the omission of words or sentences would distract from the flow of reading, these omissions have not been indicated, and conjunctions have been added.

The letters and especially the diaries are filled with abbreviations and numbers, which are spelled out in this text. Luella's diaries, which she kept daily in pen from 1912 to 1921, through all the times of stress, are contained in two "A Line a Day" leather volumes (actually five lines). In order to squeeze in the events of the day, her entries were written in condensed form. Articles and verbs omitted from the original entries have now been added. As time wore on, Irving and Luella more frequently inserted Spanish words and phrases into their writing, evidence of their growing identity with Mexico. These have been left, with translation provided only for uncommon words.

Every effort was made to produce a book that will be pleasurable to read while remaining true to the spirit and meaning of the original documents. After this volume is published, the unpublished materials will be given to the Bancroft Library at the University of California, Berkeley, where they will be available for consultation. They contain much more information than has been presented here, especially for the 1920s and early 1930s, when Irving and Luella frequently wrote to Robert about events in Mexico.

Introduction

This book offers an intimate portrait of the relationship between the foreign colony in Guanajuato, Mexico, and a broad cross section of Mexican society during very interesting times. Covering the early years of
the twentieth century, a time referred to as the Porfiriato in Mexico (named after the president, Porfirio
Díaz, who ruled from 1876 to 1911), the Mexican Revolution (1910–1920), and its aftermath in the 1920s, it
charts the emergence of the modern Mexican nation
from the perspective of two generations of an American family, the Herrs. Irving Herr, a mining engineer
recently graduated from Harvard, was the first member of the Herr family to travel to Mexico, arriving
shortly after the turn of the century first to become
mill superintendent and then acting mine superintendent of the El Cubo mine, located near the city of
Guanajuato. Eventually joining him in 1904 was his
wife Luella Herr, whose letters and diaries, along with
the correspondence of her husband, provide the reader
with the perspective of the first generation. While in
Mexico, the Herrs raised a family, and the reminiscences (Chapters 1, 4, 11, and 16) of their middle son,
Robert Woodmansee Herr, represent the view of the
second generation. Also forming part of that generation is Richard Herr, the youngest son, who also has
contributed to this book. Taken together, the writings
of the Herr family afford us a glimpse of a part of
Mexico both before and after the Mexican Revolution;
they allow us to ponder the ways in which that seminal
event changed and shaped the Mexico of today.

The book you are about to read, then, is partly

crafted by a historian (Richard Herr), partly a retrospective account by someone who lived through some of the experiences discussed (Robert Woodmansee Herr), and partly a selection of the writings of two people closest to the events, who wrote at the time that these events were taking place (Irving and Luella Herr). The story brings together multiple points of view as represented in the "winnowed" primary sources of the first generation and shaped by the selective memory and professional standards of the second. Such a multilayered text both challenges and rewards the reader.

First the challenges. Much of the book is composed of long excerpts taken directly from the correspondence and diaries of Irving and Luella Herr. These parts of the book can be utilized by readers as they would any primary source — that is, they are the raw materials from which we can draw our own conclusions concerning the assumptions, beliefs, and actions of those living in the past. Yet, as with any work of history based on documents from the time period being written about, in this material a process of selection has taken place. Some readers may be inclined to ponder about what has been omitted that might be important to understanding the Herrs, that might give more insight into why or how they reached certain conclusions or formed various opinions. The Herrs, however, have addressed this issue, and those interested in evaluating the diaries and correspondence in their entirety will be able to consult these materials at the Bancroft Library, located at the University of California at Berkeley.

A challenge of a different order is apparent in those sections written by Robert Woodmansee Herr, which also must be regarded as primary in nature. Robert Herr's views on race and gender, for example, especially the idea that one's behavior can be attributed to qualities inherent in each "race," provide more of an insight into how his generation, or at least some members of his generation, viewed the world and the place of themselves and others in it rather than an explanation for the actions of those historical actors he considers. The same is true of his understanding of the revolutionary process in Mexico as when, for example, he states that Emiliano Zapata continued fighting for Francisco Madero's principles. Such explanations of the revolution tell us more about how Robert Herr's generation (including many of the historians who formed part of it) interpreted the events of the revolution, perhaps seeing it more as a political movement whose leaders were motivated by ideals recognizable to or shared by Americans, than about recent revolutionary historiography. Despite the use of some secondary sources to provide a chronology of events between 1910 and 1931, this book, as brother Richard emphasizes, is not a history of the Mexican Revolution.

Robert Herr's account also reminds us that contemporary concerns often help shape historical memory. An apologetic tone occasionally emerges from the book, as he confronts a stream of writing (beginning after the revolution and continuing to the present) in which American exploitation is seen as the cause of the revolution and people like his father and the company he represented are identified as the main targets of revolutionary ire. Statements about "loyal" employees and others that portray Mexicans as "happy people, accepting their poverty with fatalism and fortitude," are, in part at least, attempts to justify his family's presence in Mexico in reaction to such writing.

Still, it is precisely these challenges that make this text so rewarding. The letters and diaries of Irving and Luella Herr offer new insights into a host of subjects concerning revolutionary Mexico. While Irving's letters outline the operation of a silver mine and reveal in great detail the life of a mining engineer and his relationship with both Mexicans of all classes, including the new working classes, and the mine's backers and promoters in the United States, Luella's diaries reveal much about the social lives of those forming the American colony in Guanajuato. Together, both chart the impact of the Mexican Revolution on their own lives as well as on the lives of those around them.

For his part, those sections in which Robert Herr reminisces about his life growing up in Guanajuato are among the most interesting in the book. Topics including courtship, daily life, festivals, and social structure do not escape his eye; his portrayal of some of the Mexican staff associated with the mining company and his family can be used to tease out class structures as well as his own assumptions. In short, the material presented in this book addresses many of the themes of greatest interest to those currently writing about the history of the Mexican Revolution.

Irving and Luella Herr arrived in Mexico just in time to witness the end of one era and the beginning of another. Drawing to a close was the thirty-five-year dictatorship of Porfirio Díaz, known as the Porfiriato, and about to begin was a decade of revolutionary violence and its aftermath, the Mexican

Revolution. While the majority of this book deals with revolutionary Mexico, the Herrs' story begins in the United States at the Columbian Exposition, a world's fair held in Chicago in 1893. Irving Herr was sixteen years old when he attended the fair; Luella's father, A. E. Winship, guided groups of visitors on tours through the fair; and Luella herself visited the exposition. In fact, this fair, with its new invention, the Ferris wheel, designed as the American answer to the Eiffel Tower that had been constructed a few years earlier for the Paris Universal Exposition, serves as a marker of modernity for Robert Woodmansee Herr, a celebration of technology that both reflected and helped shape the ethos of his parents and, indeed, that of their entire generation. Robert's insight is a perceptive one, and it enables us to better understand how the Herrs, taking up residence in Guanajuato, were imbued with their own sense of modernity as well as with the expectation that, at the same time, they were helping to usher in Mexico's.

Moreover, it is an insight that should not be limited to Americans of that era. In Mexico, as well, members of the Mexican elite saw world fairs as opportunities to claim for their country its place among the assembly of modern nations. At fairs like the Columbian Exposition and the Paris Universal Exposition, Mexico's rulers commissioned the construction of pavilions and displays that demonstrated Mexican competence in new sciences like criminology, statistics, and anthropology as well as new ways of governing based on these "scientific" methods. Above all, modernity was to be achieved through embracing new technology, especially the railroad, the epitome of progress. Not only was the railroad portrayed in Mexican landscape paintings at such expositions, but it was also being constructed across the length of Mexico. Guided by the motto "Order and Progress," President Porfirio Díaz presided over a regime determined to bring about Mexico's economic, political, social, and even cultural modernization. While "order" was to be imposed both by force, as in the state's new rural police force known as the Rurales, and by creating virtuous citizens and peaceful and working people by means of, among other things, the school, the army barracks, and the modern penitentiary, "progress" in all realms was premised upon economic development and modernization.

As foreign investment seemed the best means to attain this bright future, Mexico's rulers facilitated its arrival. Between the early 1880s and 1910, some nineteen thousand kilometers of track were laid (much of it well traveled by the Herrs and others), thereby establishing major trunk lines and the country's modern railroad network. This was made possible by a thirtyfold increase in foreign investment in the country during the Porfiriato, much of it from the United States and up to one-third in railroads. Although the consequences of the arrival of the railroad varied by region, in general its construction led to the concentration of landholding, the expansion of export agriculture, stagnation in the production of foodstuffs, the beginning of Mexico's industrialization, and, most importantly for the Herrs, a tremendous boom in the mining industry.[1]

The Herrs, then, arrived in Mexico, part of a wave of Americans and American capital that was transforming the country while tying it more closely, economically, to its northern neighbor. Part of this wave, in addition to the railroads, was the mining industry, as a number of circumstances on both sides of the border spurred the arrival of American mining promoters and smelter operators. First, in contrast to the silver ore found in the American West, much of the silver ore in Mexico tended to be high in lead content. As a mix of such ores made for an efficient smelting process, American smelter owners in Denver, Pueblo, Omaha, Kansas City, and San Francisco provided the demand for ore that helped rejuvenate the Mexican mining industry in the late nineteenth century. When Colorado lead-ore miners succeeded in having a prohibitive duty, the McKinley Tariff, imposed on the import of lead ore in 1890, American capitalists established the Mexican lead-silver smelting industry by building a number of smelters in northern Mexico. Second, changes in Mexican law — specifically, new mining codes in 1884 and 1892 and new tax codes — helped make the industry more attractive to foreign investors. Finally, changes in technology, both within the mine and in the processing of ore, enabled the profitable mining of ores of lower quality than in the past. Yet, this could be accomplished only with access to ever larger amounts of capital. As a consequence, by the end of the Porfiriato, the mining industry was predominantly foreign-owned, with American companies controlling nearly three-quarters of active mining and 70 percent of the metallurgy industry.[2]

This concentration of ownership was noticeable in the Guanajuato mining district, where El Cubo, the mine managed by Irving Herr, was located.

Founded in the mid-sixteenth century after the discovery of silver in what is now central Mexico, Guanajuato became one of the richest silver mining districts in the Spanish empire in the eighteenth century. Even at that time, in mines like the Valenciana, discussed by Robert Herr and still famed for its riches, mining was a large-scale proposition requiring thousands of laborers, hundreds of mules, technical expertise, and substantial investments of capital. Flooded and greatly damaged during Mexico's struggle for independence between 1810 and 1821 when Guanajuato was a center of insurgency, Guanajuato's mines were the site of substantial British investment during the nineteenth century, much of it with disappointing results. At the end of the nineteenth century, British investors were bought out by Americans; and by the end of the 1890s, a single group of American mining promoters came to dominate mining in the Guanajuato district. Uniting with another group of American promoters in 1906, they formed the Guanajuato Development Company, a holding company that came to control fourteen mining companies along with valuable timber and cattle properties. Part of this group also organized the Guanajuato Reduction and Mines Company, comprised of some of the most famous mines in Guanajuato, including the Valenciana.

Although the mine at El Cubo that drew Irving Herr and his family to Mexico was also purchased by Americans just after the turn of the century, it, by contrast, was one of the few mines in the district to be operated independently from this group of American promoters. Purchased from the British-owned United Mexican Mining Company in 1902, the El Cubo Mining and Milling Company was chartered in New Jersey and under the direction of H. L. Hollis, a consulting engineer involved in a number of mining ventures in Mexico. Given that Irving Herr arrived in El Cubo in 1901, he must have been evaluating the property prior to its purchase and was part of the management team from its inception as an American company. With a change in management in the summer of 1905, another person was named mine superintendent. Herr then left Guanajuato, but he returned in 1910 to resume his duties and take on new ones at El Cubo.

As the site of extensive mining operations during the colonial period (especially in the eighteenth century), the Guanajuato region was covered with tailing dumps, the initial reason for the American interest in investing in properties there. Tremendous technological change characterized both the mining of ore and its refining in the late nineteenth century, making it possible to mine profitably ores of a much lower grade than previously and, of greater initial importance, to extract silver from dumps and tailings previously considered to be little other than waste. Cyanidation was a relatively new process for recovering precious metals (it had been patented only in the 1880s) and had been used extensively to recover gold from ore in South Africa. After the turn of the century, mine owners in Mexico demonstrated that the technique could also be applied to silver. The process worked by first crushing the ore into a powder (thus the need for stamp mills), adding water and cyanide, and then stirring the mixture until the cyanide formed a compound with the particles of precious metals. Once zinc was added to the solution, the precious metals precipitated out and could be recovered. Experts writing for the *Mexican Mining Journal* estimated that the use of cyaniding plants, combined with the availability of cheap electricity, had led to a fourfold increase in the production of precious metals in Guanajuato in the first decade of the present century. Most sources date the arrival of cyanidation in El Cubo to before 1907,[3] perhaps as early as 1904.[4] Flotation, another way of separating precious metals from ore, worked by finely grinding the ore and then mixing it with air, oils, and chemicals. Metal particles would cling to the oil when it floated to the surface as a froth; once the water was filtered out, a concentrate of precious metals remained. As the flotation process was not perfected until after 1910, the usual pattern was for cyanidation to give way to flotation, a common occurrence in the 1920s. Moreover, a shortage of cyanide during the revolution, especially after 1916, compelled some companies to experiment with this method at this time. In Chapter 8, Richard Herr talks about the cyanidation and flotation process being used in El Cubo in 1919.

As these technological changes depended upon the availability of electrical power, one of the first undertakings of some of these early American investors was the hydroelectric plant, which eventually became the Guanajuato Power and Electric Company, mentioned occasionally by both Irving and Luella Herr in their writings. Once cheap electricity became available in the Guanajuato mining district, the American companies there, including the El Cubo Mining and Milling Company, constructed stamp mills to crush ore and cyanide plants to recover the precious metals from it. The cyanide plant at El Cubo, for example, had an initial capacity of 50 tons, which later was increased to 100 tons.

Cheap electrical power also helped revolutionize work inside the mine as well as out. Replacing the old methods of mine work—sledges and steel bars for drilling, black powder for blasting, and the motive power of humans and animals to transport ore—were pneumatic drills, dynamite, and electrically operated winches and hoists. Irving Herr arrived in Guanajuato just as these changes were taking place, and his correspondence offers a glimpse at the old methods as they gave way to the new. Still at work, for example, even as late as 1920, were women in the patio of the hacienda outside the mine sorting the ore, a task that the new technology with its need for large quantities of low-grade ore would make redundant. Also described are the laborers working with sledge hammers and sharpened steel instead of pneumatic drills, whom Robert Herr remembers seeing at work, probably in locations where small quantities of ore made pneumatic drills impractical. Such mine workers possessed their own culture and skills, like the language of whistles noted by the author.

Mining engineers trained like Irving, however, found little use for the mine workers' traditional skills, such as the ability to prospect for deposits of rich grades of ore. Disparaging the Mexican style of mining as "gophering," by which they meant the unscientific search for the richest ore deposits with no systematic plan for the development of the mine, American mining engineers, by contrast, viewed their own methods as sound, rational, modern, and efficient. By the time of the outbreak of the revolution in 1910, most mine workers in Mexico worked in large-scale mining operations run by such trained men. These extractories, where a single mining company controlled all facets of mining and, sometimes, the milling of ore as well, looked very much like El Cubo. Although all mining companies were not always so isolated, most did come to employ hundreds of workers in mines, mills, machinery shops, and associated activities such as the more than six hundred men at El Cubo, whose very community of about two thousand depended on the mine for its existence.

Working in an extractory, however, did not necessarily mean that mine workers automatically adopted the work habits considered necessary by the foreign mine managers. In fact, perceptive readers will note the constant struggle between managers and workers over the inculcation of the time and work discipline of industrial capitalism documented throughout the book. To begin with, working in a mine or for a mining company did not necessarily lead a person to define himself, or, in the case of a woman sorting ore above ground, herself, primarily as a mine worker. In fact, El Cubo almost closed every May, as most of the workers left the mine that month, just before the start of the rainy season, to prepare their fields and plant corn. As in many mining areas in northern Mexico, much of the workforce combined subsistence agriculture with waged labor during the slack periods in the agricultural cycle, often leaving the mines to plant or harvest. Such people were as much peasant cultivators as mine workers. Nor was mine work the only opportunity to earn a wage — many alternated work in the mines with stints helping to build the railroads that were being laid across Mexico; some traveled farther north in Mexico or even to the southern United States to work in mines or on railroad construction crews there, often drawn by the promise of higher wages or fleeing dangerous or dirty jobs in search of more acceptable working conditions. Throughout northern Mexico a veritable floating population existed, a population that seemed wedded to the agricultural cycle rather than to the six-day industrial work week so desired by managers.

There are also hints in the book that even those not being called away by pressing agricultural chores were less than enthusiastic about a six-day work week. When asked how many men were on the company payroll, for example, Irving Herr responded that as the "average" workman only worked four days out of the six-day week, he employed 450 men to cover two shifts of 150 men for the full six days. Such comments help us to remember that notions such as "full-time" are inculcated or imposed (and often resisted), rather than inherent. To people accustomed to working as the task demanded, perhaps from sunup to sundown at critical times like planting and harvesting and less at others, a constant six-day work week made little sense. Nor were higher wages always enough to motivate adherence to the industrial schedule. Many workers in the Mexican north were what might be called "target earners," people who quit work after they had earned a certain predetermined amount. Raising wages, then, sometimes meant that workers stayed on the job even less time than before, as this target could be earned more quickly at the higher rate. Managers throughout northern Mexico thus resorted to other strategies to coax their workers to remain on the job, sometimes paying a bonus for a full week's work.

Although Irving Herr does not discuss the use of higher wages as a strategy for cultivating a reliable labor force at El Cubo, much of his correspondence does, nevertheless, highlight the struggle between managers and workers over work habits. In references to the *peon* class (the accepted term for un-skilled Mexican workers at this time), for example, the majority of the workforce at El Cubo and the members of which he characterizes as "very much like children," Herr bemoans, in his opinion, the excessive number of holidays and fiestas as well as the manner of their celebration — the excessive gambling, drinking, and visits to the Catholic church. To him, such activities made regular attendance at work impossible. The issue of work habits is also at the center of the many discussions of *contratistas* found in the book. *Contratistas* were men who brought their own crews to carry out various as-pects of work in conjunction with mining, including drilling, blasting, tim-bering, and, at times, even the entire mining operation. Rather than a daily wage, *contratistas* were paid by the task accomplished, for example, an agreed-upon amount for each meter of ore dug. Carrying out mining operations on the *contratista* system, then, placed the onus for working on the contractor and the men under him. Managers often preferred this because it relieved them of the need to constantly supervise to ensure that work was actually being carried out, as the amount paid to workers would only correspond to the amount of work accomplished rather than the amount of time spent in the mine.

Finally, and although it may not appear so at first glance, the interest of management in knowing the number of families supported by mine workers at El Cubo may also have been a question related to work discipline. Else-where in northern Mexico, managers, believing that "men of family" (as such men were called at the time), that is, those supporting other family members, were less likely to float from one job to the next, and they would only hire men who had their families with them. It is not clear, however, and is perhaps doubtful, whether this was also the case at El Cubo.

Irving Herr's focus on the habits of Mexican workers, to which, as you will see, some American mine managers could simply not adapt, also helps reveal the existence of important divisions within the Mexican labor force and, indeed, a critical fault line within Mexican society generally at the time. In fact, both generations of Herrs comment extensively on the economic, social, and cultural divide separating skilled from unskilled workers. Not only did the Herrs note that skilled workers were better paid and that they lived in areas of the town removed from *peones*, but they also describe them as possessing a "measure of refinement," that is, they were culturally distinct from the rest of the workforce. Representatives of this "better class," as the Herrs call them, emerge in the text, such as José Velásquez, the electrician who wore a felt hat instead of a sombrero and dressed in a shirt and tie on Sundays, and José Padro, the master mechanic who threw New Year's Eve parties attended by foreigners and Mexicans, "all well behaved." Such cultural characteristics and moral values — clothing, dedication to work, participation in American sports, sobriety, rejection of gambling and other popular pastimes, and marriage customs — critically marked one's possession of *decencia*, a complicated concept that described one's behavior and characteristics that served to separate the people who had it, the *gente decente* (decent people), from those who did not. They were especially important attributes for these artisans and skilled workers, so closely identified with the world of manual labor, yet so desperate to be accepted as members of the world of "decent" and "refined" people.

Such social divisions were clearly demarcated in space in Mexico, especially in the city centers, and what might be called a social and moral "geography" emerges from the letters and reminiscences presented in this book. We learn, for example, that *peones*, both before and after the revolution, were expected to step off the sidewalk and doff their hats when approached by their supposed social betters. And, despite the fact that, for many, the Mexican Revolution had meant that the world had been turned upside down and social hierarchies reversed, even after the revolutionary decade the open area in front of the bandstand in the Jardín de la Unión in Guanajuato was still off limits to those not considered to be *gente decente* — people wearing straw hats and serapes watched the *gente decente* enjoy the performance from the other side of the street. Not documented in the book is the existence of a moral reform movement that swept much of Mexico during the Porfiriato and continued after the revolution. The existence of whorehouses, mentioned by Robert Herr, and the various negative references to alcohol and bars by Irving Herr, leave out the fact that many of this type of establishment, along with those dedicated to gambling, were moved out of city centers and into zones of their own during the Porfiriato in an attempt to reshape the moral geography of the city center to claim it solely for the *gente decente*. Adherence to moral reform became an essential means of defining one's membership in the *gente decente*, a distinct and separate cultural category from those *peones* who, it was believed, indulged in these traditional vices.

Indeed, an important new insight provided by this book is the self-conscious role of the foreign colony in modeling these new cultural and work values, if the Herrs can be judged typical in this regard. While the various foreign colonies in Mexico have been the subject of recent research, especially their economic activities, interactions with elite Mexicans, and even their celebrations (such as the Fourth of July), all interesting topics, the example of the Herr family makes a strong case for a consideration of their self-appointed redemptive role as well. Irving Herr is explicit about this—he speaks Spanish with an "American" accent on purpose so that people will know he is not Mexican but from the United States, and he sees himself and his family (and perhaps all Americans) as "setting an example in sobriety, steadiness, and law-abidingness" for Mexicans, these "quick-blooded" people, as he describes them. Robert Herr, as well, discusses the importance of an American's "living up to one's station" by conducting himself honorably, dressing well, and maintaining his "emotions and equilibrium," values he sees as "Spanish," indicating, perhaps, that each nationality influenced the other. That this "redemptive" work was colored by the Herrs' understandings of "race" is also apparent, as, one's race could apparently be overcome by embracing these morals and values. As Irving Herr puts it when discussing their Mexican housekeeper of long duration, "Angela is one of the Mexicans who are white in everything but color." Historians need to continue to assess the interrelationship between race, nationality, morality, and class as they figure in the interactions of the foreign colony and Mexican society, a task that will be aided by books such as this one.

That the concepts of race, nationality, morality, and class were also shaped by and, in turn, helped shape ideals of gender also can be teased from the material presented here. Luella's strong voice throughout the book provides us with her insight into the interactions both within the foreign colony and between foreigners and those Mexicans whom they employed and observed. Also evident are descriptions of what she considers "picturesque" about Mexico, such as the blessing of animals by the priest. These accounts not only provide us with some idea of events that those living there might have taken for granted and not written about, but they also show what initially came to terms with the Huerta regime, hoping for a restoration of Porfirian law and order, personal loyalties, circumstances, and Huerta's unwillingness to negotiate forced others, most notably Pancho Villa in Chihuahua, Venustiano Carranza in Coahuila, and Alvaro Obregón in Sonora, to declare themselves in opposition to the new regime.

Thus began the Constitutionalist revolution, an uneasy, often fractious, mixture of urban, respectable opposition bent on a national campaign to overthrow Huerta, with Carranza identified as its First Chief, combined with the reassertion of popular revolutionary movements motivated by the desire to right local wrongs. Nowhere was this more evident than in the state of Chihuahua, where popular movements reappeared, urged on by the presence of Pancho Villa, to control much of the countryside in that state by the summer of 1913. The same popular mobilization, spurred on by agrarian grievances, characterized the state of Durango, to the south of Chihuahua, leading to the rebel capture of Durango, the first major city to fall to popular forces, in June of that same year.

For those comprising the U.S. business community in Mexico, however, Huerta was welcomed, by contrast, as the new strongman whom the nation supposedly needed. Americans in Mexico were sorely disappointed when recognition of the regime from the United States was not forthcoming. Feeling that she spoke for all her compatriots, Luella Herr expressed disgust with the leaders in Washington, especially President Wilson, for the failure of the United States to do so. As she states, "All Americans in Mexico are for Huerta as against Wilson." Whether actually intervening in Mexican affairs or not, the U.S. government seems a constant presence in the book, ready to act at any moment to alter the course of the revolution. Some scholars, using sources very much like those in this book, have reached conclusions as to the importance of the United States in shaping the trajectory of the Mexican Revolution. Students and scholars should be careful here, however. While U.S. governmental actions, such as embargoes, recognition or lack thereof, and the occasional recall of the American ambassador, do need to be considered when evaluating the revolutionary decade, these actions, or the threat of them, did not determine the outcome of events.

What these actions did result in, however, was the outburst in Mexico of kinds of anti-Americanism that were profound and traumatic

she considered to be exotic and different about Mexico. As for the social life of the foreign colony, numbered at some two hundred twenty-five in Guanajuato, luncheons, bridge parties, tennis (for the men at any rate), piano lessons, dances, dinners, the cinema, weekends in town, and social calls helped knit this community together; readers will note the growing importance of the telephone in facilitating such get-togethers and providing a sense of community at a very early date.

Likewise, a domestic sphere emerges, as Luella comments on her dealings with family, servants, and staff, such as her need to keep an account book to track how much she is owed by Mexican employees and others who are in the position of being able to make claims on her as a *patrona*. Many of these insights have to do with social and domestic life, subjects often not commented on by male travelers or writers, as they were considered to pertain more to the domestic sphere. Yet, Luella also has plenty to say about the Mexican Revolution and international politics, especially U.S. policy toward Mexico. Expecting U.S. intervention in Mexico to occur at any moment, Luella had strong words for then-president Woodrow Wilson, revealing the links that she saw between masculinity and politics. When U.S. troops finally landed in Veracruz in 1914 and then advanced no farther but instead asked South American countries to help mediate the situation, Luella saw it as a "disgraceful page to U.S. history." To her, President Wilson and his secretary of state had not finished a fight that they had started and then asked someone else to help them get out of their own mess. Their only accomplishment, she thought, was to endanger the lives of Americans in Mexico, including her family.

Luella's preoccupation with American intervention underlines the fact that a great part of this book is concerned with the Herrs' encounter with the Mexican Revolution. While it would be neither possible nor desirable to attempt to explain such a diverse and complicated phenomenon as revolution in the space of a short prologue, it is possible to offer some general comments that might help make sense of their experience. To begin with, the Herrs were not always present in Mexico during the years of some of the greatest hardship and famine associated with the revolution, the period between 1914 and 1918, when many of the five hundred thousand to two million people who are estimated to have gone missing during the revolution perished or emigrated. In the period when the Herrs were mostly present, during the first half of the decade of revolt, a series of revolutionary springs is evident, associated with the leaders Francisco Madero in 1911, Pascual Orozco in 1912, Pancho Villa, Venustiano Carranza, and others in 1913, and again with Villa in 1914. Although during these times the Herrs clutched their copies of the *Mexican Herald* in hopes of making sense out of what was going on around them, many of the most important changes were the unforeseen result of local responses to local grievances rather than changes brought about by the plans and pronouncements of those appearing in that newspaper or any other.

The Madero revolt, which began in November 1910 and resulted in the downfall of Porfirio Díaz in May 1911, is a case in point. By focusing on Francisco Madero, the Herrs cast the revolt as the work of one great man, out to redistribute the wealth and the resources of the landowners and Church to the lower classes, only to be betrayed by lesser men who then moved the revolution in a different direction. Two problems are apparent here. First, this characterization of Francisco Madero is closer to that of the hero created by official myth than that of most historians, who see Madero instead as someone much more concerned with bringing about liberal democracy than with redistributing resources. Second, this emphasis on the man masks the fact that many of those with whom the Herrs dealt on a daily basis were inspired by Madero's call, which, however, they interpreted in their own way. In much of Mexico, including Guanajuato, workers of all types expected Madero's political slogan of "Effective Suffrage, No Reelection" to result in meaningful changes in the workplace and in local relationships of power as well as in national politics. This revolt and others led to the formation of unions, workers' movements, and a new attitude on the part of labor that was more important in bringing about long-term change than the statements of political leaders. That they formed unions and struggled for gains under these circumstances is testimony to how much the climate of politics and of society in general had been changed, beginning with the Madero revolt.

Faced with an incredible demand for appointments and favors once the Díaz regime had been toppled, Madero responded by passing over many of the military and popular leaders who had joined him in revolt, favoring instead civilians from the middle class for political and administrative posts.

One such leader who felt slighted was Pascual Orozco who, in March sided with many local groups that had turned against Madero in the The Orozco revolt, which caused Luella and her family to leave M February and March of that year, was yet another example of movement composed of rural folk, bandits, cowboys, and village whom had initially fought with Madero for the overthrow of rather than being created by a leader, carried one along. Nor wa face of Orozquismo. The Orozco revolt was an uneasy coa' included many elite conservatives, who feared that Madero to protect peace and property.

Centered in the far northern state of Chihuahua, O quickly through March of 1912, succeeding in controllir April and, after some successes against the federal arr ened as far south as Torreón, where federal troops General Victoriano Huerta awaited. Plagued by a and facing a well-entrenched federal army, Orozco' series of encounters in May 1912. As Huerta mo ever, the revolt changed from one capable of m the Madero government to a guerrilla movem weakened Madero's authority by forcing him handed manner while helping to drain the r participated in the revolt spent the summe and property in the mountains of wester boring state of Sonora, and continued while, the federal army, and the conc these operations, Victoriano Huerta,

Just how dangerous became ap treacherously prolonged and mani involved elements of the federal a as the Ten Tragic Days, brough time, led to the death of Made Huerta's assumption of the the counterrevolution, whic militarization of Mexican and the eventual outrigh for the Herrs and other U.S. nationals living and working there. In fact, if one looks at the times during which the Herr family, or members of it, were forced to leave Mexico during the revolution, what is striking is that it was not the reality or threat of violence at the hands of rebel groups or workers that motived their departure but, rather, one of these episodes of anti-Americanism generated by U.S. government policy. The first departure, that of Luella and her family in February and March 1912 during the Orozco rebellion, while mostly motivated by fears of isolation due to loss of train service, also coincided with anti-American feelings that were then being vented because of an arms embargo imposed by the Taft administration. The second departure, in August 1913, which lasted until December of that year, was before many of the major battles in the fall of 1913 and spring of 1914 associated with the Constitutionalist revolution. These took place beginning in October 1913 with Villa's victory in Torreón, which he then left to return north to Chihuahua to take the major cities there in November of that year. It was in the spring of 1914 when the major battles of this phase of the revolution (most important, Villa's capture of Torreón and San Pedro in April of that year, which heralded the end of the Huerta regime) took place — that is, after Luella had returned to El Cubo. Thus, although the taking of Durango in June 1913 before she left had been accompanied by its sack and riots that horrified many of the elite, both Mexican and from the United States, what motivated her departure in August 1913 was a wave of anti-American agitation that reached its height in July of that year, stirred up by Huerta in response to the failure of the United States to recognize his regime.[5]

By far the most serious of these intermittent episodes of anti-Americanism was that prompting their third departure in April of 1914, in response to the U.S. occupation of Veracruz on April 21. This time, the entire family, along with most of the American colony in Guanajuato, left, the Herrs that very day while others followed later in the month or in early May. This episode, beginning with the Tampico incident in early April and culminating in the landing of troops in Veracruz, is described in detail in the book. Ill-conceived by President Wilson and his advisers as a means of preventing war materiel from reaching Huerta and of removing him from power, the invasion failed to do either of these things and, instead, drew upon him the wrath of those U.S. citizens who had been placed in jeopardy and forced to leave Mexico — all for nothing, in their opinion. Of great value in this book, then, is the discussion of the Herrs' interpretation of these events and of how the invasion affected their lives.

Of perhaps even greater value, in terms of contributing to our understanding of revolutionary Mexico, is the realization that while there were episodes of anti-Americanism, such as those in 1912, the summer of 1913, and following the invasion of Veracruz, they were fairly limited, mild (despite the trauma suffered by the Herrs), and confined to specific events. The events discussed in this book do not support the existence of a virulent anti-Americanism caused by economic dependency on the kind of enterprises that Irving Herr represented. Finally, the event that caused the Herrs to depart revolutionary Mexico for good—the murder of seventeen mining engineers in Chihuahua in January 1916, known as the Santa Isabel massacre—only to return once the revolutionary decade was over, was so shocking precisely because it represented such an exception to past revolutionary practice. We learn a great deal, then, about the nature of the Mexican Revolution by carefully attending to exactly what circumstances made the Herrs feel threatened enough to leave the country, or their American employer believe it advisable to tell them to leave.

Despite these identifiable episodes of anti-Americanism, it is important to note that at no time were foreign companies such as El Cubo the particular targets of revolutionary ire. As late as early 1915, for example, Luella stated that while she was "hopelessly disgusted" with the chronic fighting between Mexicans, no foreigners were bothered. To the contrary, rather than cause revolutionary discontent, the dominant impression left by the events at El Cubo is that the availability of jobs sopped up revolutionary sentiment. It was when companies, faced by shortages of supplies and the lack of transportation, were forced to close, throwing men out of work, that they faced trouble from their former workforce. While Irving Herr considered the actions of his own workforce in warning him of advancing parties of rebels as evidence of their "loyalty and respect" and thus of his own special, somewhat exceptional, relationship with workers, a different interpretation is possible. Given their dependence on earning a wage, workers had a vested interest in the continuation of the mining operations of the major foreign companies and became even more dependent on these companies for the provision of basic necessities as the revolutionary decade progressed. Contrary to what some have argued, there was no special proclivity for urban workers or workers in foreign-owned industries, like mining, to join the revolution inspired in the countryside — to the contrary, rural revolt often meant lost jobs.

Having left Mexico at the time of the U.S. occupation of Veracruz, Irving Herr returned to Guanajuato in August 1914 in time to witness the demise of the Huerta regime. With Villa's capture of Zacatecas, the site of Huerta's last stand, Huerta departed the country for exile in Spain, and Mexico City prepared to receive the rebel army of Carranza and Obregón, to which it unconditionally surrendered in August 1914. Writing to his wife, Irving remarked that, for the first time since the revolutions had begun, Guanajuato was experiencing its first real taste of the unpleasantness of revolution. Luella, who returned to Mexico in December of that year, may have been in time to read about the occupation of Mexico City by the forces of Pancho Villa and Emiliano Zapata that month in the *Mexican Herald*. It now became apparent that the violence would not end with the downfall of the Huerta regime; Carranza and his forces retreated to Veracruz and prepared for the battles against Villa that would eventually become known as the war of the winners. By early 1915, Villa dominated in central and northern Mexico, although Carranza's forces had not been eliminated. Then, in April and May 1915 and again in July, in a series of encounters in the Bajío region, not too far from where the Herrs lived and worked, Obregón defeated Villa's celebrated army, eliminating Villa as a serious contender for national power. It was in the midst of these battles in June 1915 that many of the citizens living around Guanajuato, cheering on Villa and fearing their loss of an escape route once Carranza controlled the railroad lines, made a hasty evacuation to the nearby town of Dolores Hidalgo, where they caught the train to the border, along with a glimpse of the northern caudillo himself.

As the scene of some of the major battles of the revolution, involving more than fifty thousand men, the Bajío experienced firsthand the deprivations that accompanied the destruction of the Mexican economy. Although the first few years of revolt had led to political change while leaving the economy more or less intact, the next few, beginning in 1913–14, began to destroy the economy as well. In the area around Guanajuato, the Herrs reported businesses operating through 1914 and the first half of 1915, but not without difficulties. Whereas the period up to mid-1915 illustrates the ability of many of the major companies to withstand the revolutionary storm and continue business operations despite the lack of a stable currency and the difficulty in receiving supplies, this was no longer possible after the war of the winners. In the pre-1915 period, in the face of hoarding, debasement, and the proliferation of currencies, companies kept several forms of tender on hand and let workers choose the one they wanted or paid their workers in company scrip, which, although illegal, often offered the only medium of circulation acceptable to workers and merchants.

When the mining companies around Guanajuato suspended mining operations in early 1915, it was in response to a government edict mandating the manner in which wages were to be paid rather than from pressure from revolutionaries or workers. This book reveals the strategies used by companies in the Guanajuato region to keep operating despite the problems caused by the Mexican Revolution, which was possible because the revolution was neither antiforeign, with the exceptions noted above, nor anti-imperialist. By contrast, in the period after mid-1915, continued operations on a similar scale were no longer possible. Not only did the country suffer from damage to the railroad system and the lack of a stable currency, but also the new Carrancista rulers seemed bent on self-enrichment rather than the amelioration of the starvation and disease that had accompanied the battles and destruction. In Herr's opinion, these were the "darkest days of the Mexican Revolution." As companies closed, or turned over their operations to caretakers, it was then that they found themselves confronted by their former workers.

At El Cubo, such "trouble" often took the form of what Herr and other company officials considered to be the theft of ore from company mines. At first, the evidence presented in this book seems overwhelmingly to support such an interpretation. In the years after 1916, former workmen and others did enter the company's various mines at El Cubo, without the permission of the company, to remove the richest ore they could find. These men were collectively known as *buscones*, or high-graders, because they were not out to systematically exploit the mine but only to take the highest grade ore they could find. This ore was then transported to Guanajuato or elsewhere, sometimes carried by women in much the same way as they would carry babies, to be purchased by ore buyers, linking workers, merchants, and others in what managers considered to be highly organized ore-theft rings. Yet, another interpretation of these practices is also possible, one not premised on legal norms and the private ownership of property but instead on long-standing beliefs and practices in the mining community, or what might be called the "moral economy" of mine workers. For these workers, any mine that was not actively being exploited by a company or individual was fair game for *buscones*. Likewise, when companies refused to pay living wages, many believed it only fair that rich pieces of ore be smuggled out in the lunch box or set aside for retrieval at some later time. And, while contemporary readers might find it hard to accept these practices as anything other than theft, the extent of these practices, implicating many in the mining communities, and their long history, enabling them to qualify as customs or traditions, made it otherwise to many who worked and lived in Mexico's mining communities.

Another consequence of revolution also can be seen in the mining communities around El Cubo, that of the formation of unions. While workers in modern foreign enterprises like the mining companies were likely to join revolutionary bands only when jobs were no longer available, such workers did not hesitate to seize the opportunity presented by the various revolutionary movements to organize and demand improved wages, better working conditions, and respect from the representatives of these companies. In some parts of Mexico, like the state of Chihuahua, this had begun with Madero's victory over Porfirio Díaz, as workers there expected the Madero revolt to result in changes in the workplace as well as in government. Many likened revolt under Madero to a "great awakening" in which workers could organize and strike for wages more in keeping with the amount they worked. Others, however, believed that workers, in demanding their own "rights," were trampling on the rights of others, especially those of managers and company officials. Managers, including Irving Herr, were extremely reluctant to tolerate what they regarded as interference with their authority. In El Cubo, and Guanajuato generally, the consequences of the Madero revolt seem to have been more muted, as Herr notes the absence of labor organizations through 1914. It was only in late 1915 and 1916 that he comments on the arrival of unions—yet another reason, he states, that he is glad to be out of El Cubo after this date.

The formation of labor unions and government legislation in favor of workers was among the transformations that Herr would have to become used to when he returned to Mexico in the 1920s to run the El Cubo Mining Company. In fact, in reviewing the major changes engendered by the revolution from the vantage point of 1920, which would include the destruction of the old Porfirian structures of authority, including the army; the creation of a new, younger, more plebeian political elite; and the mounting of a challenge to the power of the clergy, one of the most important would have to be the support given by the postrevolutionary state to workers in their struggles to organize and demand increased wages and better working conditions. On this point the Herrs, both father and son, are clearly of two minds. While they acknowledged that these policies were necessary to improve the lives of mine workers, they expressed their frustration at having to accept that the relative power of workers had increased vis-à-vis that of managers. Thus, while in 1926 Irving Herr can state clearly and directly that working conditions had greatly improved in the 1920s "due to labor unions and labor laws," six years later, in the Great Depression, he can make the following complaint: "I feel as though our Company, instead of being a business concern, were simply a sort of institution for the purpose of supplying work to a lot of down-and-out Mexican workmen." Readers will have to decide for themselves if this ambivalence is simply part of the process of adjusting to the changed circumstances or a contradiction in the text and, if so, what it might mean.

Perhaps Irving Herr, given his view that the Catholic Church represented one of the "greatest evils of the peon class," was not so ambivalent about another aspect of postrevolutionary policy in the 1920s, official anticlericalism. Although not originating with the Mexican Revolution, the conflict between Church and state was exacerbated during the revolutionary decade by the identification of the Church with counterrevolution. As a response, during the revolution, Carranza began seizing Church properties and turning them over to labor organizations. During the 1920s, postrevolutionary state-builders, continuing in the tradition of those of the late eighteenth and nineteenth centuries, identified the Catholic Church as an antinational institution that stood in the way of the molding of the new revolutionary citizen, in competition with the nation-state for his, and especially her, loyalties. Ironically, the other major institution considered by state-builders to fulfill the same role as the Catholic Church was the large foreign mining extractory, such as the one Irving Herr represented at El Cubo. While these companies faced labor legislation and a changed work environment, the Church-state conflict culminated in the outbreak of the Cristero Rebellion in 1926. These disturbances, which began spontaneously after the Church stopped public worship and withdrew priests from churches in response to the anticlerical measures of the government of President Plutarco Elías Calles in August 1926, grew to involve tens of thousands of the country people of Mexico's central states, including Guanajuato, lasting until a compromise was reached between the Church and the state in 1929. Perhaps as many as ninety thousand combatants died during this struggle.[6]

Another change that Irving Herr noted from the vantage point of the 1920s was that the arrival of automobiles and the construction of roads seemed as important as the revolution in "modernizing" and "civilizing" life in Mexico. His statement is interesting in two regards. First, it reminds us that all change that occurred after the revolutionary decade was not necessarily caused by the events of the revolution. Second, it also alerts us to the possibility that there existed a great deal of continuity between pre- and postrevolutionary regimes. In many ways, for example, postrevolutionary leaders hoped to instill the same developmentalist ethics that so enamored Porfirian rulers. Memorable, for example, are the use of mottoes and the construction of clock towers to inspire proper behavior from the armed forces stationed in Guanajuato, as discussed by Irving in 1931. So, too, did a prominent role remain for foreign investment in the export sector, as in mining, although, as discussed above, some changes were apparent. Readers will have to decide for themselves which of these changes can be attributed to the revolution and what remained unchanged.

William E. French

Notes

1. Robert M. Buffington and William E. French, "The Culture of Modernity," in Michael C. Meyer and William H. Beezley, eds., *Oxford History of Mexico* (New York: Oxford University Press, forthcoming).

2. On the Mexican mining industry at this time, see Marvin D. Bernstein, *The Mexican Mining Industry, 1880–1950: A Study of the Interaction of Politics,*

Economics, and Technology (Albany: State University of New York, 1965). For a case study of a mining region during the Porfiriato and the revolution, see William E. French, *A Peaceful and Working People: Manners, Morals, and Class Formation in Northern Mexico* (Albuquerque: University of New Mexico Press, 1996).

3. Juan Luis Sariego dates it to 1907 in *Enclaves y minerales en el norte de México: Historia social de los mineros de Cananea y Nueva Rosita, 1900–1970* (México: Centro de Investigaciones y Estudios Superiores en Antropología Social, 1988), 40.

4. Bernstein, *Mexican Mining Industry*, 46.

5. Alan Knight, *The Mexican Revolution*, 2 vols. (New York: Cambridge University Press, 1986), vol. 2:71.

6. For a brief discussion of the 1920s including the Cristero revolt, see Jean Meyer, "Mexico: Revolution and Reconstruction in the 1920s," in Leslie Bethell, ed., *The Cambridge History of Latin America*, vol. 5 (Cambridge: Cambridge University Press, 1986).

Chronology

1902 — Irving Herr first goes to the mine at El Cubo.

1904 — February 10: Irving marries Luella Winship.
— December 8: Son John born at the El Cubo mine residence.

1906 — Son Robert born in Stent, California (Herr family had left Mexico).

1910 — January: Family returns to El Cubo.
— April 15: Francisco I. Madero nominated for president of Mexico to succeed Porfirio Díaz.
— June: Díaz declared reelected. Madero, in the United States, declares Díaz election invalid.

1911 — February: Madero reenters Mexico to lead rebellion against Díaz, supported by Pancho Villa and Pascual Orozco in the north and by Emiliano Zapata in the south.
— May 21: Díaz resigns and escapes to Paris.
— June 7: Madero enters Mexico City to take over government.
— November 6: Madero formally elected president.

1912 — February 7–March 19: Because of unrest in the north in opposition to Madero, Luella and her two sons move to San Antonio, Texas.
— March 3: Orozco openly rebels against Madero in Chihuahua.
— September: General Victoriano Huerta, with Villa's help, drives Orozco north of the border.
— October 12: Félix Díaz, nephew of Porfirio, rebels at Veracruz and desists after one week.

1913 — February 9: Coup d'état against Madero fails. Rebels occupy arsenal in Mexico City and fight Madero's forces under Huerta.
— February 18: Huerta arrests Madero.
— February 22: Madero is assassinated and Huerta assumes presidency.
— March 25: Venustiano Carranza in the north declares against Huerta and, as leader of his Constitutionalist party, enlists Alvaro Obregón and Villa to lead armies south.

—August 18: Because of rebel activity, Luella and her two sons leave for the United States via Veracruz.

—December: Villa sets up headquarters in Chihuahua City. Obregón advances south on the west coast, and Zapata is active against Huerta in the south.

—December 20: Luella and the boys return to El Cubo.

1914 —April: Villa captures Torreón for the Constitutionalists.

—April 9: U.S. Marines are arrested in Tampico. The United States demands an apology.

—April 21: United States occupies Veracruz. The Herr family leaves Guanajuato for the United States via Mexico City and Veracruz.

—July: The Constitutionalists reach León and Querétaro, surrounding Guanajuato. Villa returns to Chihuahua.

—July 15: Huerta departs for Spain. On August 1, Irving returns to Veracruz, en route to Guanajuato, where he finally arrives on August 23.

—August 15: Obregón enters Mexico City, followed by Carranza on August 20.

—October: Convention at Aguascalientes appoints Eulalio Gutiérrez as provisional president.

—November 23: U.S. troops withdraw from Veracruz.

—November–December: Carranza moves to Veracruz with Obregón, refusing to recognize Gutiérrez.

—December 6: Villa and Zapata enter Mexico City to install Gutiérrez as provisional president.

—December: Luella and the boys return to Mexico via El Paso, arriving in Guanajuato on December 25.

1915 —January: Villa leaves Mexico City. Gutiérrez moves his "government" north to Nuevo León.

—January 28: Obregón reenters Mexico City with the Carranzistas.

—March 10: Obregón heads north for a showdown with Villa. Fighting erupts in the Guanajuato area.

—June 12: Herr family leaves for United States via Dolores Hidalgo.

—October 19: Carranza recognized by United States as de facto president.

- November: Villa effectively eliminated in Sonora.

1916 — January 8: Irving Herr arrives at the El Cubo mine, returning via Laredo. He leaves again shortly after the Santa Isabel massacre.

- January 10: Seventeen American mine workers in Chihuahua are killed in the Santa Isabel massacre.

- March 9: Villa raids Columbus, New Mexico, prompting the United States to send General John J. Pershing with an expeditionary force to pursue Villa, to no avail.

- April 14: Carranza returns to Mexico City.

1917 — January 31: New constitution proclaimed in Querétaro.

- March 11: Carranza formally elected president.

1920 — January 16: Irving Herr returns to Guanajuato and El Cubo, followed by Luella and their sons on March 8.

- April-May: Rebels gather in various parts of Mexico in favor of Obregón over Carranza's nominee in the coming election.

- May 5: Carranza prepares to move to Veracruz.

- May 21: Carranza ambushed and murdered en route to Veracruz.

- May 24: Adolfo de la Huerta appointed provisional president.

- September 5: Obregón elected president.

- November 30: Obregón assumes office.

1921 — August 29: John and Robert, accompanied by Luella, leave Mexico for schools in New England, arriving in Boston on September 4. They would return each year for summer vacation with one exception: five years for John, six years for Robert.

1922 — April 7: Son Richard born at El Cubo.

1923 — President Obregón selects Plutarco Elías Calles to succeed him in 1924 election.

- December: Adolfo de la Huerta declares against Calles and starts a revolt, opposing Obregón's regime.

1924 — Obregón's federal forces eliminate de la Huerta. Order is restored and Calles is elected president.

1925 — March: Santa Teresa Country Club organized for Guanajuato golfers.

- October 3: Hotel Luna in Guanajuato opens new addition.

- December: Mexican Congress passes alien land and petroleum laws to give effect to constitutional provisions that limited land ownership by foreigners and reserved subsoil mineral rights to the state.

1926 — February: Catholic Church repudiates the Constitution of 1917, and government orders nationalization of Church property. In response, the Church suspends services. Start of Cristero revolt.

— October 30: United States warns Mexico not to deprive American owners in Mexico of their property rights in land and oil.

1927 — November 17: Mexican Supreme Court declares confiscatory petroleum laws unconstitutional. Friction with the United States is temporarily averted.

1928 — February: Federal troops dismantle statue of Christ on Cubilete Mountain. Cristero Revolution grows hotter.

— June: Robert's last summer vacation at home in Mexico.

— July 1: Obregón (Calles's man) reelected president of Mexico.

— July 17: Obregón assassinated. Emilio Portes Gil made provisional president; Calles remains in control.

— December: José Padrón leads rebels, now turned outlaws, in Guanajuato area. Threats of kidnapping for ransom.

1929 — February 9: Irving and Luella celebrate their twenty-fifth wedding anniversary with a party at the Guanajuato casino.

— February 20: Two American men in Guanajuato area are kidnapped and murdered.

— June 21: Agreement between the Church and state. Churches to reopen in July.

— July 6: Guanajuato troops capture Padrón — dead. Order restored.

— August 31: Herr family moves from El Cubo to a rented house in Guanajuato.

— November: Pascual Ortiz Rubio elected president. Calles's policies remain.

1930 — December: Irving, Luella, and Richard tour southern Mexico, anticipating possible shutdown of mine.

1931 — February: Silver drops to twenty-seven cents per ounce, reflecting the Great Depression in the United States.

— August: Authorization secured to shut down El Cubo mine.

1932 — June: Herrs leave Mexico for a new life in Cincinnati, Ohio.

PART I

Eruption, 1910–1920

CHAPTER I

Reminiscences I

We were in Mexico, my brother John and I, in 1910 when we started to remember things. Odd things, like making "slime things" — we spent hours doing this. Or playing "cutting-out elevator," or running on the parapets of great concrete vats ten feet deep that were empty now but once held deadly chemical solutions. It was great fun too to climb around huge pieces of idle machinery with gears larger than we were, or go down to the blacksmith shop and watch men shape drill steel with a hammer on an anvil, to be sent back into the mine. The mine "motor" would come out of the tunnel bringing both ore cars and men who were through with their work, and would haul the sharpened drill steel back into the mountain.

Mostly we were by ourselves in the big hacienda that enclosed the outside end of a silver mining operation in the little town of El Cubo. The cyanide mill that extracted silver and gold from the ores had once been located inside the hacienda too, but had now been moved upriver, so the old mill site with its mechanical ghosts was a part of our playground. I was "Robertito" to the Mexicans, and many of them were our good friends — the gardeners, the hostler, the gatekeeper, the blacksmith, and some of the mechanics who worked in a small machine shop where the mill had stood. When the mechanics stopped for lunch and unfolded the napkins holding their frijoles and tortillas and queso (wonderful goat's milk cheese), the inevitable "¿Usted gusta?" often enticed us to share in these delicacies. That was against our house rules, but we never told.

The "slime" was the leeched ore crushings that were discharged from the old mill after the cyanide solution had dissolved the silver and gold and been filtered out and pumped to the recovery room. Much of it still lay around the patio and when it was slightly wet it made a wonderful modeling clay, much better than plasticene. So we made "slime things."

One of the relics of the mill was part of a Pachuca tank, perhaps half of it still standing. A Pachuca tank was a tall cylindrical tank some thirty or forty feet high with powerful air jets at the base. In it the finely crushed ore was blended with cyanide solution and the whole potful agitated with the air jets until the cyanide had swallowed up the precious metals and the goop was sluiced off to the filters. Bolted to the side of the tank was a vertical iron ladder. One of my earliest recollections (I must have been four or five) was climbing gaily up this ladder with my teddy bear in one arm until I was perhaps fifteen feet up, when I chanced to look down. I froze and bellowed. They tell me it was almost dark when at long last Dad came up the ladder and rescued me.

But to get back to "cutting-out elevator," our house was built in a corner against the wall of the hacienda that looked out on the town street. The wall also served as the back wall of the house with barred windows. The house was strung out in an L shape, one room deep, with a tiled veranda that ran its length on the inside of the L. A flower garden in front with little stone-lined paths completed a square. At the end of the veranda, broad flagstone steps went down one full story to the doors of the mine office, which housed the bookkeepers and the engineers. The telephone was here, the old-style verti-cal wooden box that hung on the wall. You rang the bell by turning the little crank. Our ring was one long and three shorts. High over the offices was a second floor reached by a flight of wooden steps that crossed over the flagstone steps at the end of our veranda. From the top of the wooden steps to the bottom of the flagstone steps was a vertical distance of about two stories, which was ideal for an elevator. John and I would tie a string to the handle of a handbasket. I would sit at the top and he at the bottom, each of us equipped with some old magazines and a pair of "cutting-out" scissors, and he would cut out pictures for me and send them up in the basket, while I would send others down to him. This game lasted for hours and lunch was an unwelcome interruption.

Besides Mother and Dad, who always spoke to us in English, our household included the Mexican servants, with whom we naturally spoke Spanish, never giving the matter a thought. There was Angela, the cook and head of the household staff, who had a housemaid and laundress beneath her. Also the company provided a gardener and a handyman – old Pánfilo, who might be catnapping as he stood over the block where he was supposed to be cutting wood.

As children we were not allowed outside the hacienda gates, nor did the Mexican kids come in. The gates were massive like those of a medieval castle, made of oak about four inches thick, and they swung open from the center on giant metal hinges. The upper gate opened out on the town marketplace in front of the church, but it was always kept bolted and chained except on special fiesta days. The lower gate was the main gate, which was open during the day to receive shipments of mine supplies, the water burro that brought drinking water from the spring up on the mountain, meat vendors who brought fresh-killed meats for the Señora to inspect (we grew our own vegetables), travelers, visitors and such. The gatekeeper had his little gate house where he was inclined to doze when things were dull, which was most of the time. John and I liked to talk to the gatekeeper. Little Mexican boys would gather on the outside of the gate and we would talk to them, too. They played a game outside called "monos," which was like pitching pennies against the hacienda wall, but they used tiny cast-lead figures or "dolls" instead of pennies. We used to play this with them outside the gate while the gatekeeper looked the other way. I still have some "monos."

Outside the wall of the hacienda were the cobblestone streets of the town of El Cubo, lined in places with plaster storefronts or walls of houses, that led to the small church whose pink calcined bell tower dominated the town. Reaching up the hillsides from the center were the small adobe houses of the miners and their families, each with a little piece of ground to accommodate their chickens and pots of flowers, and perhaps a dog. Houses near the church would be the homes of merchants, minor authorities, and perhaps a few of the skilled workers and contractors who worked in the mine. The people of Cubo accepted their way of life and were not asking for revolution, but were caught up in it, as we shall see.

The mine was seven miles from Guanajuato, the only city that could be reached without first going there and taking the train. The road from Cubo to "town" ran up and down and around the mountains that lay between, and we did it on horseback, although the Mexicans mostly walked or rode their burros. It was a wagon road of sorts over which heavy mine machinery had been hauled by large teams of mules, but we took short cuts with the horses. As early as I can remember, John and I always rode our own horses to town. We used regulation saddles and shortened the stirrups so that we could reach to put our feet in the loop of the straps from which the stirrups hung. It was some time before we could reach the stirrups, but the horses knew we were there. About halfway to town there was a level stretch that passed the ruins of an old sheep corral whose fieldstone walls ran for perhaps half a mile. John and I always raced our horses here, leaving Mother and Dad (if they were with us) far behind. Our horses knew the race was coming and were as eager as we were. On the rougher short cuts we gave the horses their heads, and even at night they could pick their way over the steeper trails.

The *mozo*, or hostler, was one of our good friends. We used to watch him groom the horses and fix the saddles, helping where we could. When we were going somewhere during the rainy season, we would ask him whether it was going to rain and he would always say no. We asked him once why he always said no, and he answered that it was time enough to worry about the rain when it actually came — in the meantime we might as well be happy. And so we were. The *mozo*'s name was Brígido and he always accompanied any of the family who rode out of the hacienda, to act as attendant and take care of the horses after we reached our destination. On these occasions he dressed in tight-fitting leather breeches decorated with embroidered patterns, a leather vest to match, and a broad-brimmed felt sombrero complete with tassel. Although slightly overweight he cut a handsome figure.

One of the great adventures was going into the mine. When we were quite young, I was only allowed to go partway into the tunnel with Dad, which was exciting enough. But when I was seven or eight, on rare occasions he would take me all the way into the workings, and that would be a great day. The tunnel ran horizontally for about a mile straight into the side of the mountain to meet the vein of ore that ran almost vertically through the mountain at right angles to the tunnel. Originally the tunnel was driven as a roadway to take the ore out and bring it to the old mill in the hacienda. In those days ore had been brought out to the hacienda patio, where it was broken and sorted by hand. Now it was mainly a service tunnel for the workmen to enter and for bringing supplies. Long since, they had driven a vertical shaft from the tunnel level to the top of the mountain, one thousand feet up, and the ore was now hoisted up this shaft and dumped at the new mill upstream. But the tracks were still there with a bare trolley wire overhead, and the mine motor still hauled occasional cars of waste out through the tunnel. You could hear it coming through the mountain and we would squeeze up against the rocky sides of the tunnel to let it pass.

As we went into the mine, Dad would let us fix our own carbide lamps. These were hand carried, with a water compartment that screwed down over the carbide container, and we had to adjust the drip of water with a hand valve until just enough of the acetylene gas flowed to give a bright, steady light. We always carried matches and candles in case the light went out. The first real sign of activity as we approached the "workings" was the throb of the compressors reverberating throughout the tunnel as we approached the compressor room, and soon we would see the electric lights around them. These were the air compressors that served the air drills in the mine, and they were housed in a cavern carved out of solid rock. After nearly a mile of dark, lonely tunnel, this was always a friendly sight.

Not far beyond was the bottom of the shaft, which was a busy place indeed. Here, one thousand feet below the surface, mine cars were coming and going regularly, bringing chunks of rock both large and small containing the silver sulphide that was pay dirt. This was dumped in huge bins at the base of the shaft waiting to be hauled up in the skip. The skip was an oblong steel bucket with eyelets on either side that rode two cables or guide ropes strung taut up the center of the shaft. It had a handle at the top with a cable in the middle that was the haul rope, and after loading it would disappear up the shaft with surprising speed. I can remember when Dad would want to check conditions on the surface he would tell us to wait, then he would take his position atop the loaded skip, feet on the steel sides with one hand on the haul rope, and up he'd go. We would talk to the loading crew or the compressorman until he came back.

But all this was just the start of a trip through the mine. From here tunnels went left and right with tracks for the mine cars to reach far up and down the vein where the ore was being mined. They were mining above this level and below this level, perhaps five hundred feet up and five hundred feet down, chuting the broken ore down from above and hauling it up from below. To reach the working faces we would tramp down these tunnels, climb wooden ladders or even wire rope ladders until we came to the drilling areas where Dad could inspect the work and take a few samples of his own. Air drills were mostly used to cut two- or three-inch holes deep into the rock for dynamite charges, and in some parts the exhaust air from the drills was the chief ventilation.

In the old days there was still some hand drilling, and the speed and precision of these drilling teams was something to watch: one man would wield a sledge with perfect timing while the other held the drill steel with both hands, giving it a quarter turn between each stroke, with no thought of a mashed finger. When the holes were drilled and the dynamite fused, everyone vacated the mine for four hours between shifts. It also would then be time for us to go, and, if we were lucky, we caught a ride out on the mine motor. That, too, was a thrill.

CHAPTER 2

A Mining Engineer

Irving Herr was a mining engineer who enjoyed his profession. For him real satisfaction would come from studying the pitch and direction of a mineralized vein of quartz and locating a new ore body. There was plenty of opportunity for this at the Cubo mine. Irving was born in Indianapolis, Indiana, in 1877. His father had come from Pennsylvania (Herr is a good Pennsylvania name) and his mother, of English stock, from Terre Haute. As a boy, he grew up and went to school in Oak Park, Illinois, a suburb of Chicago, where his father published the local *Oak Park Reporter*. Irving delivered papers and breathed the air of the smalltown newspaper office. In later life, when he had leisure, he would try his hand at short stories, and his letters would reflect his love of words and images. But his career would be in applied modern technology; he shared the spirit that sparked the development of the United States in those years.

Eighteen ninety-three was the year of Chicago's Columbian Exposition, and Irving was sixteen. Not to be outdone by Paris, which had just celebrated the centenary of the French Revolution by commissioning the bridge-builder Gustave Eiffel to create a structure taller than anyone had imagined possible, Chicago hired the American engineer George W. C. Ferris to construct a giant wheel, two hundred fifty feet in diameter, that carried cars holding forty passengers upward in a majestic arc to look out dizzily over the city and the lake, and down again to skim the solid earth. Irving earned pocket money selling "smoked glasses" to the visitors at the fair and was undoubtedly impressed by the feats of modern engineering.

Irving was the valedictorian of his class at Oak Park High School. He preserved the text of his speech, written in a fine, regular hand. Entitled "The Question of Immigration," it warned of the growing danger from "the crowded centers of foreign population, . . . whole colonies of wretched, ignorant useless creatures living in squalid filth." Irving set off to college well versed in the nativist spirit of the Midwest.

In 1895 he enrolled in the University of Michigan at Ann Arbor, but after one year he decided that he wanted to go to Harvard and study engineering. However, with four children in the family, father Isaac could not afford an eastern college for his son. Irving spent a year working at a bank to build up his resources, and in 1897 he boarded a train for Cambridge, Massachusetts, and presented himself at Harvard as a candidate for admission. As he tells it:

> In the Fall of 1897 I arrived in Cambridge and took examinations for entrance to Harvard, though I had already passed my Freshman year at the University of Michigan. I flunked practically all the examinations that I took, and was requested to return to my home in Chicago, as I could not be admitted. It was impossible for me to return to Chicago, and the upshot of the matter was that I was admitted as a "special student on trial." I think Professor Smyth of the Mining Department will vouch for this.[1]

The fact is that he did not have enough money to return home, and after he presented his case to the Admissions Department it was decided that he could stay and work part time in the Astronomy Laboratory to help pay his way, subject, of course, to his future grades. Just before Irving left for Cambridge, news had arrived of the discovery of gold in the Klondike. Thousands of people were rushing north to Canada and Alaska. Irving would later recount that the Alaska gold rush made him decide to become a mining engineer.

Irving proceeded successfully through his courses, and by his senior year he was on a scholarship. In June 1901 he received his bachelor's degree in mining engineering, magna cum laude. Fifteen years later he would write for his class report:

In July 1901, after a hard struggle not to be turned down on account of lack of practical experience, I was appointed to take care of the development of a copper mine at Terrazas, Chihuahua, by Mr. H. L. Hollis of Chicago. In the summer of 1902 I was transferred to the Cubo Mining and Milling Company, of Guanajuato, by Mr. Hollis, and there I have done the major part of my mining work. I began in Guanajuato as engineer and occupied positions as mine superintendent, mill superintendent, and general superintendent. In 1904 I returned to Somerville to be married to Luella Parker Winship, whom I had met during my last year at college.[2]

While working in the Harvard laboratory in the summer of 1900, he found time to go north on holiday. According to a photograph in the family album he met Luella at her vacation home in Bayville, Maine. She had just completed her freshman year at Mount Holyoke College. Her father was Albert Edward Winship, who lived in Somerville, adjacent to Cambridge. Luella remembered all her life that when she was a young girl the family moved into a three-story clapboard house in Somerville that had its own lot, so that she could run right around it. Even in those days it was an advantage to be a daughter of A. E. Winship. A Civil War veteran (at least of five months' guarding a prisoner of war camp in Indiana — he was considered too young to go to the fighting front, much to his chagrin), Winship switched early in life from the ministry to become the editor of the weekly *Journal of Education*. Before 1875 he had traveled as far as the Rockies as a correspondent for the *New York Herald*, and in 1883, when Luella was three, he had taken his wife on the train across the Southwest to the end of the line in Chihuahua, Mexico. Ten years later he led tours to the Chicago Columbian Exposition, and in 1895 he took a tour group to Europe. As editor of the *Journal of Education*, he traveled throughout the United States, spending almost as many nights in Pullman berths and hotel rooms as in his bed at home. Many American teachers admired him for his talks in school auditoriums and before school boards, where he urged teachers to arouse the curiosity of their students, and school boards to raise the salaries of their teachers. His children knew from early on that a wide world existed outside Boston.

Although his higher education had been limited to one year in normal school and another at the Andover Theological Seminary, Winship wanted his children to have a broader educational background. When Luella's turn came, being adventuresome, she chose Mount Holyoke College, away from home. This was against her father's better judgment because he believed that it could not equal Harvard or Radcliffe, but he at length consented, provided Luella could pass the entrance examinations for Radcliffe — which she did.

At college, Luella pursued her studies conscientiously, as befitted her origins, but she also dreamed and played and schemed with her contemporaries, joined a sorority, and made lifelong friends among her classmates. Her independent spirit, which had moved her to go to school away from home, matured and strengthened during these years. She loved her family dearly but was not tied to them. Also she had tasted other climes. Her father had taken her and her mother on one of his tours of the Columbian Exposition, as Luella described in excited letters home to her sisters. When Irving received his degree in 1901 and took his first job in Mexico, Luella was baited by her college friends. "It is certainly romantic to have a suitor in Mexico, but what is the good of a man that you will never see?" and "How do you know he doesn't have some Mexican girl, or even a Spanish señorita, to keep him company when you are far away?" Lue said, "Not Irving. He would tell me right away if he had another girl. And besides, he'll come back. Just wait and see. Maybe he'll even take me to Mexico some day." To prepare herself she studied Italian, for Mount Holyoke offered no courses in Spanish.

The company books show that Irving had begun work at the Cubo mine for 150 pesos a month, soon raised to 200. (Most of the Mexican miners were paid 1.25 pesos a day, while some made only one peso, the more skilled one peso fifty.) The Cubo village presented little to distract Irving's pocketbook, and by 1904 he had saved enough to return to Somerville and marry Luella. The wedding on February 10 befitted the daughter of A. E. Winship. Photographs of the couple have not survived, but one of sister Edith resplendent in a lush white gown testifies to the elegance of the event, as does the gold pendant watch inscribed with her initials and the date that Luella received from her father. For their honeymoon, the newlyweds boarded a Pullman train to Mexico. The last seven miles from Guanajuato to Cubo were traveled on horseback, probably the first time Luella had ridden a horse.

Their first son, John, was born that December at the Cubo mine beside a small fireplace in the bedroom of the ancient L-shaped residence of the mine superintendent. Edith came to be with Luella, but Luella must have missed her Somerville home that first Christmas in this strange land with a strange language. Luella would later communicate regularly with her family by letter, and in her stoic bearing she would always be a worthy New England lady. She later admonished her daughters-in-law, "A wife must follow her husband where his work takes him." She lived by this rule, in spite of many worries and hardships. There were often times when her advice and counsel were an important contribution to Irving's achievements. They were in fact a team, deeply devoted to each other.

After a change of management at Cubo in the summer of 1905, Irving resigned and took Luella and young John back to Somerville, Massachusetts. His next job took them to Esparta, Costa Rica, on a mining venture that proved a dud. Luella was sorry, for as she wrote during their stay, "Irving and I both wish very much that there would be a good mine here, for we would like very much to settle here for a number of years. We could have a truly delightful home here if we were to stay."[3]

A short assignment in Nicaragua proved equally disappointing, and Irving came back to Boston where Luella and young John were living temporarily. He was out of a job and wondering where to go next when he received a telegram from H. L. Hollis, who managed the Cubo mine, asking him to come immediately to his office in Chicago. Hollis was a consulting engineer who managed properties for the Potter Palmer Estate of Chicago, which owned the Cubo mine and had extensive mining interests not only in Mexico but in the United States and Canada as well. Upon Irving's arrival, after the usual inquiries about Irving's doings and his family, Hollis disclosed that he was acting for Harry Selfridge, a prominent Chicago businessman who was about to embark for London, where he would establish his well-known department store. Upon Hollis's advice, based on the reports of two engineers, he had just purchased a promising new gold mine in Stent, California, from a Colonel Thompson, who represented the miners who had opened it. Now was the time to put the mine on a paying basis, and Hollis had decided that that undertaking needed someone more vigorous than Colonel Thompson. He concluded by offering Irving the position as new manager.

Hollis and Irving went out to Stent, and Hollis had a long private conversation with Thompson, in which he informed him that Irving, still not thirty years old, would be taking his place as manager of the New Calico Mine. Despite the news, the two men emerged in a warm and friendly spirit. What happened next so marked Irving that he later wrote a memoir and a short story about it.[4]

Thompson retired to San Francisco, Irving took over, and Luella and John came out to Stent to settle into what promised to be the permanent home Luella longed for. It was time, for John's sibling was due in a few months. Stent was a busy mining town near the entrance to Yosemite Valley with a two-story hotel and a street full of stores, far more advanced than the mining camp at Cubo. Irving and Luella obtained a small house of their own, and Irving began building the mill for the mine.

He also began to sample the ore. Although to his eye it did not look promising, the samples sent to the assay office in San Francisco showed high values. One day a Welsh miner, sensing his suspicions, tipped him off that something was fishy. Irving then secretly cut and sent his own samples to be assayed. The reports showed values of only a few cents a ton.

Hollis at first responded to Irving's telegrams by accusing him of not knowing how to sample, but when the assays continued to be negative Hollis suddenly wired that he was coming out at once. What puzzled Irving was, if the sampling had been salted to fool Selfridge into buying the mine, why the tampering should continue once the sale was completed. Hollis now made this clear. Thompson had kept his share of the mine, and Hollis had personally agreed to buy it in sixty days contingent on the continued satisfactory showing of the mine. Hollis had arrived on the fifty-ninth day. Irving's sampling and telegrams had saved him from a scam. Hollis went to San Francisco to catch Colonel Thompson. He found him, but he discovered that California justice disliked eastern investors, and Thompson was safe — not only safe but ready to crow to Hollis about how his men had injected gold dust in the samples at night before shipment to San Francisco. On his side Irving learned that practically all of the townspeople of Stent were quite in the know about what was being done down at the Calico Mine from start to finish.

An oldtime California miner had managed to swindle a capitalist of world stature, who was advised by a leading mining consultant in Chicago, who had sent out two trusted engineers to check out the mine. Although he had not been apprised of any urgency, Irving had uncovered the swindle within two months. Why had the Welsh miner tipped him off and not the other engineers? The answer may lie in a trait that separated him from the ordinary run of eastern engineers. "I might also add," his memoir says after commenting on Thompson's evasion of justice, "that the graduate mining engineers from eastern colleges were also held more or less in contempt. We were popularly known as Yellow Legs on account of the wearing of high yellow leather hobnailed mining boots by the majority of the young engineers who came out from the east. This was a practice I never indulged in, knowing how most of us were regarded by the old time western practical miner. It was my custom always to wear a disreputable pair of broghans when on a job in that part of the country." Irving's lack of pretension would serve him well later in Mexico.

Robert was born in Stent on September 2, 1906. Irving had to run two and a half miles to Jamestown to get a doctor while Luella was in labor. The New Calico Mine was abandoned. Saving his employers from an expensive scam had provided nothing for Irving's own immediate future, although it established for him with Mr. Hollis a reputation for integrity that served him well in later years. Luella had again lost her hopes for a quiet home. A few years later a catastrophic fire destroyed Stent, and it is today hardly more than a few houses and a roadside bar.

Irving's next adventure took the family to the Trinity River on the West Coast. When Robert was six months old Luella traveled with the two boys by train to Redding, in northern California, and by stage coach from there to Weaverville near the Trinity River. She described the all-day stage coach ride as the dirtiest and dustiest she had ever experienced. In Weaverville she stayed in a boardinghouse with her two boys while Irving was gone for days at a time on horseback inspecting mining properties along the river. After other assignments, ranging from the Bonanza mining area of Nicaragua to Tonopah, Nevada, Irving received an offer from Hollis to return to the Cubo mine. Irving accepted, and he traveled to Guanajuato, Mexico, in January 1910, taking his family with him.

Of this move he wrote to his then-employer from Tonopah:

I wired you this morning as follows — Am resigning. Will mail you full explanation by first mail.

The explanation is that I have received an offer from my old employer Mr. H. L. Hollis of Chicago to return to Guanajuato, and take charge of the Cubo Mining and Milling Company's property.

You may recall that I spent about three and a half years at this property while it was under the management of Mr. Hollis, and occupied a number of positions there ranging from Engineer to Superintendent. The property was bonded to an English company who sent another man out to take charge of it, and I left shortly after because my position became unpleasant. I always hoped that I would have an opportunity to return there, both because I had a great deal of confidence in the worth of the property, and also because it is a much pleasanter place for my wife and family than any camp in the States that I have yet been in.

I had a talk with Mr. Key Pittman, and he agreed with my view entirely. . . . Our present balance in the bank here is $134 and this will be reduced still further by checks already drawn. Therefore it will be necessary to draw what salary I have due.[5]

Their return to Cubo was more than welcome to Luella.

IN HIS FIRST ten years out of Harvard, Irving had moved from mine to mine and country to country, employed, as he wrote, in "a number of positions ranging from Engineer to Superintendent." What kinds of activities and expertise did these occupations call for? Among the papers that he left is a bound "Record Book" with leather backing and corners in which he made notes during his early years. Later, when the Mexican Revolution had forced him to move to the States, he had some articles accepted by *The Engineering and Mining Journal*. These writings are a window to his concerns and abilities. Drawings of steam valves and connecting rods, bracing for mine tunnels and shafts to prevent any collapse that could bring death, plans for headframes above the shaft to hold the pulleys and cables that drew up the skip filled with ore and tipped it into small cars that ran to the mill for crushing show an engineer in charge of developing the mine and keeping it running smoothly.

How much of this had he been taught at Harvard? Probably not very much. The fledgling engineer learned on the job, and much of his success out in a mine site away from libraries and teachers depended on his imagination and ingenuity. However, his Harvard program had stressed the techniques of surveying, and this was an essential skill of the mining engineer. When one entered the main tunnel into the Cubo mine, one came to a place where it made a zigzag to the left. The men who had dug the tunnel had come from opposite directions. Instead of meeting, they had become aware that each team could hear the other at work off to one side, and they had had to dig across to meet each other. The preparatory surveying had been sloppy. Irving was much more careful. On one occasion he had to determine where to sink a shaft in a hillside above the mine so as to hit the tunnel below. The task required sighting out along the mine tunnel to the entrance, then to a hill across the small Cubo River, then back to the hill above the mine, a total distance of several miles with a number of points on the way. To reduce his error, Irving went through the process a number of times. The shaft, when sunk, was one foot off target at the bottom.

However, what separated the sheep from the goats among mining engineers was the capacity to find a new ore vein and judge its worth, for from this came the knowledge to evaluate and develop a mine site. A case in point occurred at the Pozo Azul mine in Costa Rica, which Irving describes in some detail. The mine had two veins, the Pozo Azul vein, which had been exploited, and a west vein. "Before reaching the property it was my belief that the west vein was the larger of the two; this conclusion having been arrived at from a short visit to the mine in 1906 and from what I had been told by others." The west vein was rich on the surface, but driving a drift toward it fifty feet below the surface from the Pozo Azul tunnel turned up nothing. "It did not occur to me at first that there might be no west vein at all. This is now my opinion." Irving judged that the so-called west vein was a continuation of the Pozo Azul vein, which a geological fault had broken in two and pushed forty feet to the west. The fifty-foot-deep drift from the Pozo Azul vein had run parallel to the fault so that it had missed the end of the west vein.[6] College lessons in geology were at work, with the help of an intuitive knowledge developed in the field.

Another indispensable skill was the ability to sample a deposit accurately, for on it depended whether or not developing a mine would be rewarded with profits. Uncovering the scam of the New Calico Mine at Stent established

Irving's eye for sampling. He became recognized as an expert, and his ability was respected by his employers and rewarded with consultancies from other owners.

The difficulty in sampling was that the bodies of ore were uneven, with high-grade masses disseminated through the main body of the ore. In 1916 Irving published an article discussing methods to avoid the common error of obtaining samples that gave too a high a reading. Here Irving's feeling for human nature complemented his technical expertise. In the end, he said, the problem of sampling lay in a psychological process:

> The sampler knows that he is liable to err on the high side, and must take precautions against it. In most cases the barren or low grade ore is harder and more difficult to cut than the richer portion. In his zeal not to slight the lowgrade, considerable time and muscle are expended in cutting this part of the sample. In fact, by the time he has broken off what is really a fair proportion of it, he has expended so much time and force that he unconsciously believes he must have taken too much. In an effort to be fair he will probably add a little more of the better ore and salt the sample.
>
> All hands, including the engineer, about a mine are glad when there is good ore on hand. If the development faces are running well the whole atmosphere around the property is more cheerful. The tension slackens a bit, and good fellowship increases. The mine foreman coming off shift drops into the office and in an unobtrusive manner glances over the assay sheet for the day. If the faces of his headings are sampling well up, he closes the book with a grin.
>
> Is it much to be wondered at, then, that the mine sampler, while aiming to be careful and conservative in his work, also wants to do the fair thing by the ore and unconsciously believes that his very precautions against too high results may cause his samples to run lower than they should, and is influenced thereby?[7]

We can imagine Irving and his small staff in the Cubo mine office.

The ultimate responsibility of a mining engineer consisted of successfully administering a business enterprise, hiring and organizing the staff, purchasing supplies and equipment, effectively running operations, and shipping the final product. He also had to represent the company in dealings with the civil authorities. These activities called for both human and professional capacities, and a commitment and dependability that could be relied on.[8] The Cubo mine offered such a challenge. It was centuries old and the center of an established community.

How extensive an enterprise Irving had to direct is revealed by an accounting that he sent to Hollis in 1916 in connection with a suit against the government of Mexico that will be discussed later. He listed the number of men under his direction at El Cubo during full employment.[9] Most numerous were those working the mine and producing the ore that represented the income of the company. To break the ore, there were two shifts of one hundred fifty drillers. This gave employment to four hundred fifty men, since the Cubo workmen on average worked only four days of the six-day week. This was true also of the laborers who did the mucking; twenty per shift meant a total of sixty wage earners. In addition were the men who did special jobs — timbering, loading the skips, running the hoist and the motor car, and sharpening the tools — all with their helpers, twenty-two men in all. Overseeing them were two bosses per shift. Listed separately were the miners assigned to development, that is to exploring new ore bodies: drillers, muckers, pumpmen, and others, another forty-six men. Outside the mine was the mill at El Tajo somewhat up the Cubo river, where the ore was crushed and the silver precipitate prepared for shipment. It employed fifty-eight men. Mechanics, another blacksmith, and employees in the assay office were twelve more. The office and storehouse gave work to five, there were ten watchmen, and finally the domestic and garden staff, nine men and women in all, of whom the cooks and their helpers were responsible to Luella. Six hundred and seventy two persons would be on the payroll in order to run at full capacity.

Hollis asked Irving also for the average size of the families of these men. Irving's response was conservative. He listed a number of them as single, and the rest with families of three or four. The total number of people supported by the mine, he calculated, was 1992. This figure did not include those whose income came indirectly from the mine, those who raised and sold crops locally, and the owners of the stores and the bar. The Mexican census of 1910 gives the population of the *mineral* El Cubo as 1447. In addition the *minerales* El Tajo de Dolores, where the mill was located, and Villalpando, where the shaft emerged, according to the census, had populations respectively of one hundred twenty-three and five hundred fifty-four. In all, 2,124 mouths.[10] Of course, Irving's figure was an estimate, and the census counts were probably off some, but they confirm what was obvious to the observer: El Cubo and its dependent pueblos existed only because of the mine. It was Irving's job to keep the mine working smoothly, make sure the workmen were trained for their jobs and did them efficiently, and avoid tensions that would hurt production. He reported to Chicago, but he was on his own, the economic lord of El Cubo. The civil lord was the *jefe político* of the village, and the spiritual lord was the priest. In normal times Irving's relations with them would be at a distant formal level, each in his own sphere, but our unfolding story will reveal them sometimes providing mutual aid, but at other times in bitter conflict in the face of trouble.

Mr. Hollis and the investors for whom he administered the Cubo Mining and Milling Company were in the enterprise for the profits they could get. Irving's report tells us the expected returns for a three-month period. The mine, he estimated, produced 150 tons of ore a day, each of which gave 360 grams of silver and 6.5 of gold. Over 90 days, this would add up to some $54,000 of gold and $85,000 of silver. After taking out 10 percent for Mexican federal and state taxes and $65,000 for wages and expenses of running the mine and the mill, the net profit for three months would be $60,000.[11] That is roughly $250,000 per year under ordinary circumstances. If one counted on a 10 percent return on capital, the Cubo mine represented an investment worth two and a half million dollars for the period before World War I.

The mine was modest but successful, and had every indication of a long future ahead of it. A survey of the Mexican mines made in the eighteenth century (now in the Archivo General de la Nación in Mexico City) lists Cubo among the mines of Guanajuato,[12] and the hacienda, with the single-story L-shaped house the Herrs occupied, the ten-foot wall around it, and the heavy gates, was no doubt already there before Mexico became an independent republic. Irving had not hit a bonanza, but he had finally made it professionally, and Luella had the quiet, comfortable home she had longed for in which to bring up her boys.[13]

Notes

1. Undated memorandum in family papers.

2. Harvard Class of 1901. Fourth Report (1916), 211.

3. Luella to her mother, January 30, 1906.

4. Irving's experience at the New Calico Mine is the subject of an autobiographical story that he submitted unsuccessfully to the *Saturday Evening Post* in 1916 and of a personal memoir written many years later, about 1946.

5. Irving to Robert Sawyer, Boston, December 18, 1909.

6. Irving, Record Book, in which he made notes during his early years at the mine (ca. 1901–09), 225–29.

7. Irving Herr, "Some Observations on Sampling," *Engineering and Mining Journal* 102:24 (December 9, 1916), 1016.

8. In October 1912, Irving received from the government of Mexico the concession to the mining rights of two lots adjoining those held by the Cubo Mining and Milling Company. Days later he explained to the civil judge of Guanajuato that he had applied for the concessions in his own name to hasten the proceeding and asked the judge to transfer the title to the company. As Mexico was a land of Hispanic law, Luella had to add her own consent to the transfer. (Copies of concessions and transfer in the office at the Cubo mine, shown to Richard by Ingeniero Oscar Manuel Pérez, March 1996.)

9. Irving to Hollis, September 17, 1916. Irving described the list as "the full crew of Mexican employees that would be used at Cubo for the purpose of running the Tajo mill at full capacity. . . . It is as nearly correct as I can make it, judging from our experience in the past."

10. *División territorial de los Estados Unidos Mexicanos: Estado de Guanajuato* (Mexico: Secretaría de Fomento, Colonización e Industria, 1914), 34, 108, 116.

11. Irving to Hollis, August 11, 1916, and enclosed "Cubo Mining and Milling Co. Calculation of Ore Reserves, Villalpando Mine, Jan. 1, 1916, and Estimate of Returns from Operation of Tajo Mill during April, May and June, 1916." Hollis asked Irving to calculate the expected income for April–June 1916, when the mine was closed because of revolutionary activity. Irving's papers do not include actual figures for the returns for 1910–13, before revolutionary activity affected operations, nor were any found in the Cubo archives.

12. Archivo General de la Nación, Mexico, D.F., Ramo Minería, vol. 11, Informes sobre estado de Minería, minas de Guanajuato (1773), fol. 21 verso.

This lists three mines at the Real de el Cubo, all abandoned at the time. Dated October 22, 1773.

13. We do not know how much Irving was earning. The mine provided income for his house and domestic help. The Cubo books show him drawing occasionally on the company account for a total of about 2000 pesos a year. (Archivo, Ledger No. 4, 1909 ff.) The rest of his salary, of which we have no record, was deposited into a U.S. bank.

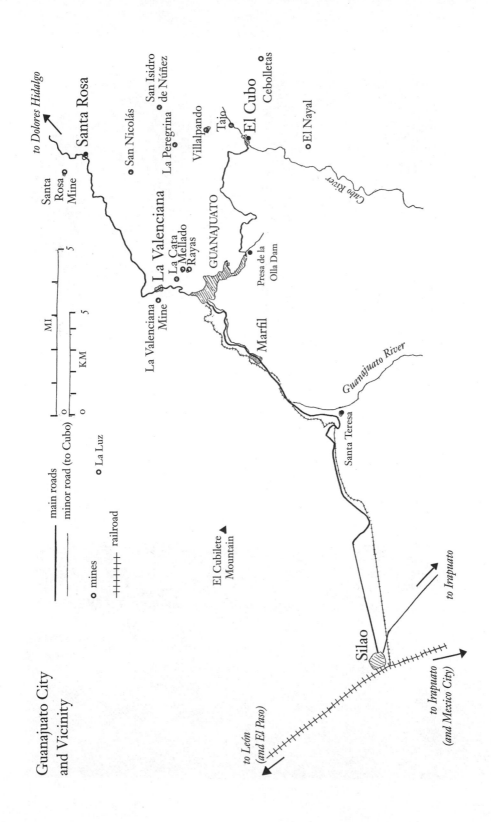

Guanajuato City
and Vicinity

main roads
minor road (to Cubo)
railroad

mines
railroad

La Luz

El Cubilete
Mountain

MI
5

KM
5

to Dolores Hidalgo

Santa Rosa

Santa
Rosa
Mine

San Nicolás

San Isidro
de Núñez

La Peregrina

Villalpando

Tajo

El Cubo

Cebolletas

El Nayal

Cubo River

La Valenciana

La Cata
Mellado
Rayas

La Valenciana
Mine

GUANAJUATO

Presa de la
Olla Dam

Marfil

Guanajuato River

Santa Teresa

Silao

to Irapuato

to León
(and El Paso)

to Irapuato
(and Mexico City)

Irving Herr, ca. 1901

Luella Parker Winship, senior at Mount
Holyoke College, 1902

Guanajuato, the state capital.
The barrel roof of the Hidalgo Market (1910) and
the massive square eighteenth-century granary,
the Alhóndiga de Granaditas, are prominent.

The Cubo house
"The house was strung out in an L shape . . . with a tiled veranda that ran its length on the inside of the L."

Irving and Luella, expecting their first child, in the Cubo garden, 1904

Head sampler and three peons, Cubo patio, 1904

"The water burro brought drinking water
from the spring up on the mountain."

Angela, our cook, 1914

*Irving's return
to Cubo,
August 1914*
"Everyone travels
first class now —
at least there is
only one kind of
tickets sold."

Robert, October 1912
"It was some time before we could
reach the stirrups."

The Cubo Sunday market
"The upper gate (of the hacienda) opened out on
the town marketplace in front of the church, but it
was always kept bolted and chained except on special fiesta days."

Angela, our cook, 1914

*Irving's return
to Cubo,
August 1914*
"Everyone travels
first class now —
at least there is
only one kind of
tickets sold."

Robert, October 1912
"It was some time before we could
reach the stirrups."

The Cubo Sunday market
"The upper gate (of the hacienda) opened out on
the town marketplace in front of the church, but it
was always kept bolted and chained except on special fiesta days."

The ride from San Luis Potosí to Queretaro, August 1914
"I ran across Mr. Gilmore and two other Americans from the power plant . . . We got into the rear of the train — an ordinary freight car." (Photo by Irving; Gilmore and Fisher in the doorway, left and right)

Luella and the boys return to Cubo
Irving photographs them on the Mexican National Railroad nearing Silao, Christmas Day, 1914.

CHAPTER 3

Madero

The city of Guanajuato rests in a hollow close to the
Continental Divide in Mexico's central mountain
range, and is flanked by the "Veta Madre" or Mother
Lode of silver, harboring many mines scattered along
the hillsides. The famous Guanajuato mines of Rayas
and La Valenciana, opened by the Spaniards in the
1700s, have been described as among the richest in
the world, and over the years the area is said to have
yielded close to one billion dollars, or about one third
of the world's production of silver. The Cubo mine was
on a vein tributary to the mother lode.

In 1910 Guanajuato was probably a city of about
35,000.* As a flourishing Spanish colonial city and
capital of the state it was well garrisoned with federal
troops and well developed, boasting many ornate
eighteenth-century churches and monasteries, the
government palace, a mint dating from 1812, a national
college, and an ornate opera house, the Teatro Juárez,
built in the 1890s. There were many well-to-do Mexicans in banking, mining, commerce, law, education,
and, of course, in government. And there was a "foreign

---

*The 1910 census figure was 35,682. There is little reason to
believe that it was less accurate than most censuses. See
*División Territorial de los Estados Unidos Mexicanos: Estado de
Guanajuato* (Mexico: Secretaría de Fomento, Colonización e
Industria, 1914), 11.

colony" of about two hundred twenty-five, including families, consisting of Americans, English, northern Europeans and others, who were the operators and managers of foreign interests in the mines, the electric power company, banking, and development. Mexican produce and manufactured goods were plentiful. Imports of fancy groceries, wines and liquors, and other delicacies for the tables of the well-to-do were available at the Canastillo de Flores (Basket of Flowers), where the distinguished Spanish gentleman, Don Francisco, welcomed customers in his shop on the Plaza Mayor. Tram cars hauled by mules circulated through the narrow cobbled streets, and one traveled to the neighboring mines on horseback over the wagon roads used for hauling freight.

Luella and Irving became active in the Guanajuato foreign colony and on weekends might ride their horses into town for a party or a game of cards, staying overnight with friends and leaving the two boys with the servants at the mine. At neighboring mines — El Tajo, Peregrina, or Pingüico — exchanges were more frequent and at times when there were other foreign children the boys would be included. During big fiestas such as Holy Week all four Herrs might take the seven-mile ride into the city and stay for a day or two at the Woods Hotel, where accommodations were certainly adequate. It was a good life for the foreigners, and for the better-off Mexicans as well.

In the mines the peon was a member of the laboring class, bound to his job by his poverty. He worked for a meager wage and lived in the surrounding area in an adobe hut with a dirt floor. At the end of the week he paid his dues to the Church and spent what little was left on corn and tequila. If he was lucky he would find a small plot, maybe 20 feet by 20 feet, on the hillside by his "house" where he would plant some corn in the rainy season to supplement his fare. He was basically a peaceful soul so long as he was fed and housed, however poorly. Centuries of domination by the Spaniards and their successors had taught him the futility of raising his voice in protest. On a city street, when he met someone of a higher class, he would automatically doff his straw sombrero and step off the narrow sidewalk to let the other pass.

Although with hindsight we know that trouble had been brewing for some time under the surface of the Mexico of Porfirio Díaz, when Irving and Luella Herr returned to Cubo at the beginning of 1910 Mexico still had an air of order and the future seemed assured. Presidential elections were in the offing, but the reelection of Díaz was assumed, and, following a brief recession, the economic indicators were good. Appearances were deceptive, however, as Irving and Luella were to discover forcibly in the following years. On April 15, 1910, Francisco I. Madero was nominated to challenge Díaz in the coming elections scheduled for June. Arrested for his audacity and then allowed to go into exile in Texas, Madero, now in San Antonio, declared the reelection of Díaz invalid and proceeded to organize a rebellion against the Díaz government. His call was picked up by various of the revolutionary cells that had been organized by Madero's supporters and by opportunists in different parts of Mexico — notably by governors of some northern states, by Pascual Orozco and Francisco (Pancho) Villa in Chihuahua, and by Emiliano Zapata in the southern states of Morelos and Oaxaca.

Madero crossed the border from the United States in February 1911 to direct his revolution with a small force of less then two hundred men, but he had the support of Villa and Orozco. On May 10, 1911, the forces of Villa and Orozco, restless and impatient for action, took Ciudad Juárez on the United States border from the Federals (the forces of the central government), acquiring customs revenues, opening the way for arms and ammunition from the north, and starting the revolution on its destructive path. Railroad trains were commandeered to carry men and horses and equipment. After the fall of Ciudad Juárez, Orozco and Villa moved rapidly south along the railroad line as Federal garrisons at key points along the way swung over to Madero's side. On May 21, 1911, the dictator Díaz resigned and proceeded with a prearranged plan — a well-prepared escape with family and possessions via railroad to Veracruz and thence to Paris. Madero's forces continued their rapid movement south on the central railroad, to shouts of "¡Viva Madero!" as they went, and on June 7, 1911, Madero entered Mexico City a conquering hero.

The early revolutionary activity had skirted Guanajuato. Its foreign colony felt no immediate threat to themselves, but the news from other parts of the country was not reassuring. Shortly before the resignation of Díaz, Irving Herr wrote from the Cubo mine to Luella, who had taken their two sons on a visit to her parents' home in Somerville:

[May 18 and 19, 1911] Monday night, [the 15th] a band of ladrones visited Peregrina [a mine half an hour away by horseback] and burned a store or two and robbed, but they did not bother the mine or the mill. Two or three of the robbers were killed. Last night we got a telephone message from somewhere that one hundred fifty Maderistas were on their way to Cubo. Before this message came, Atenedoro came up to the house just as I was finishing supper and said a band of robbers was just coming down off the hill into Cubo. He was scared stiff and made a bee-line into the mine with what little money there was here. The Jefe politico also lit out for Guanajuato posthaste.

We Americans got together in front of the office and I guess were a pretty nervous bunch. We waited around until 9:30 and nothing happened, although we were told by phone that a bunch of about fifty were passing through Villalpando toward Cubo. I sent our women and servants into the mine and got the Jefatura in Guanajuato on the phone and reported what was about to occur. We waited until 11:30 and nobody came. About 4 A.M. a bunch of cavalry reached Cubo from Guanajuato and scoured Villalpando and surroundings but could locate nothing.

On the following day Irving wrote from Guanajuato:

[May 19, 1911] Today the first train came in from Silao [railroad junction for a short branch line to Guanajuato] since last Sunday [May 14]. The Maderistas got control of Silao and had Guanajuato cut off all week. I came in town this morning partly to hear news and partly to get a license to carry arms and on a little other business. I am trying to arrange today for some gendarmes to go out with the payroll tomorrow.

The installation of Madero's provisional government in Mexico City brought an end to the disturbances, and it was thought that business could return to normal. Luella and her two sons returned to Mexico in July, coming by steamship to Veracruz, where they were met by Irving. Back in their home at the Cubo mine, Luella wrote to her sister Edith in the States:

[August 4, 1911] Irving met us when we landed [in Veracruz] at 8 A.M. The city of Vera Cruz was a very pleasant surprise to me. It was very clean and attractive for a little while — I imagine there wouldn't be much to do there after the first day. Also the hotel was clean and the food good. We took the evening train and went as far as Orizaba where we spent the night. There, there is a first class hotel, French and very foreign and charming. . . . We wanted to ride to Mexico city by day so we took the train from Orizaba at 10:25 A.M., and at 12:30 we ran into a landslide and were held up until 7 P.M. with no luncheon (the eating station was just the other side of the slide — about 10 miles away — and there was no Pullman on our train). We landed in Mexico City at 1:30 the next morning. We spent the day in Mexico City visiting friends, and took the train that night to Silao as I had no desire to stay longer with the boys.

Trouble is expected everywhere throughout the Republic during elections but it is not expected to take an antiforeign turn.

Being an idealist and a visionary rather than a practical man, Madero insisted on a free election for the presidency, and in the meantime he disbanded his revolutionary armies and allowed the government to continue under the Díaz bureaucracy, even allowing the defeated Federal forces to remain in control. By the time Madero was elected president and assumed office on November 6, 1911, opposition groups had formed to defend the interests of the landowners and the Church.

For the moment life in the Guanajuato mines continued serene. Business was normal and Luella rode her horse freely over the surrounding mountains visiting the wives of other foreign managers at nearby mines. At this time she began to keep the first of two five-year diaries (1912–1916, 1917–1921). Brief entries read:

1912 - January
16 — Mrs. Truax [wife of the local mill superintendent] and I rode over to Peregrina in the afternoon and made ten-minute calls on Mrs. Seifert and Mrs. Hopkins.
[Today's reader must pause to realize that these American ladies so far from home addressed their neighbors as "Mrs."!]
24 — Irving and I went to town in the afternoon and I did some shopping while he closed a deal for some land.

However, in the north, Pascual Orozco, dissatisfied with a secondary role in the Madero government and supported by the landed interests, was plotting a counterrevolution against Madero's regime, and on March 3, 1912, openly rebelled. Early in February, as reports came in of Orozco's men attacking various properties across northern Mexico as far south as San Luis Potosí, foreigners became uneasy. On February 7, the Herrs were advised that the men in the foreign colony of Guanajuato were sending out their wives and children the following day. Irving and Luella decided that she and the boys should go too.

The railroad line from Mexico City to the border divides one hundred fifty miles to the northwest at Celaya. From here the shorter line goes east of the continental divide through San Luis Potosí and Monterrey to Nuevo Laredo on the Rio Grande. The longer line goes to the west of the divide through Irapuato, Aguascalientes, Zacatecas, Torreón, and Chihuahua to Ciudad Juárez, across the river from El Paso, Texas. Guanajuato lies between the two lines, but closer to the western route. It is tied to it by a fifteen-mile spur that takes off from Silao, north of Irapuato. To take the eastern route north to the United States, one had to go back toward Mexico City to Celaya and change trains, or, in an emergency, one could go across the mountains by horse about thirty miles and get the train to Laredo at Dolores Hidalgo. The western line went through Orozco territory, so the decision was made for Luella to go south to Celaya and take the eastern line. She and the boys went via Nuevo Laredo to San Antonio, Texas, where she wrote her mother:

[February 10, 1912] We came away on twenty-four hours notice — hadn't thought of such a thing five minutes earlier. Practically all the American ladies around Guanajuato came this time. . . . I shall stay here awhile and await developments. What we all fear is U.S. intervention. It seems inevitable to us and then the saints preserve all the husbands left behind! It may be a needless scare and Madero may prove competent to handle the situation but he hasn't yet shown any signs of it.

[I was five years old at the time. My hair was in a "Dutch" cut, bangs and long over the ears, and my only real recollection of San Antonio was when we boarded a streetcar and the conductor asked me whether I was a boy or a girl. Mother saw the point and that afternoon I had a boy's haircut. Otherwise, although we knew what was going on, John and I had no real worries. I can remember no sense of fear or alarm coming down from our parents, and to us every move was an adventure.]

From the mine at Cubo, Irving wrote to Luella in San Antonio:

[February 27, 1912] The citizens of El Cubo have organized a home guard—about forty men so far and they expect to get about eighty before they are through. The Governor has given them so far fifteen old single-fire rifles and they expect more. This guard is to defend the town against bandits. A watchman is stationed every night in the church tower and some of the guard patrol the town each night. It sounds very businesslike.

Today's paper states that conditions around Torreon are becoming critical and it is expected that Ciudad Juarez will surrender to a rebel army very soon without making a fight. This army then expects to start a march south toward Mexico City. At the same time the Federals [now Madero's forces] seem to be getting the best of the Zapatistas [in the south]. The situation is very puzzling, but I hope we can see our way to have you come back within the month.

Luella wrote from San Antonio:

[March 1, 1912] Mail continues to come daily over the Laredo route— that by which I came out. The El Paso route has been out of commission for a month. [Orozco's doing.]

Irving, to Luella from Cubo:

[March 5, 1912] The war news is coming faster now, and the following has become established. Chihuahua now is held by the rebels [now opposing Madero!] who have been joined by Orozco, and it is said that Orozco with 5,000 men is headed south. Torreon is surrounded and has had no railroad communication for nineteen days. The Minister of War [General José González Salas] has resigned and is going to take the field on Madero's side in the north of Mexico.

Another carload of American women is leaving Guanajuato tonight. Madero has issued a call for volunteers and this is in the form of posters to be circulated all over Mexico. Things seem to be getting interesting and I wonder what the finish will be.

The Americans in Guanajuato have a plan all ready in case of an emergency, which could not be detailed over the phone—all anyone talks about in town is guns and where to get them. . . . I think the

Guanajuato bunch is more scared than there is any reason to be. Out here things seem to be going on the same.

Madero sent Victoriano Huerta, who had been a general in Díaz's army, against Orozco. He proved more effective than González Salas, Madero's Minister of War, who ended by committing suicide in Torreón, leaving Huerta to face Orozco. But things were quiet in Guanajuato and Luella returned to Cubo via Laredo, arriving on March 19 without incident and on schedule. All was not well, however. From her diary:

1912 - March

21 — Find things in a good deal of a mess. My trunks arrived and I had several things stolen out of one.

28 — Federals were defeated in four days of fighting north of Torreon. Things look rather bad.

1912 - April

11 — American conductors and engineers are leaving the service of the Mexican railroads.

12 — No mail because the Guanajuato-Silao train was held up by bandits last night and robbed and the conductor murdered. A vicious business.

13 — Papers and mail arrived to our surprise as we understood the railroad refused to run trains on the Guanajuato branch for the present.

15 — The Rurales (four) left Cubo and I feel uneasy because of the holdup of the Guanajuato-Silao train.

17 — Five Winchester riot guns arrived for the hacienda against a possible holdup.

20 — Guanajuato people are worried over possible U.S. intervention — it makes us all uneasy.

28 — The Mexican Herald is full of intervention talk and Irving said he thought I better go to the States again, but we decided to wait a few days.

30 — I feel nervous and worried over this intervention talk and am wondering if I ought to leave the country again.

However, she did not leave, and on the same day, April 30, she and Mrs. Truax once again "rode over to Peregrina to see Mrs. Hopkins." On

May 6 she and Mrs. Truax rode in to Guanajuato "to do some shopping." Her diary continues:

1912 - May

11 — Reports that a big battle is on around Torreon [about 350 miles to the north].

12 — Another holdup of a train just north of Silao.

13 — Our four Rurales have been sent down to Silao to join a force to hunt down the bandits.

14 — Newspapers are full of a big battle north of Torreon — so far reported to be a Federal victory. Rumor has it the Rurales met the bandits and were defeated. Bandits were too many for them.

On May 25 news was received of "a big Federal victory at Rellanos," where Orozco was defeated by Madero's forces under General Huerta and Pancho Villa. Apparently the Federal government maintained good order in the interior, because one week later on June 1st Irving left Guanajuato for Mexico City "to buy himself some clothes," returning at 9 P.M. on June 4 as "per schedule much to my joy."

Heavy rains in June 1912 did more damage in central Mexico than revolutionaries. Mines were flooded, and on July 1 Luella reported no mail had arrived because the railroad was washed out between Guanajuato and Mexico City.

Early in 1912 Pancho Villa had joined Huerta's campaign against Orozco, and in September they ran Orozco north across the U.S. border. Huerta became alarmed at Villa's growing strength and popularity and had him arrested on a minor charge and sent to prison in Mexico City. If Madero sensed that Huerta himself was getting too strong, he was in no position to remove him. Having temporarily quieted the threat from the northern revolutionaries, he was faced almost immediately by an attack from the Right. On October 16, 1912, Félix Díaz, a nephew of Don Porfirio, declared himself a rebel and occupied Veracruz.

Luella's diary reports:

1912 - October

17 — Received news that General Felix Diaz has started a new revolution and has captured Vera Cruz — i.e. the Federal garrison there went over to him voluntarily.

Also on October 17, the *Mexican Herald*, an English-language newspaper published in Mexico City, printed a Manifesto of Félix Díaz, stating: "La Tribuna, a new independent afternoon daily, yesterday printed what purported to be the proclamation of General Díaz to the Mexican people," and followed with the text of the "proclamation." The first paragraphs are enough, but illuminating:

> Mexicans—in these moments of supreme trial for the country, I come to lift my voice to ask the help of all men of good intent, who may be desirous of bringing about among us the rebirth of an era of peace and concord.
>
> It is no longer possible to bear in silence such ills as have originated in and continue to be brought upon the republic by the unspeakable administration, the outgrowth of the revolutionary movement of 1910.
>
> Stripped now of the mask of democracy and altruism which it used meanly to deceive the people, [etc., etc.] . . . .

On the same day, October 16, 1912, the Boston Red Sox defeated the New York Giants 3 to 2 to win the World Series of 1912, an item that also made the front page of the *Mexican Herald*. Luella continues:

1912 - October

18 — We're all interested in the new revolution and hoping it will win out.

24 — News received that the revolution of Felix Diaz collapsed as suddenly as it sprang to life. Vera Cruz is in the hands of the Federals once more.

[Which is interesting, since it was the Federal garrison in Veracruz that "went over" to Díaz "voluntarily" one week earlier. And some three months later on February 9, 1913, according to the history books, Díaz was "released from jail" in Mexico City by the army group leading the revolt against Madero. We might well wonder whether Félix Díaz may have had an "understanding" with Huerta, and whether perhaps Huerta sent a message to Díaz in Veracruz, telling him to bide his time.]

Although rebels had not yet been cleared out of Chihuahua, Huerta now appeared to be in control and business in Guanajuato continued as normal.

The Herrs planned a vacation with Luella's family in the States and left Guanajuato on November 25, 1912. They sailed from Veracruz on November 29 on board the steamship *Esperanza*, and returned aboard the S. S. *Morro Castle*, landing in Veracruz on January 11, 1913. Although there were "stories of Zapatistas," they left for Mexico City at 7 P.M. on the same day, and after a day of visiting in the city reached Guanajuato without incident at 6 A.M. on January 14. One trunk was missing, which went to Guadalajara and finally came back to Guanajuato on January 22. "Praise be!" wrote Luella to her mother three weeks later. "Everything was in it and in good condition."

Shortly afterward the situation in Mexico City began to deteriorate. Here the Díaz sympathizers, including army men, were working out a plot to overthrow Madero, and on February 9, 1913 attempted a coup d'état but were unsuccessful. The rebels took possession of the Cuidadela, the midcity arsenal, and from there battled government forces with artillery and rifle fire in the streets for ten days. Huerta, the former Díaz general, was in command of Madero's government troops, and it appears that he deliberately prolonged the fighting to create an emergency and manipulated behind the scenes in favor of the rebels. On February 18, Huerta turned on Madero, had him imprisoned, and four days later arranged his murder on false charges of "attempted escape," the well-known Mexican *ley fuga* (law of the flight, i.e., shot trying to escape). Huerta thereupon assumed the office of President of Mexico.

Luella's diary reports:

1913 - February

4 — Newspapers full of revolution and bandits.

9 — Mexico City said to be in a state of riot — and the military prisoners, including Felix Diaz, to have escaped.

11 — Exciting revolutionary news from Mexico City, but no newspapers. Robbery in Don Pedro's store in Cubo last night and ten "loafers" sent to jail today.

12 — We are all excitement over the state of affairs in Mexico City. Received two Mexican Heralds, of the 10th and 11th. Diaz and Madero preparing to fight in the heart of the city.

13 — No more news from Mexico City, except that they are fighting there with artillery and doing much damage.

Despite the fighting in Mexico City, things continued as normal around Guanajuato and order prevailed. Of the Huerta violence in Mexico City Luella wrote to her mother from Cubo:

[February 16, 1913] We are getting uneasy to know when and where it will end. It is lasting too long and the fighting with artillery in a capital city of a country without giving women, children, and noncombatants warning to get out is barbarous. The feeling hereabouts seems to be that it is simple bull-headedness on the part of Madero — though he has more support from the army than anyone would have predicted. But we can none of us get over the fact that they are really bombarding each other in the very center of Mexico City!

Our news is too limited to satisfy us. This is Sunday evening and our last authentic news is a Thursday morning Mexican Herald — which by the way is the only newspaper in the City that is even attempting to get out an issue. Rumors are very plentiful but no one has any way of sifting the true from the false.

Every day we hope to hear of some definite outcome. If not, the U.S. troops will be here — of that I feel convinced — for the present condition in the City can't be allowed to continue indefinitely. But I am not at all sure now that there would be any resistance to U.S. troops and the thought doesn't worry me as it did a year ago. The rest of the country is strangely quiet — all awaiting the outcome of things in the City. We are getting daily mail from the north, as always, and everything here is peaceful as one could wish.

Her diary notes:

1913 - February
18 — News came late in the evening that Madero is made a prisoner by General Huerta.
19 — General Huerta is made provisional President of Mexico.
21 — Mexican Heralds succeeded in coming through again and we all rejoice at the chance of getting authentic news.
23 — Madero and Pino Suarez murdered (?) in the night which has caused much excitement — also indignation.

25— John and I went to town. Found people disgusted with the state of
    things in Mexico.

Madero sought to bring about change by legal means without disrupting
the nation. His targets were wealthy landowners and the Church; he sought
to redistribute their resources and their wealth among the lower classes. Society was little changed, business was not seriously affected, railroad, telegraph and mail services continued in an orderly manner, and police protection was maintained to a large extent, except in the north where Pascual
Orozco was in revolt, disrupting communication above Torreón and causing
concern to foreigners in the central parts of Mexico.

Madero tried. But he was not equal to the rough and tumble of revolutionary politics and upheaval. His backers duped him. Orozco proved to be a
turncoat of the first order. Having been among the first to give armed support to Madero's cause, he soon became a general. A year later in 1912 he was
in revolt against Madero, only to be driven out of Chihuahua by Huerta.
Huerta likewise proved extraordinarily "unreliable." It would seem that he
played along with Madero as long as necessary to work up a covert organization adequate to ensure Madero's overthrow in favor of a return to the social
order of Porfirio Díaz and protection of the vested interests.

CHAPTER 4

Reminiscences II

Before covering the details of later revolutionary activities as seen by Irving and Luella, it may be of interest to see how they appeared to me as a boy of eight or nine. As I remember it, the political revolution in Mexico rocked along, and Dad set up a code with the mine owners in Chicago who were in close touch with Washington. If anything developed that looked like trouble for us, the owners were to wire Dad: "You may draw on Chicago for funds," and we were to get out — fast. But meanwhile, of course, Chicago knew little about what was really going on. Bands of revolutionaries were organizing in the mountains north of Mexico City, all the way from Guanajuato to Chihuahua, under various leaders, and finally Francisco (Pancho) Villa and Venustiano Carranza emerged as the two main contestants. Before it was settled they chased each other in and out of the hills around our mine and the neighboring towns in the state of Guanajuato as well as farther north. Chased is a good word, because if the Carranzistas were occupying a town and word came that the Villistas were moving in, they would load up their pack animals, pots and pans, camp women, and all, and take to the hills in the opposite direction to wait for a chance when they could "strike" back to better advantage. And vice versa.

When a band was running short of food or tequila they would raid our mining town, galloping in over the cobblestoned streets and shooting pistols into the air.

With all the lights out and the curtains drawn we would sneak a look out our window in the back wall of the hacienda and watch them entering the stores across the street, taking what they wanted. The hacienda gates were locked and barred. But there were times when a larger force would come, led by officers in some sort of uniform, looking for supplies. There was always some advance warning of this from hill people who had spotted them coming hours before. Our horses and saddles would be taken from the corral and hidden in a small garden behind a wall near the mine entrance, all but one or two that could be spared if it came to that. Guns and ammunition were likewise hidden except those that were carried by the men. The foreign women and children (ourselves and one or two other families that were working for Dad from time to time) would be rushed into the mine tunnel, sometimes as far as the compressor room if there was time, and Dad and his men would wait outside in the hacienda for the inevitable visit. I can remember being awakened from a sound sleep in the middle of the night, having a blanket wrapped around me as there was no time to dress, and being taken into the mine on the motor before I knew what it was all about. I must have sensed some of Mother's concern but I don't remember being frightened. It was quite an adventure.

If such a visit was in the daytime Dad would leave the lower gate open. Business as usual. And the officers of these groups were usually courteous — courteous but insistent. The first problem for our men, in order to have the right answer to the usual question "¿*Quién vive?*" (Whose side are you on?), was to make sure in advance whether the visitors were Villistas or Carranzistas. (One answered "¡*Viva Villa!*" or "¡*Viva Carranza!*") It was very important to be on the right side, and loyal mine employees would find this out and pass the word. Dad would ask that they leave their men in the patio of the hacienda and invite the officers up to the office, or even to the house if they seemed sufficiently important, where he would bring out the cognac. They needed horses and guns, to support the revolution of course, and they must count on their friends to help. "But alas, *mi comandante,* so many have already been taken, and I must have at least one horse to carry on the business of the mine." And so the bargaining would begin. More than once they settled over the cognac for one horse and a saddle, or perhaps an old Mauser rifle and a few rounds of ammunition, or a few hundred pesos to help the cause along. I doubt that there were ever any serious threats and certainly no gunfire.

But to make sure that there would be none, Dad and his group of three or four Americans and Englishmen made a great point of target practice with rifles, good Winchester .30-30s. Every Sunday they would march out of the hacienda to the top of a hill outside where everyone could see, and practice with their rifles against the wall of the Panteón, or cemetery. And it was well known that they were excellent shots.

As the revolutionary armies grew and became better organized each side took to printing its own currency. It was better to pay for things that were "requisitioned" if you wanted the support of the people, and the printing press was a simple solution. So we had Villa money and Carranza money. All hard money had disappeared. At the pay window every Saturday the miners could choose either Villa money or Carranza money. The paymaster had both. Nearly all took Villa money, which was all right because they could spend it in the town. With our cook, Angela, it was another matter. She chose Villa money too, but she was saving all her money for the day when she could return to her home and family and their pigs and chickens, near Mexico City. She often spoke of them. As it finally turned out, Carranza won with the help of political pressure from the United States. Villa became a bandit and her savings were worthless. But to the people of Guanajuato, Villa was the hero who had broken down the Establishment, who would lift the burden from the peons and give them back the land. We learned his marching song:

Con las barbas de Carranza	With Carranza's beard
Voy hacer una toquilla	I'll make a hat band
P'a poner en el sombrero	To put on the hat
Del Señor Don Pancho Villa.	Of Señor Don Pancho Villa.
La Cucaracha, la Cucaracha	The cockroach
Ya no puede caminar	Can't go any further
Porque no tiene, porque le falta	Because he has no
Marijuana que chupar.	Marijuana to puff on.

On April 21, 1914, the telegram came: "You may draw on Chicago for funds." We packed what we could, including two trunks full of Mother's choicest possessions, wedding silver, linens, and other things that she would not want to part with. At least these would be saved. When we got to town we found that other foreigners were leaving too. The word was that President Wilson had ordered the U.S. Marines into Veracruz. The Gringos were enemies of Mexico. And so it was decided that we would leave on the morning train with an English family, the Wallaces, and that we would be English too. Mr. Wallace would do the talking; he spoke excellent Spanish with a fine British accent.

The morning train was quite late in leaving — so many wished to go, and there was so little room. But finally we took off, with our trunks checked and carefully watched to see that they got aboard. We traveled down to the junction at Silao and on to Irapuato to wait for the Mexico City train. When it came after several hours more it was already full, but we crowded in, too. However, before it got underway the car door opened, a squad of soldiers moved in with their guns at the ready, and ordered everyone out. We were escorted up the station platform with Mother, John holding her by one hand and I by the other. Dad was with Mr. Wallace, who was sizing up the situation. Dad sensed that the officer in charge had had a few drinks, and at length said, "Where are you taking us?"

"To the jail."

"Why?"

"Those are my orders, Señor."

Whether by convincing him that we were English, with his clearly British accent, or by sweet talk with a little "grease" (after the manner of such negotiations), I wouldn't know, but before we reached the end of the platform the order came to put us back on the train and in the Pullman which had come through from the west. It was late at night and before long John and I were stretched out on two Pullman seats given up by some of the men who had to stand in the aisle. We were assured afterwards that there had been gringos hung from telegraph poles along the way.

I remember the Hotel Geneve in Mexico City, where Mother paced up and down the lobby. Dad had gone out to check on their trunks, and Mother was beside herself. Where is Dad? He should be back by now. Maybe he hasn't heard that today's train will be the last to take any foreigners out of the city to Veracruz. Why doesn't he hurry? When he came he had heard all right, but he said, "We can't take that train unless we leave the trunks behind. I couldn't find them in the baggage room. No sign of them anywhere."

And Mother said, "Damn the trunks. Let's get out of here." The Wallaces went too.

Part of the way to Veracruz a bridge had been burned out and a section of track torn up, but with a burst of efficiency that was hardly expected the railroad had brought up another train to meet us on the other side of the break. We crossed on foot to the other side, carrying our bags, and went on our way.

I remember pulling into the station at Veracruz, where we were met on the platform by U.S. Marines. One of them gave me a Hershey bar and I felt much better. This had not been a happy time. The marines lined up the refugees, for we were certainly that now, and escorted us through the cobblestone streets to one of the hotels. There was one room for perhaps ten or twelve of us, and we spread out on the floor while some of the ladies heated food over Sterno canned heat. In the very early dawn the marines came for us again. More marching through the streets, a guard stopping us every few blocks with "Who goes there?" just like in the storybooks. At the docks a motorboat took us out to the harbor where we boarded the Ward Line steamer *Mexico* that was standing by to rescue people. Several days we stood by. We had our suitcases, and that was all. And when we landed in New Orleans some time later, Dad had to wire Chicago for funds.

We went back to the mine again before a year was out because things had quieted down momentarily. Mother found everything in our house at the hacienda just as she had left it. Nothing had been disturbed. Our cook, Angela, had seen to that. She would let no one touch anything of the Señora's and all we had lost was what had been packed in the trunks.

CHAPTER 5

Huerta

A few weeks after he had dispatched Madero, at the formal opening of the Mexican Congress in Mexico City on April 1, 1913, Huerta addressed that body in glowing words, here quoted in part from the *Mexican Herald* of April 2, under the headline "Ovation Follows Plain Soldierly Talk by Huerta":

> . . . the chief executive delivered an informal, man to man, straight from the shoulder talk. It was an address to the Mexican people and was meant to carry farther than the walls of the chamber of deputies. . . . He did not address them as deputies and senators but as brothers, Mexicans, and fellow citizens. . . . [He said,] "We are face to face with a mission committed to us. The eyes of the nation, of all humanity are upon us. We are, and we may as well admit it now as later, in the presence of God. . . .
>
> "The force of circumstances has placed me at the head of this nation, but I assure you that the proudest moment of my life will be when I turn that responsibility over to a man duly elected by the Mexican people, and again can take up the sword like a good soldier to uphold the honor of the fatherland. . . .
>
> "My friends, I call upon you to lay aside all personal aims and grievances, and work with me for the welfare of this our fatherland, unfortunate as she is rich. . . .

"Now, amid these difficulties, these dangers and reefs about the ship of state, I swear to you," and General Huerta struck his breast with his white-gloved hand, "on my honor as a man and a soldier, that there will be peace in the republic though it be bought even at the cost of my life." As the chief executive turned to leave the tribune, a storm of applause burst from the floor and galleries, and from the doorway came the first strains of the national hymn. . . .

Interesting, from a man who later escaped to Spain with what remained of the federal treasury. General Pascual Orozco, whom Huerta, as Madero's man, had run out of Chihuahua in 1912, was among those in the Chamber of Deputies contributing to the ovation for Huerta.

Victoriano Huerta was an Indian (probably with a dash of Spanish blood) who had come up through the ranks. He first appeared on the revolutionary scene as a general in the army of Porfirio Díaz. When Díaz prepared his escape from Mexico City in May 1911, it was Huerta who ably assisted in making the arrangements and who bid Díaz *buena suerte* when he boarded his special train for Veracruz.

Soon after Huerta's assumption of the presidency, opposition to him developed from revolutionary followers of Madero. In the north, Venustiano Carranza, one-time Minister of War for Madero and now Governor of Coahuila, declared against Huerta and proclaimed himself "First Chief" of revolutionary forces, enlisting support from disgruntled leaders in other parts of Mexico. On March 25, 1913 he promulgated his revolutionary program in his Plan of Guadalupe and proclaimed a new party of reform, the Constitucionalistas. Alvaro Obregón in Sonora would lead Carranza's forces there. Pancho Villa, a strong believer in Madero's cause and committed to improving the lot of the Mexican poor (of which he was one), took up arms against Huerta's Federals in Chihuahua and soon joined Carranza's party. In the south, Emiliano Zapata would not accept Huerta and continued fighting for Madero's principles.

Irving had now spent nearly eight years at the Cubo mine, and Luella had been with him all but the first three. Irving was now thirty-six, Luella thirty-three; John and Robert were going on nine and seven. During their years outside Mexico they had settled down nowhere—the longest stay was in

Stent, California, where Robert was born. If they could call any place "home," it was the L-shaped house inside the wall of the hacienda of the Cubo mine. But a home in a foreign land in turmoil could be very fragile, as the next years would show.

During March 1913, as Huerta prepared his address to the congress in Mexico City and Carranza was writing his Plan of Guadalupe in Coahuila, conditions in central Mexico were reasonably stable and the foreign colony of Guanajuato was not seriously concerned. Luella wrote from Cubo to her family:

[March 17, 1913] Mail continues to be minus — the line has been cut again and we are quite hopeless. We have just come home from a very gay time in Guanajuato. Saturday evening we were in a box at the opera, and it was really a good troupe — Spanish of course — and the music and costumes were very good.*

THE STORY CONTINUES in her diary:

1913 – March
23 — Still no U.S. mail and revolution in the north grows worse.
30 — At last — after 31 days — came a few letters.

1913 - April
2 — A few magazines came at last. More letters coming in since March 30.
3 — Peons started roughhousing in town in the evening — mildly — and Irving sent to town for soldiers.
13 — Mail from the United States stopped coming again and now there's no communication with the United States by rail.
14 — Exchange rates have gone up so high as to be prohibitive. Business in this country is rapidly going to the dickens.
15 — Mr. Gisholt [the Cubo Company accountant] left to take a position in Guerrero — we hope he'll be back, however, as that part of Mexico is full of revolution [Zapata territory].

---

*Unless otherwise noted, Luella's letters quoted in this chapter were addressed to her mother but intended for the entire Winship family.

18 — Still no U.S. mail and no knowing when there will be. Things continue to look bad for Mexico.

1913 - May

1 — Irving received a telegram from Mr. Gisholt saying he would return to Cubo.

2 — First mail from the U.S. since April 12 — all two or three weeks old.

3 — Ore is running high these days so Irving is feeling good. There seems to be a general optimism about the future of Mexico.

20 — More or less uneasiness as railroad traffic daily becomes more uncertain — all freight hauling was stopped for a few days because of scarcity of oil.

1913 - June

4 — The town of El Cubo was held up by a band of bandits (from 60 to 75 of them) at 9:15 P.M. Irving and I saw them enter Don Pedro's store. Then I took the boys and went in the mine. The men stayed outside to receive invaders. However they didn't tackle the hacienda. They left town at 10:20 and I came out of the mine. Soldiers arrived at 3 A.M. [I remember this well. As we have said, the rear wall of our house was one of the walls of the hacienda and our dining room window (which was barred) looked out on the cobblestone street that ran along the outside of the wall. Don Pedro's grocery store was across the street opposite our window. At 9:15 John and I were in bed. We had heard the horses on the cobblestones outside. With the dining room lights out we could see them through a crack in the window shades. There were quite a bunch, many still mounted and some of them brandishing revolvers. We were rushed off to the mine entrance and into the tunnel on the electric mule, about a quarter of a mile. John and I knew the mine tunnel well and did not find it scary.]

5 — The day was spent by everyone in talking over last night's affair. We went out in the town and viewed the ruins. The bandits made quite a cleanup from stores. There is much nervous tension in the air and much uneasiness. No soldiers are available to guard the town.

6 — The town is calming down somewhat but various improvements are being made inside the hacienda for greater safety.

7 — A third night watchman has been put on inside the hacienda for greater security.

30 — Reports of outrages committed by rebels in the recent capture of Durango are reaching us, and Irving and I are getting the blues again about things in Mexico.[1] He has even mentioned the possibility of sending me and the boys out again.

But no alarm was sounded yet. The American colony in Guanajuato thought it quite natural to celebrate on the Fourth of July, and Irving and Luella went into the city with the boys, returning that afternoon. Luella wrote:

[July 7, 1913] On the Fourth of July the American colony of Guanajuato had a picnic luncheon. There was a big crowd there including many children. There were also many firecrackers and the noise was, at times, rather deafening.

But underneath, their nervousness remained. Luella continues in her diary:

1913 - July

30 — Irving received a telegram from Mr. Hollis, "If you think it advisable send Mrs. Herr to the States at Company's expense." Quien sabe.

1913 - August

7 — Have about decided I'll not go to the United States at present unless matters take a decided turn for the worse. We are all more than disgusted with the United States because it will not recognize Huerta as President of Mexico. President Wilson is sending an unofficial representative.

9 — We are all much tickled because President Huerta has issued a statement saying that President Wilson's "personal representative" will be persona non grata. All Americans in Mexico are with Huerta as against Wilson.

[It was to be expected that foreigners in Mexico would favor Huerta, because to them it meant a return to law and order, as in Díaz's time. To Mexico's upper classes it meant security in their privileged status.]

From Luella's diary:

1913 - August

11— Letter from Mr. Hollis made us decide I'd better go to the States after all, so we wired for reservations for August 21.

18— Left Cubo at 1:30 and took the night train from Guanajuato for Mexico City.

19— Reached Mexico City at 9 A.M. after having been escorted in by two troop trains from Tula.

21— Reached Vera Cruz safely. Sailed at 5:30 P.M. on board the "Monterey." Irving saw us off.

In the fall of 1913, Carranza and his rebel forces under Villa and Obregón were consolidating their position in the northern states of Mexico. Huerta's Federals were still in control further south, and in December Luella returned with her sons from visiting her family in Boston, coming via Veracruz where she was met by Irving. They arrived in Guanajuato "on time," and at Cubo she found "everything fine and clean."

Of her return trip she wrote from Cubo to her family in the U.S.:

[December 20, 1913] As we entered Vera Cruz harbor last Wednesday at sunrise, there were battleships and a cruiser or two representing the United States, Great Britain, France, and Germany all about us, but the scene itself was as quiet and peaceful as one could wish, and there was no report of any serious occurrence in the interior.

Our trip up to Mexico City and thence to Guanajuato was through equally tranquil country, and the trains were running on schedule as they have been right along, they tell me. Mexico City itself is a panicky place and everyone expects something definite and final and disastrous to happen — and they have been expecting it ever since the bombardment last February, and are no more panicky now then they were when I came through there four months ago.

The Wilson administration is blamed on all sides for the seriousness of the situation. "Everyone of intelligence" — to quote the American wife of a prominent Mexican who came south with me — "supports Huerta, realizing that he is the only man in sight who is capable of handling the situation." President Wilson did have a few supporters, few, very few, here, when I left for Boston, but they have deserted him now. But Huerta is bound to lose — or rather, not to completely win out — while the United States lends its moral support to the Constitutionalists. That the Constitutionalists, on the other hand, will win out is not generally believed in this part of the Republic, although the unexpected has a way of happening in Mexico nowadays. However, their successes are by no means so complete nor extensive as one gathers from reading the press dispatches in the States. The press agents are doing good work from their point of view, and the telling of the true state of affairs bothers them not at all.

On the other hand, Huerta is by no means at the end of his rope. Financially, he will get money inside of the country if he cannot get it outside, and there is still much to be had. He is the type of man who "sticks," and the more he is told to get out by one whose authority he sees no reason for recognizing, the more tenacious is his hold. And those of us who are within the territory that he controls and are enjoying comparative peace can only hope he may hold on long.

The money situation from the standpoint of business is very unsatisfactory, for the peon class is getting suspicious of the bank notes, and with good reason, since some of the small merchants in Guanajuato have been taking advantage of their ignorance and discounting bills for them at fifty percent, telling them that was all they were worth, and they, knowing no better, have permitted the merchants to do it.

The result is a hoarding of silver and small change and so taking it out of circulation, and it is quite difficult to do business on a cash basis. I have opened several accounts where formerly I paid cash, because when they amount to $5 or $10 I can pay with bills, but if I try to make a $1.50 purchase, more or less, and try to pay with a $5 bill I meet the unfailing rejoinder, "No hay cambio" [There is no change].

Mexican pesos, I mean a Mexican peso having more actual silver in it than it is valued at the present rate of exchange, the government has been calling in by the thousand and making into "tostones" (fifty cent pieces) for the very good reason that more than two "tostones" can be made from one peso.

Aside from the money situation and the fact that the cost of living has jumped — due to Federal taxes and the rate of exchange — and the scarcity of American goods, which were formerly so easily obtained, life in Guanajuato is going merrily along in the same old way. All the mines are running at full capacity; nearly all the women and children are here, and the social life is in full swing; and it is hard for us to realize that there is any adequate reason why friends and relatives in the States should be worrying themselves over us and secretly putting us down for reckless children.

Luella continued from Cubo in a letter to her younger sister Edna:

[January 17, 1914] Mail from the States is surely slow — there has been no mail for a week. . . . The great trouble nowadays is shopping — *and* paying for your purchases. There simply is no silver to be had — it is all cached away by numerous individuals. The American dressmaker alone in town has 4,000 silver pesos cached away and I suppose that is just a sample of what most Mexicans of any means are doing. The result is it is simply impossible to get any change and shopping is a trial. The State of Guanajuato has just gotten out treasurer's certificates for 50¢ and one peso to take the place of silver and I am wondering if these will really pass as change — these storekeepers are the most independent people you ever saw and one really can't blame them with no one knowing which banks, if any, are sound. Huerta has declared a bank holiday until March 31st — which means there can be no run on any bank until that date, so if the banks aren't sound they have that much time to tide themselves over.

Though rumors of bandits in the area persisted, life pursued its normal course in Guanajuato for a few weeks longer. Luella wrote:

[February 23, 1914] Anything sent as a letter seems to come through without delay — packages seem to be mostly minus, though I believe they do get through in the course of several months. Two lines of railroad have been opened to the American border for a couple of weeks — we only wish they could continue so but have little hope.
Tuesday afternoon I took my sewing over to Peregrina and drank tea

with the ladies there. Thursday I rode to town to do some errands and had luncheon and spent the afternoon with the Wallaces. Friday the boys and I spent the day with Mrs. Knotts of Pingüico [another nearby mine].

Luella continued in a letter:

[April 13, 1914] This past week [Holy Week] has been rather a festive one for us as we were in Guanajuato from Thursday noon until Sunday evening and they were great gala days with the Mexicans so that Guanajuato itself was very gay with its numerous band concerts and many booths erected for the occasion with fascinating pottery and such to sell. . . . There is a new Mexican hotel recently opened in town and it is much the most attractive place to stay that there has ever been there. . . .

[During these quieter days in Cubo, Mother continued her regular practice of holding classes for us boys each weekday morning. John was two years older than I but we always did everything together, and if he went to school I went to school. Actually we didn't go anywhere. We had school at home. Through her sister Edith, who was now an editor of schoolbooks with the World Book Company in New York, Mother secured the texts that were suitable for our age, and she was the teacher. We had regular hours, an hour and a half each morning, when we sat at a round, rustic table on the veranda and did our lessons, with Mother hearing us recite and helping us over the rough places. There wasn't any homework. But there were many evenings when Mother would read aloud, usually something that Dad would enjoy listening to also such as *David Copperfield, Ivanhoe, Martin Chuzzlewit*, and sometimes continued stories in the *Saturday Evening Post*, which was pretty good in those days. At one time we were even subjected to *Little Women*.]

Early in 1914 Villa had moved south along the central railway and in April he captured Torreón, defeating Huerta's Federals. By July, after some bitter fighting along the way, the Constitucionalista armies had reached León and Querétaro. Guanajuato was abandoned by Federal troops. On the west coast Obregón had captured Guadalajara. Carranza, alarmed at Villa's growing strength and popularity, maneuvered to favor Obregón's advance in the west and sought to delay Villa's progress to the south. After reducing Zacatecas in

June, Villa returned to Chihuahua to consolidate his position, leaving the way open for Obregón to move on toward Mexico City.

The U.S. government refused to recognize Huerta as the rightful president of Mexico. Mistakenly assuming that Mexico could somehow put together an honest "free" election, and influenced by Carranza's well-placed representatives in Washington, President Wilson managed to support Carranza with arms and ammunition across the border and to obstruct deliveries of arms and money to Huerta's government. On April 9 the "Tampico Incident" occurred, which was reported by the *Mexican Herald* on April 18 as follows:

> One of the American war vessels at Tampico sent Marines ashore in a launch for gasoline. They landed at a point that Mexican soldiers claimed was within the firing line and were all arrested and marched off to jail.
>
> Claiming that the Marines were entirely within their rights Admiral Mayo demanded their release, an apology and the firing of a salute to the American flag. The men were released and apology has been offered, but Mexico has declined to fire the salute.
>
> In addition to this Washington complains that a mail carrier from the fleet at Veracruz was arrested and temporarily detained in the port and that a dispatch addressed to the embassy here was held for examination before delivery.
>
> In view of these instances that Washington says are happening only to representatives of the United States[,] and as Mexico declines to offer the salute in honor of the American flag, a demand by the admiral that has been supported by President Wilson, the remaining available vessels of the Atlantic squadron not already in Mexican waters, accompanied by a further contingent of marines, have been ordered to the Gulf coast of Mexico.
>
> Informal negotiations, looking to some adjustment of the principal point at issue, have not altered the situation to date and President Huerta's answer to American newspapers that requested a statement from him is to the effect that Mexico is acting strictly within her rights and that the coming of the American squadron to Mexican waters would in no way modify the serene course of his government.
>
> The salute has not been fired and the American squadron is on the way.

The family's "escape" from Mexico at that time, as told by Robert in his reminiscences (Chapter 4), is described in detail by Luella:

[April 20, 1914] We received two telegrams from Mr. Hollis, one Thursday [the 16th], saying to send me and the boys to Vera Cruz, and one on Friday saying it wasn't necessary. But yesterday — Sunday — came a third reconsidering the second telegram and again advising that I "be sent.". . . We have known more or less of what happened in Tampico for two or three days but no one could seem to learn the outcome until the [Mexican] Herald printed it insofar as it has developed. We may be going down to Vera Cruz tomorrow or the next day. I do not anticipate a long stay however, as — the way things are told down here — matters will either develop with a rush or be smoothed over. Personally I am looking for a backing down on the part of the U.S. government as has happened on every other occasion when it has clashed with Huerta. No one for an instant expects Huerta to retreat from his present position for he just plain "doesn't give a hang." And I can't have any serious idea that this particular incident is to develop into intervention. But no one knows and hence I go with the boys to Vera Cruz — presumably.

Events of the next day suddenly changed the entire situation. On April 9, 1914, President Wilson had ordered the U.S. Marines to take Veracruz, which they occupied on April 21. Mexicans could not forget that the last time the marines occupied Veracruz in 1847 they marched up to Mexico City and captured it also. In the ensuing peace treaty, Mexico lost what is now the Southwest of the United States. Such memories could be used easily to make any Mexican look upon the "gringos" as their natural enemies.

Luella's diary reports:

1914 - April
21— Tuesday. The United States occupied Vera Cruz this morning. We rode in from Cubo in the early afternoon and had supper with the Endweiss's. Left for Mexico City at 7:20 with nine others from Guanajuato. Learned in Silao that the mob was after Gringos, so kept on to Irapuato. There we were arrested and Irving's gun taken away and pocketbook stolen and altogether it was a fearful night, but we were allowed to go on to Mexico City at 2:30 A.M. Wednesday.

22 — Reached Mexico City about 1:30 P.M. Very uneasy all morning for fear we'd not get there. Things in the City are in a rather terrifying state and I got beside myself with actual terror and decided we'd leave for Vera Cruz on the special train at 6 P.M. Our trunks were left behind, unclaimed.

23 — Spent the day on the train — many delays and much trouble for those in the first section of the train. We are in the second. Reached break in the railroad about 2:00. We walked a mile and took another train. Reached Vera Cruz about 4:00 and the U.S. Marines looked good! We went on board the S.S. "Mexico" in the evening.

24 — There are only eight of us from Guanajuato aboard ship, including four Herrs. Two stayed in Vera Cruz. We are fearfully worried about those left behind and it is hard to realize we are actually safe.

25 — More refugees came aboard from Mexico City and also the Isthmus. Disturbing rumors and tales from the interior continue to reach us. Battleships and the hydroplane and the many lights and signaling make it interesting here.

The next day she wrote to her family from on board ship:

[April 26, 1914] We are safely out now, but for once there has been most decidedly something to worry about and that we are out of it all and all together when so very many are still in the interior and unable to get out and so many other families separated, is at times hard to realize. We have lost our trunks and of course everything else we had in Mexico but that is such a minor consideration when so many have lost — or are in danger of losing — their lives and members of their families that we can't stop to regret them just yet. We have our three suitcases, packed for a couple of days — as we supposed — and that is what we have been living on since Tuesday noon, the 21st, and until - ?? There are four others from Guanajuato here and they are all in the same fix except that Mrs. McDonald also has left behind her husband and son. Truly the tragedies that we all fear will be the outcome of it all will make the Titanic look like a very small thing. It makes us all feel so sick that we can't talk of it. Practically everyone was left in Guanajuato intending to leave Wednesday morning — we left Tuesday evening — and ours proved to be the last train out of Guanajuato; a thing none of us suspected at the time. Trains are running again we understand but will carry no Americans — this order is being strictly enforced. Neither will they send telegrams for Americans. All American stores, hotels, and clubs in Mexico City are closed and most of them stoned and looted. All other nationalities are left alone — allowed to go about their business (only there is *very* little business) and get out of the country if they wish, and they are coming as fast as trains can bring them — only there are no trains except two run under the protection of the British Embassy. We came on the first of those, which one was permitted to bring Americans — the second was allowed to carry no Americans, although a few came through on it under guise of being British or German and had a mighty uncomfortable time doing it, but they got here safely and that is the main thing. I have been so very thankful that I was here [in Mexico] as that is the only thing that brought Irving out. If I hadn't been there to make him feel that he should come out at that time in order to get me and the boys out he never would have come until later — and then he couldn't have come out and personally I don't believe he would ever have gotten out alive. The feeling is decidedly more bitter than we ever thought it would be — and we thought it would be bad.

Here in Vera Cruz we are refugees aboard the Ward Line steamer *Mexico* at the expense — also the disposal — of the U.S. authorities. We are hoping to be sent to some U.S. port — two days ago we were told that we were leaving that day for Galveston — yesterday word went forth that we were to leave at 10 P.M. — for New Orleans — and here we still are and can now find out nothing at all about when and where we go.

On Tuesday, April 28, at the mouth of the Mississippi River, en route to New Orleans, the refugees were placed in quarantine for four days as a routine health measure. A bulletin printed on board ship for the benefit of its captive audience read (in part) as follows:

S.S. *Mexico* — Captain E. J. O'Keefe
Published at the New Orleans Quarantine Station, April 29, 1914

Veracruz, Mexico, April 28

Fifth Army Brigade ready to land men in Veracruz. Rear-Admiral Fletcher formally raises the American flag over the captured Mexican port. American refugees will be allowed to come through from Huerta capital, where the situation is reported more quiet. Many rumors of dynamiting railroad bridges. Four army transports with the fifth brigade on board are docked at the port ready to land the men. The other transports bringing the fourth army brigade, comprising the fourth, seventh, nineteenth and twentieth infantry regiments and under Brigadier General Fredrick Funston, were made fast to the dock before ten o'clock this morning. The troops were brought ashore afterward to relieve the marines on outpost duty. General Funston, accompanied by Captain Harry Huse, chief of staff of Rear-Admiral Fletcher, immediately came ashore to confer with Rear-Admiral Fletcher before calling on Rear-Admiral Badger, Commander-in-Chief of the Atlantic Fleet.

Two hundred and fifty American refugees whom reports indicate are entrained at Mexico City, will be permitted by General Huerta to come through to Veracruz, according to information cabled here today by Sir Lionel Carden, the British Minister to Mexico, and now in the capital. It is also said in the cable that the arrival of the refugees at Veracruz will be facilitated by General Maas as soon as their train reaches his lines, which point begins beyond Soledad Station.

A train reached here this morning bringing many English, Germans, and French refugees but only five Americans. None of them came through from Mexico City. Some had been prisoners of the Federals at Cordoba, and others at Soledad. These people brought news of a battle near the capital, where the rebels are said to be gaining ground.

Veracruz, Mexico—

According to reports given by a staff correspondent of "El Imparcial," the principal newspaper of the capital, Huerta sent the following message to the people of the city. "I will not resign. I will take to the mountains with my men and my Cabinet, and I will fight." This would mean, in the opinion of the best informed men here, that all efforts at mediation by the A.B.C. powers will fail.

Denver, Colorado

In a clash between strikers and mine guards late today at the McNally mine of the Colorado Fuel and Iron Company, one mile west of Walsenburg, the camp was taken by the strikers, several were shot and four buildings were burned. This constituted the principal indication that Colorado's industrial war is still on.

After disembarking from the S.S. *Mexico* on May 2, Luella wrote from New Orleans:

[May 3, 1914] We feel now that no lives will be lost for all foreigners left Guanajuato on May 1st and we have heard of their safe arrival in Mexico City. I fancy for refugees we had a more comfortable trip out than those who are following us. We really were quite comfortable despite the poor meals and some of the men had no bunks. We four were fortunate in all being in the same stateroom. Most families were divided — women put in together and men likewise.

But don't ask our opinion of Wilson and Bryan. We are too disgusted to talk! To start all this and make us go through what we've been through and then talk of mediation! It is too insane and a disgraceful page to U.S. history. The United States has gotten herself into a mess and then asks South American countries to help her get out of it!

From New Orleans the Herr family returned to Massachusetts to await developments in Mexico. Irving would stay until July. Luella's story of their flight from Mexico in April 1914 was printed in the *New York Sun* on Sunday, May 17, 1914:

Word of impending trouble first came to Guanajuato on Thursday, April 16, through a telegram sent to the manager of one of the mining companies there advising him to send his wife and children to Vera Cruz. Just what could be the occasion for alarm we had no idea. A strict censorship had recently been placed on all cables into Mexico and the newspapers were permitted to print only such news as the Government officials were giving out. We had received warning so many times and had had so many scares that it was well nigh impossible to get properly disturbed this time. It was the old story of the boy and the wolf.

The first group of Americans to leave Guanajuato went on the following Tuesday and we were only a mere handful, numbering eighteen out of a foreign colony of about 225. It was on that Tuesday, April 21, that the United States seized the custom house at Vera Cruz, and by 4 o'clock in the afternoon word had penetrated throughout that large central section of Mexico that the fighting had begun in Vera Cruz. The people of the city of Guanajuato were not excited, however, and they let us depart in peace, giving no outward manifestation of resentment. So we started out with nothing to warn us of what might be ahead.

Guanajuato is situated off the main railway line and is reached by a local branch line which joins the main road at Silao. Here we left the local train, intending to take the through night train from Zacatecas to Mexico City. We had scarcely stepped off the train before the Mexican ticket agent told one of the American men in our party that the Pullman on the train we were waiting for was to be cut off by a mob at a station a little distance north of Silao. He advised us to continue as far as Irapuato, where we could catch the night train from the west in case the one from the north did not come through. We took his advice and reached Irapuato safely an hour later.

There we waited until 11:30 P.M., when the train from the west pulled in, and at the same time we learned that the mob had in fact cut off the Pullman of the Zacatecas train and had demanded all the gringos. Meanwhile a small crowd of Mexicans in Irapuato had decided that they would hold the five resident Americans there as hostages. However, these Americans had been warned by a friendly Mexican and the Federal authorities sent an armed detachment to escort them to the station. At the same time the Federals sent a force of mounted rurales to guard the train while in the station. These rurales lined up two feet apart on either side of the track.

The train was held until the train from the north, minus the Pullman, arrived at 2 A.M. Then we thought surely we should be allowed to proceed. But not yet!

After we had taken seats in the car a Mexican lieutenant and a force of soldiers entered and announced: "We have no orders to carry Americans." Then he and his men questioned us as to whether we were Americans. We were told to come with them and also to turn over to them all arms and ammunition. I thought it was the end of our chance of getting out of the country and possibly the end of us for all time. They took us off the train and led us up the station platform to a colonel who was standing outside. He looked at us and said: "You are to go on this train but are to ride in the Pullman." Can you imagine the rush of new life that swept over us?

As soon as we were in the Pullman the commander of the Federal forces in Irapuato, who was a good friend of the Americans, came aboard and said the order to leave the train and the taking of our arms and ammunition was all a mistake. He had with him the revolvers and pistols which our men had given up and explained that he would leave them with the Pullman conductor, who would take care of them and return them to their owners when we reached Mexico City. He was taking this precaution, he said, so that no one would be tempted to use his pistol in case of trouble and so cause further complications.

Two of the men with us had planned to return to Guanajuato after seeing the women folk safely on the train for Mexico City. They were not permitted to stay behind, however, for the Mexican authorities insisted that all Americans at the station must get on the train and stay there. A troop train was sent ahead and a heavy armed escort was on our train all the way from Irapuato to Mexico City.

The rest of the trip to Mexico City was made without mishap. All the next morning we ran through as tranquil a country as one could find anywhere. The people were going about their various tasks as undisturbed as if the great country north of them had never been heard of.

As we neared the city limits the conductor carefully pulled down all curtains in our cars, explaining that this was done so that no one might be tempted to throw a stone or other missile at us. When we reached the station in the city he requested us to keep our seats while he went out to see that all was quiet. He returned at once to say that there was no trouble, and we left his protecting care with a grateful feeling.

The automobiles of the American Embassy were at the station to meet us and carried us to the embassy building, and from there we were taken to the Hotel Geneve. This hotel, a little way out from the heart of the city, was situated in the concentration camp and under the protection of the British Embassy.

We reached Mexico City about 1 o'clock in the afternoon, and the next four or five hours will always be more or less of a nightmare to me. No one knew what to do or where to go. Every one had a different idea and every one had a new tale of horrors or the possibility of horrors.

On Wednesday night a train was to leave the city under the protection of the British and German flags and Huerta had promised protection as far as the Federal outposts. Many preferred to stay in the Mexican capital rather than to take their chances in the train, but eleven of our party decided on the latter course. The mob in Mexico City had made several demonstrations on Tuesday evening, had broken the windows of the American Embassy and the American Hotel and had insulted pedestrians. Personally I preferred to make a try at getting out of the country at the quickest possible moment.

You must understand that at this time no one in the interior of Mexico doubted for a minute that intervention had come and that the United States troops would very soon be fighting their way to the city. The only question was, "How long will it take them to get there?"

We pulled out of Mexico city about 8:30 on the evening of April 22. Secretary Hobler [*sic*] of the British Legation, wearing his military uniform, traveled with us and all the trainmen and every one else were under his instructions.[2] Our engine was flying the British and German flags. Again the curtains of the cars were closely drawn. There were frequent cries of "*Mueran los gringos*" (Death to the Americans) and jeers from crowds at the stations until we were some distance from the city, but no shots were fired or stones thrown.

When we came to Esperanza, where the train starts down the mountain and descends 2,000 feet in two hours, the authorities gave us two inexperienced engineers and two engines that were quite useless in holding back our heavy train. Fortunately for us we had with us the superintendent of motive power of the Mexican railroad and another railway official, and they were up all night, getting out at every station to see what engines and engineers we had and looking after things generally. They refused to let the train proceed until proper equipment and men were provided, and after a positive refusal on the part of the authorities and a delay of two hours the equipment and engineers were furnished and we proceeded.

Later these railway officials were arrested, taken from the train, and led away by a detachment of ten men; but through the friendship of one of them for Commander Azueta of the Mexican navy they were promptly released and allowed to board the train again and continue to the coast.

At another point during the night men boarded the train looking for "gringos," so they said. They demanded all arms and then departed. Again the next morning the train was held up for a long time while the authorities went through all the cars hunting for newspaper men who were said to be aboard.

We reached the break in the railroad about 2 o'clock in the afternoon and all got out, carrying hand baggage, which was all we were allowed to bring with us, and walked over the destroyed section of the track under a large flag of truce. This stretch proved to be only a mile in length. The Mexicans had removed the spikes, had carried the rails a little distance away, and had taken up the ties and burned them.

At the end of the mile we found a little engine flying the British flag and I fear that to some of us the United States flag will never look quite so good as that flag of Great Britain did then. It meant safety, whereas the Stars and Stripes would have meant danger. For two days we had dreaded to have our nativity known.

The marines were everywhere in evidence here and they certainly "looked good" to us. They were a fine, manly, well disciplined body of men — men any country should be proud of.

Perhaps hoping to contribute to U.S. policy toward Mexico, Irving also wrote an article, "Present Conditions in Mexico," which appeared in *The Advance* magazine on May 28, 1914:

In discussing this question [present conditions in Mexico], the first fact to be considered is that Mexico is a large country and that conditions in any particular part of it may be decidedly different from those in other parts.

The writer, although he has lived in Mexico for the past twelve years, feels that he is really competent to judge only those conditions existing among the mining population — a not inconsiderable portion of Mexico's laboring class, since mining forms one of Mexico's foremost industries.

The state of Guanajuato, although largely agricultural, is also a great mining state, and the principal mines are located in the vicinity of the city of Guanajuato, which is the state capital.

The mines of Guanajuato really support the city and employ thousands of laborers. Throughout the past three years the state has been practically free of revolutionary troubles and the laboring class has remained steadily at work, apparently taking no interest in political questions. They have been content to have Huerta for their president, and insofar as they are able to think at all upon large questions, have wondered what the trouble is between Huerta and the United States, and why their countrymen of the North are fighting and killing their brothers of the South.

By this time everyone knows that Mexico has three social classes. The largest in number is the laboring class, often called the peon, numbering probably 75 per cent to 80 per cent of the total.

Following this is a large middle class comprising the small shopkeepers, skilled laborers, business and professional men.

Finally the top layer, the wealthy land-owners and leisure class.

It is with this peon class that the writer is most familiar. In Guanajuato, at least, these are not the down-trodden, exploited, suffering people that they are often painted, especially in the United States.

They possess little, as a rule living in adobe huts with mud floors, their principal earthly possessions consisting of a blanket and sombrero, a few cooking utensils and a happy, carefree disposition. They have no care or thought beyond the present and provide nothing for tomorrow. They are very much like children and we treat them as we would children.

By nature they are docile and obedient, and as a rule have an inborn politeness and graciousness in their dealings with each other and with their superiors.

This trait, however, seems to be on the decline, especially since the revolutionary troubles began.

The greatest handicap to the material and moral advance of this large class of people is not their political condition, nor the dictatorial form of government under which they live and suffer. Liquor and the Catholic Church are, in the writer's opinion, far more responsible for their low condition. I include the Church, because this makes no attempt to discourage the use of liquor among the peons, and also fails to encourage thrift and steady labor. Innumerable fiestas or holy days are observed in Mexico and the laborers warned not to work on those days by the priests, whereas in civilized countries they are not observed by the Catholic Church by direction of the Pope.

On these days, after an early attendance at Mass, the balance of the day is usually devoted to drinking, and in addition a day's wages are lost.

The wages paid by the mining companies are good, and many a peon could have his little plot of land and a small home of his own if he saved his earnings, instead of squandering them in drink and gambling.

Of self-government they have no idea whatever. They are used to being governed by the iron hand, and in fact admire and respect that kind of government. If they have any idea of liberty, it is that liberty means license and the right to do as they please.

The peon does not hate the foreigners. I am quite sure that as a rule he would rather work for a foreigner than for a Mexican, because with all his ignorance, he has a shrewd mind and realizes that the foreigner treats him much more justly than a native Christian master.

He is, however, very easily influenced, and one or two labor agitators, or political agitators, can work havoc in a well-ordered community, if allowed free rein. Unfortunately he will believe for a time at least anything he hears, especially anything that gives promise of a better future for him, or an easier living.

It is for this reason that it is so easy to recruit forces for a revolution. A few promises on the part of an unscrupulous leader, the prospect of loot and an easy free life is enough to make a patriot fighting for his country out of a great many of the lower class.

Of real patriotism there is practically none in Mexico, and I speak now of this nation as a whole.

The press talks in high flown language of the beloved fatherland, the love of country that fills to overflowing the loyal hearts of Mexico's valiant sons, urging them to shed their last drop of blood to repel the hated Yankee, the Colossus of the North, etc. But it is all talk.

Patriotism there is not.

The anti-foreign feeling is excited artificially by the lying press of Mexico. Lies so gross, so palpable as are unimaginable by an American are printed and are believed not only by the laboring class, but by many of the middle class as well.

That Mexico contains within herself the elements necessary to establish and maintain a democratic form of government I do not believe. The very men strongly supporting Madero during his candidacy for president turned against him as soon as it became apparent that they could not have all their personal desires satisfied. It is the old question of the outs wishing to be in and the ins to stay in, and any means to gain their ends are used even though it may mean killing and wounding of thousands of their fellows.

For such a people democratic government is not possible, except they grow up to it; and this means a matter of years, and of struggle. The beginning should be made at the bottom, and not at the top.

Let the small community first learn to elect the jefe-politico, or local police-mayor, and to abide by the rules of the election. In time the state could elect its governor. In this way during the course of years the meaning of democracy would be learned.

In the meantime the central government should remain a military one, for it is the only one that can maintain order, and there must be order.

Regarding this episode in Mexican-American relations, we have commentaries by Luella and Irving in retrospect some twelve years later:

As to my feeling about Wilson in April 1914 it was this. His method of handling the Mexican problem was utterly futile. For instance – the marines took Vera Cruz because Wilson said a Hamburg-American liner should not land the arms and ammunition it had brought over from Germany. Result – many, many Americans, residents of Mexico, were in danger of their lives and went through a great nervous strain and lost property and money so that many have never fully recovered – but the Hamburg-American liner just went down to Puerto Mexico (or some port south of Vera Cruz), landed the arms and ammunition, and Huerta got them with only a little delay. All losses and suffering were on the part of Americans. And the fact that on the refugee ship we were treated like sin verguenzas [scoundrels] and Bryan came out publicly and said no one need waste any sympathy on us – we were all down here "to get rich quick" – didn't make us any more enthusiastic Americans.

The United States took over all the Ward Line boats (four only) for the American refugees. When we got to Vera Cruz after about 52 hours without sleep on my part we found all the boats full of Mexicans who had gone there from Vera Cruz for safety (of course paying the officers for the privilege) and when we were ordered out of the hotel and onto the steamer by the American commander about 10:30 at night and got on the "Mexico" the purser said there was no room for us. When Irving and Mr. E. MacDonald each produced a $10 bill he decided he was mistaken — he did have one room for the women and children. Of course we were sore and still are.[3]

Irving then added:

In the case of Wilson intervening in Mexico this was certainly not for the protection of American lives or property. It was decidedly for the purpose of dictating the internal morals of Mexico, and of forcing Huerta out of the presidency. The immediate landing of troops was in connection with the prevention of landing of war munitions for Huerta. According to what was brought out at the Pan American 6th Conference this was against principles of International Law.[4]

"Liquor and the Catholic Church" — Irving's upbringing in Middle America still colored his vision of Mexico's ills. He judged the peon to be putty in the hands of a labor agitator, but Irving found him shrewd and believed him capable in time of learning the habits of democracy. He noted that "as a rule" the Mexican peon "would rather work for a foreigner than for a Mexican" because he "realizes that the foreigner treats him much more justly than a native Christian master." This was one of the keys to the relative tranquility surrounding the mines during much of the revolutionary activity. Around Cubo the local workmen were loyal to the *gerente* and kept him posted on surrounding dangers. When rebels came to the hacienda at Cubo they were looking for horses and guns, not sabotage, although Irving made sure that his men were sufficiently armed to make a show of resistance if necessary.

Irving was known by the Mexicans for his fairness. There had been a serious accident in the mine when a large piece of the "hanging wall" or overhead rock caved in near a crew of drillers. This was quite rare in these mines and the men were caught unawares. One of them lost his leg under the falling rock and was pulled away, leaving the leg behind. Two days later three Mexican women, relatives of the injured man, came to see Irving in his office. José was going to be all right, but they had a petition to present to the *gerente*.

Would he please arrange to have the missing leg recovered so they could give it a proper burial?

"And why is this necessary, since José will be all right?"

"Because, Señor, if we do not give the leg a proper burial with the blessing of the priest, José will not have it when he gets to Heaven and will be without it for Eternity."

The leg, of course, was covered with tons of rock. Irving pondered a while. "Señoras, the leg is deeply buried now, in the mine. Would it meet the requirement if you went with the priest to the place of burial inside the mine so that he can hold the funeral service there and bless the ground?"

So it was arranged and everyone was satisfied.

It was noticeable too that Irving spoke Spanish with an accent that was clearly American, although his command of the language was excellent. I asked him once why he did not at least make an effort to pronounce it correctly. "Because," he said, "I want them to know I am an American." In business this gave him an advantage because they trusted Americans.[5]

HUERTA MADE FUTILE remonstrances to the United States over their intervention in Veracruz. Momentarily the American aggression provided him some popularity among the Mexican public, but the armies of Villa and Obregón increasingly threatened in the north and west. Huerta saw the handwriting on the wall, and on July 15, 1914, he departed from Mexico City with what monies remained in the federal treasury. Five days later he sailed from Puerto México on a German ship bound for Spain. Carranza's forces under Villa and Obregón moved rapidly toward the nation's capital.

After Huerta's hurried departure, the office of the Cubo Company in Chicago advised Irving to return to Mexico, and he sailed from New York for Veracruz on July 23. He returned to Guanajuato under severe circumstances, which are documented by his correspondence with Luella in New England, where the family had been weathering the storms in Mexico.

From Veracruz he wrote her:

[August 1, 1914] We landed here this morning and I have now some better idea of the situation in Mexico. The sum total of my conclusion is — pessimism — and that things are on the ragged edge.

I went around to the American Consulate and got no satisfaction there — the tone of that place was very pessimistic. I ran into our old friend Mr. Kyle and he advised me strongly not to try and go to Guanajuato. Later I saw Mr. Armstead who had just come down today from Mexico City. He was quite pessimistic also and thought it foolhardy to try and go to Guanajuato. It seems communication with Guanajuato has been cut off and trains are running only a matter of fifty miles north from Mexico City. Guanajuato is either in the hands of the rebels or perhaps there is a battle going on. This latter I do not believe.

Mr. Armstead is also expecting trouble in Mexico City but not for a week or two. My latest plan is to go up to the City tomorrow morning and talk things over. Then I think it very likely that I will come back to Vera Cruz.

From the Hotel Iturbide — Mexico City:

[August 8, 1914] The political situation here does not seem to clear; on the contrary it appears to be getting worse and I do not like the looks of things. This town is the same old rumor factory that it has always been and one can hear about anything one chooses.

Mr. Endweiss is going down to Vera Cruz tomorrow and is going to try and go from there to Guanajuato via Tampico. There is no communication of any kind between here and Guanajuato, either rail or telegraph. We have heard via New York that Jesus Carranza had been in Guanajuato and had allowed the Development Company to issue company scrip with which to pay off the men, and that everything was quiet.

I do not like staying here in the City because I do not feel safe. At the same time I do not like to pull out and go back to Vera Cruz especially because I am in telegraphic communication with Mr. Hollis and we are trying to effect a settlement on the past three months shipments. . . . I think there is a grave chance of the railroad to Vera Cruz being cut any time, but am hoping for the best. . . . In case anything should happen to me, which I very much doubt, you may know that I was thinking of you at the last. I do love you heaps and miss you the worst way.

On August 15, 1914 General Alvaro Obregón rode into Mexico City at the head of the Constitucionalista forces, declaring Carranza the provisional

President of Mexico, and promising that a new president would be chosen at a convention representing all revolutionary parties, to be held at Aguascalientes. Five days later Carranza staged a triumphal entry to the city and assumed dictatorial powers. Villa, back in Chihuahua, had by now lost faith in Carranza's commitment to the principles of the revolution, but was placated by the promise of a convention at Aguascalientes.

The only way to reach Guanajuato from Mexico City was by train. No other transportation was available to cover the one hundred eighty miles over mountainous terrain. The rail line, however, was cut off, as Irving had learned. His only alternative was to make a long circuit via the Gulf of Mexico and into Guanajuato by rail from the north. Taking his responsibilities seriously and no doubt personally concerned to learn the state of his company's mine, on August 15 he left Veracruz by steamer for Tampico. From there a railroad line ran to San Luis Potosí, where it joined the line coming down from Laredo. On August 18, Irving reached San Luis Potosí and wrote Luella describing how the revolutionary wars had democratized travel:

[August 18, 1914] I have now reached San Luis Potosi, and we had a great trip getting here. We expected to travel in a freight car, but we had a fond hope that it would turn out to be at least a third-class passenger car. But it didn't and we rode from 6:30 A.M. until 1 A.M. (19 hours) in a box freight car with only a plank a foot wide on each side to sit on and a double width plank down the middle. Everyone travels first class now — at least there is only one kind of tickets sold, so we had all sorts of traveling companions — from peons up to middle class, and the car was quite full when we left Tampico. My vis-a-vis for several hours was a middle class? merchant who had the spitting habit, and his idea seemed to be to see how close he could come to my suitcase without actually hitting it.

The first three hours quite tired me out — for the springs on a freight car are most conspicuous by their absence, and at the rate we traveled it seemed as though the train would surely jump the track, as well as dislocate all my organs. After that I got my second wind and began to enjoy the trip.

Each car had four little windows besides the door in the middle, and as these were all preempted there was a fine chance to see any scenery. After lunch the car thinned out a little and I got a chance to stand up on the seat and look out of a window, and I stuck there all afternoon and watched the scenery. There is a place where the road climbs from the coastal plain up onto the plateau and the scenery is as good as on the Mexican Railroad.

We passed over several small rivers where the bridges had been blown down with dynamite, and we saw them toppled over in the river. For a long stretch the railroad stations were destroyed and bunches of burned freight cars — nothing left but the wheels could be seen. The roadbed itself seemed not to have been disturbed at all over most of the line, and I was quite surprised at that. I think it will not take much work to put this particular line into good shape. I also think the reason for there being no passenger cars is that the Federals took almost all the passenger cars with them as they retreated south.

The trip up here was not bad and on the whole I rather enjoyed it. After dark it was more tedious as the car was dark except for one dim lantern. The passengers were all very well behaved. One poor peon woman was just out of the hospital with a baby about a week old. The mother was one of those clean faced women you don't see very often and was quite weak, and the baby wrapped in scarcely more than a rag was covered with heat rash and cried most of the time. There was a girl also belonging to the woman about ten years old who held the baby most of the day. It was really a pathetic sight.

I bought the girl a bottle of soda water — sold on the train — and her face quite lit up. She gave it first to her mother before she took any herself. How many American children would do that?

Tomorrow we continue our trip to Queretaro — maybe in a third-class coach — maybe in a boxcar.

Querétaro lay near the junction of the eastern and western railroad lines coming from the north. If Irving could get there, he might catch a train going north to Silao and thence to Guanajuato. Exhausting as he found the trip, he wanted Luella to know he was safe, and he found time and energy to write. How soon his letters would reach her, he had no idea. From Querétaro he wrote:

[August 20, 1914] We are safe in Queretaro, where we arrived at 7 o'clock last night in a rain. We are supposed to leave here for Irapuato at 4 P.M. but it will probably be later before we get away. We left San Luis yesterday morning at 7 o'clock. In the San Luis depot I ran across Mr. Gilmore and two other Americans from the power plant who were going on the same train with us. They had come down from Laredo in stages and had laid off several days in San Luis because one of them was knocked out.

We got into the rear of the train – an ordinary freight car like the rest of the train, but occupied by the train crew only, so it was not crowded and full of peons like the other cars.

Traveling is a very triste proposition just now. It makes one sad just to compare it with travel four years ago. The rebels are not all to blame. They have no cars or engines to speak of. I guess the Federals took all the passenger trains with them when they retreated to Mexico City. But there is no system to anything and it is all so crude. No sanitary arrangements of any kind. Passengers had to squat at the sides of the train for relief, and not even drinking water on the train. We will probably not reach Guanajuato until sometime tomorrow – possibly not then – but I guess we will be all right.

The cities we have been in are quiet and orderly enough but they look triste. The few soldiers we have seen are a sorry-looking bunch – perhaps partly because they have no uniforms up this way. All the foreigners I have seen are pessimistic and believe the grand finale is still to be enacted. I hope not.

I have learned that all our horses were taken by the rebels, as well as all other horses around Guanajuato. The Power Company lost theirs also.

I have been keeping cleaner on this trip than I expected to. At every hotel I get in a good sponge bath and have had plenty of changes. . . .

It seems that while there is no actual looting going on – that is in an open way – there is a great deal of insidious looting. Rich Mexican families are having their stuff confiscated in a quiet sort of way. I was told – but don't believe it – that 800 pianos have been sent up to Laredo from San Luis – by the Constitutionalists, and that the American authorities have seized them until the shippers can prove ownership.

He reached Silao the next day but waited to write until he could report a safe arrival in Guanajuato. Two days later he gave up.

From Silao:

[August 23, 1914] We landed in this place on Friday morning. It is now Sunday morning and we are still here. The train service here is fine. There is *one* train which plies between Irapuato, Queretaro, Leon and Guanajuato. One day it starts out from Irapuato, goes to San Juan del Rio and back to Irapuato. The next day it runs up to Leon, back to Silao, up to Guanajuato and back to Irapuato. But on Friday it got back from Leon so late that the run up to Guanajuato was cut out, and we were left stranded here.

We could have gone up on burros or in a coach, but there is a bunch of bandits on the road from here to Guanajuato and we thought we would not take chances. . . .

The last part of this trip has really been disgusting. From Thursday until Sunday night to get from Queretaro to Guanajuato and I shan't be sure we will get to Guanajuato today until we are actually there. . . .

I am very skeptical whether this letter will ever reach you anyway. I think the main object now is to sell stamps, and to hell with the letters. You notice two stamps on my letters — one is not acceptable to the Constitutionalists, and the Constitutionalist does not go in the United States so we have to buy one of each kind.

Finally he was able to write from the mine at Cubo:

[August 25, 1914] We are back at Cubo again. We finally got into Guanajuato on Sunday afternoon and found Dr. Karr's mozo waiting for us at the station. [Dr. Karr was the resident physician in Guanajuato who served all mining interests.] Dr. Karr took us to supper at the Hotel Luna and after that we went to see the moving picture at the Juarez Theater. . . . According to Dr. Karr the Constitutionalists had about cleaned up all that we had left in Cubo, but I found after I got out here that many of the things he thought had been taken had been hidden away by Angela and were all right.

Beginning about August 1st about 3,000 soldiers came through Cubo, passing at different times, so that for several days the place was not rid of them. The first bunch took all the horses, and hunted the house for fire-arms. They also took all the feed from the almacen, saddles, ropes, and blankets from the house. The next bunch was accompanied by General Jesus Carranza, who spent the night here and slept in our bed. He was entertained by Atenedoro in our living room, and the Victrola was on duty until about 3 A.M. according to Angela. He left things just as he found them, and nothing was taken. But later other bunches came in, and then it was that Angela hid away most of our things, as these last took anything they wanted. All the clothes we left are practically gone. The dishes and chafing dish, percolator and your set of painted saucers are all here, and nothing in the living room seems to have been disturbed. Of course the serapes were put away by Angela, but none of the vases or pictures have been harmed.

Guanajuato is a triste place. There has been fairly good order kept, but sub rosa a whole lot has been done I guess. The stores have been pretty well cleaned out. I am beginning to debate whether I will not resign very soon and get out while there is time. Really I cannot see any finish to this question down here. It is not settled yet for a minute. Everybody feels the same way about it.

Huerta's regime was a partial attempt to return to the Díaz days of law and order, with "business as usual," but the revolution would not be quelled. This year and a half was a time of increasing disturbances that were complicated by the intrusion of the United States. Though Huerta maintained a semblance of government based on the old Díaz bureaucracy, Carranza and his revolutionary generals were pressing hard from the north, spreading havoc and desolation as they went. In the south Zapata and his followers, still true to Madero and fighting for his program of land distribution, were making it hot for the hacendados, or landowners. United States intervention at Veracruz completed the disruption, and its support of Carranza finally sealed Huerta's doom. Obregón took Mexico City for Carranza in August 1914. The Cubo mine, with Irving back in command, would have to wait and see what Carranza's victory would bring.

Two years later Irving summed up his experiences in these years for his Harvard classmates:

In January, 1910, I returned to Guanajuato as general superintendent of the Cubo Mining and Milling Company. There I have remained ever since, excepting those times when for political reasons the Americans had to leave the country. My wife and children have been sent to the United States and have come back so many times that their journeys can be compared to a shuttle. Yet, in 1914 after the taking of Vera Cruz by the United States naval forces we were among the "refugees" and went from Guanajuato to Vera Cruz during the midst of the excitement. That is a story in itself, but suffice it to say that we were scared, thoroughly and completely, and it made an impression on my older boy that he will never overcome.[6]

Nevertheless, he was back at the Cubo mine.

Notes

1. In April 1913 Federal forces defending Durango had executed rebel prisoners of war in cold blood. When the anti-Huerta forces captured Durango on June 18 they took revenge. In the words of the U.S. consul: "Scenes following the rebel entry beggar description. Business and private houses [were] thoroughly sacked; [the] main business section burned; prisoners liberated. . . . Foreigners . . . suffered equally with [the] natives. Absolute anarchy prevails." Quoted in Charles C. Cumberland, *Mexican Revolution: The Constitutionalist Years* (Austin: University of Texas Press, 1972), 42.

2. Mr. Hohler, the British chargé, took the train of British, Germans, and Americans to Veracruz on April 22–23, 1914. See Edith O'Shaughnessy, *A Diplomat's Wife in Mexico* (New York: Harper and Brothers, 1916), 4, 307. His name appears incorrectly as Hobler in Luella's account.

3. Luella to Robert, December 21, 1927.

4. Irving to Robert, March 1, 1928.

5. Regarding the favorable feeling and lack of enmity toward Americans, see Alan Knight, *The Mexican Revolution* (Lincoln: University of Nebraska Press, 1990), 1:296, 320, 428–29, 2:160.

6. Harvard Class of 1901 — Fourth Report (1916), 211–12.

CHAPTER 6

Villa–Obregón

After Obregón took Mexico City, he declared
Carranza the new president. His tenure was presumably "provisional" until the promised convention
of revolutionary forces in Aguascalientes should pick
their man. Nevertheless, the new Carranza regime was
opposed both by Villa in the north and by Zapata in
the south. Villa soon started moving south, routing
Carranzista forces in towns and cities along the way,
and using paper money printed in his name to replace
Carranza's "Constitucionalista" bills. U.S. troops continued to occupy Veracruz, and Irving remained at the
mine. He described the situation around Guanajuato
in the summer of 1914, writing from Cubo to Luella a
few days after his return via Tampico:*

> [August 28, 1914] So far there have been no trains
> from Mexico City except an occasional military
> train and this has looked rather suspicious. There
> are some who think the train service is being held
> up purposely in order to give this bunch in this part
> of the country a chance to "get theirs" without
> there being any means to go to Mexico and make
> complaints at headquarters. These fellows [Carranza
> men] are artists and are making hay while the sun

---

*All of Irving's letters quoted in this chapter were addressed
to Luella.

shines. The American companies are not suffering and we stand very high with the new Government—quien sabe how long it will last. Don Ponciano Aguilar, the geologist and mining engineer of Guanajuato who was in charge of the Reduction and Mines Company's property while the Americans were away, has been in prison ever since the Constitutionalists came in, because he was a National Diputado under the Huerta regime.

The Guanajuato Development Company has been issuing Vales or Bonos [scrip] for the past month because there has been no way to bring any money here. They have issued probably 150,000 pesos of these, and it is about the only money that circulates. Nobody is sure just what banknotes are good. It seems the Constitutionalists are willing to honor all State and National Bank bills issued before Huerta became President and have put the ban on all after that time. But I don't think they can make it stick.

I went out to Nueva Luz Thursday and stayed overnight. They had the worst time of anybody around Guanajuato. When the rebels [Carranzistas, opposing Huerta] first put in an appearance on the hills north and east of Guanajuato and demanded the surrender of the Plaza, it was refused and Cuellar sent up some Federal soldiers from Silao to defend the place. Desultory fighting at long range went on for a couple of days (two men killed) and then the Federals retired.

A large number of Constitutionalists were in the hills back of Nueva Luz and when they made their advance into Guanajuato some came past Nueva Luz and began firing at the house (in sportive mood). Wallace [the manager, with whom we had left Guanajuato in April] and his American helper were on the front porch watching the bunch and didn't know at first that they were being fired on. When they discovered it they went into the house. The firing continued and the soldiers got down into the patio and some bullets were shot into the house from a distance of 50 or 100 feet. Mr. and Mrs. Wallace got into the closet under the stairs in the big room that used to be the office, and Wallace says that if the soldiers had come into the room he intended to open fire and make a last stand. However, instead they went to the stables and took the horses, and decamped.

Then while it was quiet, the Wallaces and his assistant took to the mine and stayed there about a day and two nights. While they were in the mine another bunch came and robbed the house and made off with a great deal of stuff, mostly clothes. Nobody else went through any such trouble as that.

I am thinking of hiding some of our stuff again, for we might have another raid.

[September 5, 1914] I have never seen people around Guanajuato more pessimistic about the outcome of things in Mexico than they are now. Nobody seems to have any hope, and all seem to think it is only a matter of more or less weeks before we will have to get out, if it is possible to get out.

I think myself part of this feeling is due to the fact that this is the first time since the beginning of the revolution that Guanajuato has had a real taste of some of the unpleasantnesses of the Revolution. It is easy to read in the paper of a town being taken, and such and such forced loans being made, etc., but when it is your own town, and your own pocketbook that suffers, things are much more grave. Then the financial situation is disheartening, no banks open, and about fifty kinds of paper money which may be good today and by tomorrow no good on account of some decree or other, and no communication with Mexico City except an occasional military train.

Mail is coming in better now and I have hopes that matters will clear up some before the end of the month. Of course the matter of vital importance is what Mr. Villa is going to do, and nobody here has the least idea.

Trains were running again in October in spite of Villa's forces advancing south, and Irving was able to go to Mexico City on business. Here he witnessed a different aspect of the revolution. Labor unions had been organizing since the days of the Porfiriato among railroad and textile workers and some miners. More radical than most union leaders were propagandists and organizers like Ricardo Flores Magón, who had gone over to violent anarcho-syndicalism along the lines of the International Workers of the World in the United States. In Mexico City the Casa del Obrero Mundial became the center of anarcho-syndicalist activity. The breakdown of order during the revolution gave its leaders an opportunity to push their line, and workers in Mexico City responded. Irving wrote from there:

[October 9, 1914] I came down here to fix up financial matters so that we could get payroll independently of the Development Company. This was done by having Hollis make a deposit in the Canadian Bank in New York, and they wired it down here. The bank here is going to ship me money by express. So that is settled for as long as there may be railroad communication between Mexico City and Guanajuato — which I do not believe will be very long.

Everybody down here in Mexico City is amazed at the idea that seems to be prevalent in the United States that things are progressing satisfactorily. Mr. Moss [another foreign representative] is more nervous than he was in April.

Yesterday all the streetcar employees went on strike at noon and there has not been a car running since. Today the coaches are out of business, having been forced to make a sympathetic strike. It is expected that to-morrow the taxis will be out of business. At the same time it is being attempted to have the lighting of the city stopped and if this happens God only knows what may result.

They say the common soldiers are about ready to mutiny because they have not been allowed to loot — whereas the officers have helped themselves to autos, houses and other things. In fact the City is on the crater of a volcano which may not boil over, but which again may almost any minute. I am glad to leave tomorrow. It makes one sick to hear some of the inside facts of things as they are here.

Yesterday after lunch Mr. and Mrs. Moss walked over to Chapultepec Park with me where there was a Police Band concert in progress, and we heard the last piece while we had a refresco at the restaurant there. They then walked down the Paseo de la Reforma with me. It was now long past dark.

If it looks like much of a revolution coming or chance of foreign complications I may recommend that we shut down the property and let us come out. But I still have faint hopes that it will turn out to be a good deal of a fiasco. But I have my doubts. If only complications do not arise. These people here in charge are already trying to get worked up because the American troops are not going until – Quien sabe quando.

When the Convention of Aguascalientes was finally held in October 1914, both Villa and Zapata were well represented, with Obregón on Carranza's side. After fiery exchanges the convention finally decreed that both Villa and Carranza should withdraw and a provisional president be appointed by the convention. Eulalio Gutiérrez was chosen as the provisional president. Irving comments about the convention (no date, November?):

> These people are such d – – children or they would get together right away and stop all the dickering. Really the proceedings at Aguas are laughable in some ways. First they sign their names to the flag and everything is lovely, and then someone gets up and says the flag is only a rag anyway, and then there is pandemonium, and they all pull their guns and are going to shoot the speaker for a traitor. The idea of wearing guns at a Constitutional Convention anyway. It reminds me of a bunch of cowboys in the wild west days.

Villa accepted the decision of the convention but Carranza ignored it. Instead, Carranza moved his "government" to Puebla, and after negotiating the withdrawal of U.S. troops on November 23, made his headquarters at Veracruz, where he was joined by Obregón. Armed forces were in confusion throughout the country. Uncertain of Carranza's next move, Villa continued south. In November his advance toward Mexico City was being felt in Guanajuato. Irving wrote from Cubo:

> [November 13, 1914] Since I last wrote there has been some mild excitement around here. Night before last all the troops who have been stationed in Guanajuato [Carranzistas] were to be sent down to Silao to join others who were there, I understand, with General Pablo Gonzales. A large bunch of those in Guanajuato decided they were Villistas instead of Carranzistas and decided to beat it. So they got a lot of ammunition and started out about midnight in the general direction of Peregrina. The Superintendent was aroused about 4 or 5 o'clock in the morning and asked for money and other things. They broke into the mine office

and tried to break open the strongbox, but were not successful. They did take the horses however, and the Superintendent gave them 50 pesos or thereabouts. They hung around Peregrina until about 8 o'clock in the morning and then went up in the hills and did some shooting. We fully expected they would be over here during the course of the day, and I was rather nervous, but they evidently decided that Cubo was not worthwhile, for the next we heard from them they had passed Cienega, and were headed for Dolores Hidalgo, where Villa is said to have a large number of troops.

Today no mail has come, and that always gets me in the dumps, for when the mail is cut off and there is no way to get any news I always imagine most anything may be happening. This time we seem to be right on the borderland between the two contending parties, and it is not so pleasant as having them off in Sonora or Chihuahua.

Before the troops left Guanajuato they set loose all the prisoners in the jail, and left the city without any government at all. Whether this is still the condition I do not know as I have not talked over the phone yet today. But evidently nothing in the way of a row has happened in town or I would have heard of it.

Yesterday morning about 4 o'clock there were several of this same bunch who came to the gate of the Hacienda after horses. The watchman on duty did not open the gate, but told them that there were puros burros [nothing but donkeys] inside and no horses, and the fellows went away.

Evidently the railroad is cut somewhere or else the trains are being used to move troops. The only thing I am worried about is that Carranza may start something down at Vera Cruz. That is a worry that is constantly with us. It would be just like him to start something if he sees he is done with the Mexicans.

As Villa and Zapata moved on Mexico City, and on the day that U.S. troops withdrew from Veracruz opening the way for Carranza to make his headquarters there, Irving continued the story around Guanajuato:

[November 23, 1914] I have not written you for a week or more because there have been no trains running out of Guanajuato. The Villa

men now hold Guanajuato, and Villa is somewhere down the line between here and Mexico City, but I do not know how far he has gotten,
or anything else that is going on. With the exception of a week ago yesterday, we have had no mail of any kind for almost two weeks, and do
not hear anything either about Mexico, or about anyplace else.

For several days Guanajuato remained without any government at all
and during that time the people were pretty nervous in town, as they
were afraid the bad element might start in and loot the town. But nothing happened, and on Wednesday last a small force of about thirty Villistas came up from Silao and took the town, and since then there has
been no alarm. These men behaved very well, and no disorders were
committed. But now I think they have gone away, and there is only a
very small force of local police in town. Villa seems to need all his men
to go south with, and has none to leave as garrisons.

The road between here [Cubo] and Guanajuato is getting bad. Night
before last four armed men, who might have been some of the band of
Carranzistas who decamped from Guanajuato, held up a bunch of workmen going in from Peregrina and robbed them and killed one. Several
peons have been held up on the road before this, but nobody has been
killed before. Robberies are becoming frequent all over.

Last night the first train out of Guanajuato for more than a week
started down to Silao and was wrecked near Marfil, not by robbers but
by careless running. The train was ditched and at least eight people
killed and a number wounded. It seems the engineer was going full
speed around a curve on the edge of an embankment.

On Tuesday I went in town to the Power Plant to get some money for
payroll, and as it was expected that day that General Angeles [a Villa
man] might come up from Silao with soldiers to install a governor, I decided to stay and see the fun. But nobody came.

I sent you a telegram Thursday night to the effect that everything
here was lovely. Everybody was feeling rather optimistic about that time,
and expected that Guanajuato at least had seen the last of its troubles.
Since then, not having been able to hear anything at all, I do not know
whether to remain optimistic or not. I shall feel better when there are a
few troops around this vicinity, and a guard on the roads.

I guess things are not going to get worse, and that very soon I can send you a wire to pack up and come down. I fear you will have to come via El Paso, because it may be quite a while before there is communication between here and Vera Cruz. But do not start until you get definite word from me. Mrs. Meiklejohn started down the line from El Paso on her own account with her two boys and landed in Aguascalientes just as Villa was starting out with his army. She had to stay there two days, and finally got to Silao where there were about ten thousand troops, and had been there four days at last account. I think by this time she has been brought up in an auto or by train.

[November 28, 1914] Here at Cubo we are living in a condition of being continually expecting to be held up or raided. La Luz was raided again last Monday. Why not Cubo next, and there is no force either in Guanajuato or anywhere else near. They say that several of those who were in La Luz raids have been caught and shot, but I have my doubts. Most of the men who robbed Mr. Wallace of nineteen boxes of dynamite have been caught; there were supposed to be eight involved, and Mr. Wallace says they have gotten either four or five. I suppose those fellows will be shot but quien sabe.

I met the Governor when I was in town this week. He is a young man who came into prominence just recently in connection with the Carranzistas. I understand he was formerly the manager of a large hacienda by the name of Santa Teresa somewhere in the State of Guanajuato, and was a Constitutionalist. At any rate he was put in charge of the troops in Guanajuato by the Carranzistas although he was rather a Villa man. At the time when the troops mutinied here in town he is supposed to have handled the situation very well and the people in town seem to think he is all right. He struck me as being a very decent sort, and there is no doubt that he is doing his best to straighten up the situation without having adequate means of doing it. He is evidently a man of some nerve, and also is not surrounded by a lot of red tape. I had no trouble at all in seeing him. Guanajuato itself [under Villa control] is very calm and peaceful, and the townspeople are not looking for trouble. The chances are that after worrying for a certain number of nights, things will pass off smoothly and I shall have had my worry for nothing.

The new Governor's name is Camarena. He was appointed directly
by Villa, who told him he could come up here and be provisional governor, but also told him he was to employ the best lawyer in town to help
him run the job, so as not to get into a mess on legal details. He was also
instructed to establish courts again as soon as possible and to shoot anyone who stole even a cigarette. Which struck me as being pretty sound
advice.

No mail is coming in yet from the States, and it is now more than two
weeks that we have heard nothing from the outside, except occasionally
like yesterday when Gilmore talked to San Luis Potosi over the power
line 'phone and got the summary of news from an El Paso paper in that
town.

I am very lonesome for you but I am glad you are not here at Cubo
right now. I do not think things will remain so uncertain very long. I
heard from this San Luis paper that the troops got safely away from
Vera Cruz on the 23rd.

After Carranza's move to Veracruz, Mexico City became a vacuum. Still
supporting the convention and its appointment of Gutiérrez, Zapata moved
on the city from the south and was soon joined by Villa, whose forces had
moved steadily toward the city from Zacatecas, routing Carranzistas along
the way. On December 6, 1914, Villa and Zapata together entered Mexico
City and helped to install Gutiérrez in the National Palace.

Villa's authority seemed to command respect. As he and Zapata took
charge in Mexico City to enforce the findings of the Convention of Aguascalientes, Guanajuato took heart, and it was decided that Luella and the two
boys should return to Cubo in time for the Christmas holidays. Irving met
them in El Paso and they crossed the border on the morning of December 23,
1914. En route to Silao on the Mexican National Railway, Luella wrote to her
mother in the States:*

[December 24, 1914] (Nearing Torreón) We are fully 12 hours late so
far, so we are expecting to spend most of Christmas Day on the train.

---

*Unless otherwise noted, Luella's letters quoted in this chapter were addressed to
her mother.

The delay, as far as we can judge, has been due to having to go very slow over some of the newly-laid track, and mostly to waiting on sidings for a train to pass us. We are now bowling along at a good rate.

After crossing the International Bridge in the early morning yesterday (Wednesday) and waiting in line, we finally got our baggage to customs inspection, and the inspector didn't look at anything — probably a twenty-five cent piece — gold [i.e., U.S.] — that Irving produced helped — and we got on the train a few minutes before it started. Others were not so fortunate and I doubt not some were left behind.

All day yesterday we could see the wheels and ironwork of burned freight trains and miles and miles of rails that were lying beside the track all twisted out of shape. That was Orozco's work. He used to hitch a chain to the rails at one end and an engine at the other and then start the engine full speed. The twists and double twists he'd get into them were wonderful to see.

I felt quite like an emigrant when it came to meal time. We had a big basket of lunch — after hunting I found one of those alcohol stoves that come with the solid alcohol (at exactly double the price they cost in Boston). The first noon I heated some of Heinz's baked beans on it. This morning I made coffee. John says he thinks "it is very satisfactory" and I agree with him.

The train is full up. In the section next to us are two children four and six whose nationality I have not been able to determine. The six-year-old talks German, English and Spanish. This I know because I have heard him. He says he also speaks Italian and I do not doubt it. He told us last evening that "the Germans fight the Russians and the Russians they fight the Germans. The Germans fight the French and the French they fight the Germans. The English fight the Germans and the Germans they fight the English and the Germans they whipped 8,000 Russians." I thought him very well informed for six years.

Irving had a horrid time getting the trunks through Customs. He went across to Juarez with them Tuesday afternoon. The man at the bridge is evidently having his first taste of getting a sight of the things inside a trunk. Formerly of course baggage went across in a train and was examined at the station. He made Irving open every box in the green trunk. He had it on the sidewalk and just dove down into it and ripped things out. Finally Irving succeeded in having it carried into the building. There they ripped out the remaining things and Irving was told to separate everything that was new. Then he was told to dump things back in and take the two trunks over to the station. So things were literally dumped. You see the baggage room had closed at 5 P.M. and if Irving didn't get them through the customs and checked that afternoon there was little chance of our being able to leave the next morning. At the station the inspector was very decent — when the bridge fellow called his attention to the new things he said, "Why those are merely the belongings of his family" (in Spanish) and put on the Customs seals. So the brown trunk wasn't disturbed. When Irving returned to the hotel he was carrying the package of tapioca I had left over from the summer as he'd been quite unable to get it into the trunk in the few minutes he had. From his description the inside of that green trunk must be a frightful mess. If everything is still in it I'll be thankful. The jar of mince meat was yanked out and the man demanded — as he did of everything — "Que es este?" (What's that?) and Irving responded every time "Yo no se" (I don't know). Irving said it was leaking but he wrapped it up in a suit of underwear.

From Guanajuato:

[December 28, 1914] I believe I got us to Silao in my letter of yesterday — at about 9:30 on Christmas night. We went to a hotel and got a room and then asked the cargador [porter] at what time the next day the train would leave for Guanajuato, and were told it was leaving in twenty minutes. So we hustled back to the station and so reached Guanajuato at 11 P.M. and went directly to the hotel and to bed. We were awakened the next morning about 7 by rifle firing and had arrived just in time to see a fight — though we didn't see much of it. When Villa gained control of Guanajuato he put a young fellow by the name of Camarena in as Governor. Everyone — Americans and Mexicans — were much pleased — liked him and felt he was the right sort to establish a good government. But he was given no soldiers and when a little later a soldier — or petty officer — confiscated a house in Leon, Camarena told him to return it and he refused, and the Governor had no way to enforce his order, so he left for Mexico City to see Villa and find out if he was Governor or not and said he'd not be back until he could enforce his decrees. Then, after he'd gone, a bunch of so-called soldiers appeared — and they were more thieves than soldiers — and robbed people on the road and demanded horses and arms and everyone wished they'd leave. This was the state of affairs when Irving left and during the time he was away. The night we put into Silao there was a bunch of cavalry there lined up at the station and later they rode off on the gallop and we were told that trouble was brewing. Camarena had gotten as far back as Irapuato and General Torres in Silao was ready for him as it was his men that were holding Guanajuato. Well what happened the next morning when the firing aroused us was the return of the Governor with eighty cavalry.

We had a corner room at the hotel and it was just around that corner the firing was going on — the cuartel, or barracks, was only a few houses down the street and the newcomers were storming it. Our first impulse was to rush to the windows to see what was going on and then Irving said we better duck as these fellows never shoot straight. So we all hustled into the corridor — barefooted and in our pajamas and nightdress — and stood along the side of the wall. . . . But Irving didn't stay inside a minute — he was back in our room looking out the window because he said he'd never seen a town captured yet and didn't want to miss the opportunity.

But it was all over in a little over an hour — the place was captured — three men wounded — one seriously — two horses killed — and about one hundred eighty taken prisoners. Camarena was with his troops and all Guanajuato rejoiced to see him back. For a while the streets were full and the soldiers rode back and forth, shouting "Viva Villa — Viva Villa — Viva V-ill-a" — first two short and sharp and the last drawn out — getting the populace to shout with them. These Mexicans are a stolid bunch at a time like that. A few of them were standing on the opposite corner from our room with their burros when the fighting began and they continued to stand there unmoved through it all — looking on as if it were just some uneventful happening. We are told there is quite a bunch of infantry on the way, and it looks as if Camarena has come to stay. Irving says things look better to him around Guanajuato right now than they have since his return in August. However everyone advised us not to go out to Cubo that day as a few of the defeated bunch might be in the surrounding hills.

From Cubo, Luella wrote to her older sister Edith:

[January 11, 1915] Things are very quiet here in Cubo and we live the simple life. There are only two white men working for Irving now, no one at Tajo [where the mill was located] and no women in any of the outlying camps. Also it seems that no women are riding now without a white man as escort so I am staying strictly at home and having no company. I talk with Mrs. Wallace every day or so however and learn what is going on in Guanajuato. . . .

None of my blankets were taken — also none of the good saddles including Bob's. The saddles were hidden in an old tank and the blankets were left on the beds but were not touched. But I find only one of my good towels, except the guest towels — those are all here.

It was during this time around Guanajuato that, aside from various *bonos* or *vales* put out from time to time for local use, there were two distinct currencies in circulation: Carranza money, or bills printed by the Constitucionalistas and used by them to pay for goods they requisitioned; and Villa money, printed in areas where he was in control that was claimed by Villa men to be the only valid currency. No one knew who would ultimately win out and which currency would in the end be honored by the government, which as we have seen posed a dilemma for the Herrs' cook, Angela, who was saving her money.

The years 1914 and 1915 were full of turmoil and confusion. Hopeful of some success for their revolutionary aims, Villa and Zapata had relied heavily on the Aguascalientes Convention to make some sense of their objectives. Neither was politically oriented, but both did what they knew how to do, which was to put their man, Eulalio Gutiérrez, in office and leave the politics to him. He failed, and Carranza's forces under General Obregón engaged in war to force Villa and Zapata out. Result — disaster, hunger, and misery. Mining operations had to be frequently interrupted.

At the end of 1914, Villa's strength was at its height. Railroads and telegraph lines in and out of Mexico City were under his control, and Zapata soon returned to Puebla. But on January 5, 1915, Villa left the city to consolidate his position in the north. Gutiérrez, fearing Villa, turned to Obregón for help, and to be on the safe side moved his office north to Nuevo León. Obregón, sensing the advantage, strengthened his force of Carranzistas and reentered Mexico City on January 28. He found a dead city, paralyzed by strikes, silent, hungry, businesses closed. For six weeks Obregón presided over a rule of terror in the city.

Luella and Irving sensed the deterioration almost at once. She wrote from Cubo:

> [January 20, 1915] Our dreams of peace in Guanajuato seem to be founded on false hopes. Governor Camarena stayed in office (also in Guanajuato) just three weeks. Within that time he and the general sent to support him developed differences as to who really was the head and on Sunday, the 17th, General [Felipe] Dussart ran the Governor out of town. There was a good deal of fighting in town all that day (3 men shot with about 15,000 rounds of ammunition) and everyone stayed indoors with windows and doors—also blinds—shut. Since then the city has been quiet. In the meantime all has continued quiet in Cubo and we tell the Wallaces (over the telephone) that they better come out here to live where it is quiet.
>
> Also, as you have perhaps seen before we did, President Gutierrez has escaped with funds and soldiers from Mexico City. Villa is cut off from the City—fighting is in progress somewhere thereabouts and it looks as if things are in more of a mixup than ever. We are of course hopelessly disgusted—but we are not worried. This fighting is all strictly between themselves and foreigners are not bothered. But we can see no end to the tangle nor how the companies can continue running indefinitely unless some freight is brought through from somewhere. Here at Cubo life moves serenely and uneventfully.

The first six months of 1915 were a time of anarchy and uncertainty in Mexico. There were four governments simultaneously—Carranza in Veracruz; the Convention Government in Mexico City, still claimed by

Zapata's followers; Gutiérrez with a diminished following seeking refuge in Nuevo León; and a separate civil administration set up by Villa in Chihuahua. There was no mail in Mexico City, no commercial telegrams or cables except as allowed by the Carranzistas through Veracruz. The generals controlled the railroads and telegraph. Newspaper reports were nonexistent or unreliable. There was monetary chaos, and in Mexico City food was scarce.

Luella's diary shows how these conditions affected her family, as developments headed toward a new crisis for the foreigners in Guanajuato:

1915 - January

17 — Fighting in Guanajuato all day. General Dussart drove out Governor Camarena. Telephone out of order so we couldn't talk with Guanajuato.

18 — Antonio [the mail carrier to the mine] sent word that he passed 100 soldiers on the road to Cubo. So we hid money, serapes and jewels and awaited them. However they went to Peregrina instead and we didn't see them.

21 — Feeling uneasy about things in Mexico — no trains. Am laying in supplies.

22 — Las Nuñez [nearby] was visited by 20 soldiers and robbed of 3,000 pesos — hence we felt uneasy.

23 — The report is that the soldiers who robbed Las Nuñez are in Guanajuato, and the Captain has been arrested and is to be shot.

29 — No mail for a week and no prospect of any. We know nothing of what is happening in Mexico, the United States, or Europe.

31 — We were visited by a bunch of cavalry (eleven men) from Guanajuato who came to take our horses and saddles — which they did — except that Bob and I succeeded in hiding his and Irving's saddles and a few bridles.

1915 - February

1 — Irving went to town with the Jefe of Cubo — riding a mule — to try to recover horses and saddles. He and Mr. Smith returned at five P.M. with one horse and the mule and two saddles.

2 — Woke up to a seemingly serene holiday. At ten A.M. a bunch of cavalry was seen coming to Cubo from Dolores Hidalgo way and we

rushed around hiding things and the boys and I went into the mine. They were Villistas and o.k. so we came out, but they told of Carranzistas at their heels so we packed up two trunks and hustled to town — Bob on a mule, John and I on one horse and Irving on foot, and landed on the Wallaces.

9 — Downtown today we saw palace furniture being moved to Leon, where the State government is to be. Also heard there is a possibility of U.S. mail — and rumors of bandits nearby.

While they were in town at their friends' house, Luella assisted members of the foreign colony to care for Mrs. Cunningham, an English woman who nearly died in childbirth. She writes from Guanajuato:

[February 11, 1915] Her husband was sent to Guadalajara on business and then all lines and telegraph wires were cut and there was no way for him to return or get any word. . . . Mr. Cunningham reached Guanajuato three days after the baby was stillborn — word having been gotten to him by telephone — messenger — telephone — and then telegraph. He came on a military train halfway, and was taken prisoner when the Carranzistas captured the train (of Villistas), and the other foreigner with him, an Arab, and two noncombatant Mexicans were shot before his eyes as they were armed. He fortunately had abandoned his gun along with all his baggage just a little while before in an endeavor to get away from the fighting and he thinks that is all that saved his life. The rest of the trip was made partly on a burro, and partly on a lame horse, and he certainly looked like a tramp when he finally reached here. Mrs. Cunningham is now far on the road to recovery but she caused us all a great deal of anxiety for a week or ten days and her poor husband was nearly frantic those days he was trying to get here and meeting with delay after delay. . . .

Everyone is quite hopeful again after two or three weeks of dark pessimism — not hopeful of permanent peace in Mexico but hopeful that we are again connected with the United States and the rest of the world (except southern Mexico) by rail and telegraph and so will be able to get supplies and mail. There has never yet been any cause for worry as to our personal safety and as a matter of fact Guanajuato has been wonderfully peaceful these past two weeks.

Concerning this time of "anarchy and uncertainty in Mexico," Luella's diary continues:

1915 - February

17 — Daily mail service established between Guanajuato and Silao again — by coach, not train.

19 — Returned to Cubo. Slow journey as some of our animals were pretty poor. . . . Many of our belongings were in hiding during our stay in Guanajuato.

21 — Everything is very peaceful.

22 — Mail is coming daily but most of it is old — of November. Irving is still getting letters from me, written before I came back in December. . . . Everything is wonderfully quiet round about.

1915 - March

3 — The Cubo Company has leased the Tajo mill and Irving will be busier henceforth.

5 — No mail again — said to be because troop trains are going north. Sixteen passed Silao yesterday.

On March 10, 1915, Obregón headed north for a showdown with Villa. Villa awaited him in Irapuato, some thirty miles southwest of Guanajuato. With Villa's men still in control, on March 28, a decree was issued in Guanajuato requiring payment of employees in silver or the equivalent value in paper, and on the 29th, Cubo and all other Guanajuato mining companies decided to shut down in consequence. The decree was suspended temporarily and operations resumed.

Luella, in town for Holy Week, continues in her diary:

1915 - March

28 — (Sunday) Much upset in the evening to learn of a decree of the Guanajuato Jefe [Villista] requiring payment of employees in silver or the equivalent in paper. All the Guanajuato mining companies are to shut down in consequence.

29 — Cubo and the other mining companies shut down and we are all rather nervous. . . . The Jefe agreed to suspend the decree for a week or two so the companies are to start up again.

1915 - April

5— Mrs. Gilmore [wife of the American manager of the Guanajuato Power Company] gave a luncheon and bridge for eight and I went up to help. She is much worried over things generally down here. A band of Carranzistas are at San Miguel de Allende.

6— Everyone is more or less uneasy—fearing a visit from Carranzistas. Irving came to town in the afternoon bringing three horses after hiding stuff at Cubo.

7— [In town]—Got very nervous over tales of eight hundred Carranzistas out Cubo way, etc., etc. Later proved to be untrue.

8— Villistas and Carranzistas are fighting in Celaya [forty miles east of Irapuato].

9— Irving with six other mine managers left for Leon to see the Governor regarding the effect of the new decree about wages [March 28] on Guanajuato mines.

10— Our husbands unexpectedly returned in the afternoon to our great joy after a successful trip.

By now Obregón's forces, the Carranzistas, had penetrated the area around Guanajuato and were facing Villa for a showdown. The people in Guanajuato had felt secure while Villa's men were in control, but were fearful of depredations by the Carranzistas, who had the reputation of being destructive looters. Luella continues the story from Cubo:

1915 - April

15— Great rejoicing over news of a big Villa victory at Celaya—which turned out to be a Villa defeat. Hence distress.

16— Irving went to town for payroll and left me with the news that I better begin packing, ready to get out if the Carranzistas come up this way. Later we found that no one else is leaving so he thought better of it. Then when Irving returned from town Mrs. Gilmore telephoned that she was packing so I packed too. Am sad and disgusted.

17— The Herr family left Cubo for Guanajuato at 6 A.M. en route to the U.S. (we thought). In town we talked matters over with others and decided to wait another day before leaving. We learned later that Villa was evacuating Irapuato and going north and there were no trains, so we can't go. [The Herrs stayed in town.]

18 — Irving rode out to Cubo and advised the other American family there to move into Guanajuato until the change of government is effected.

19 — The former Villa Jefe of Guanajuato [Camarena] returned with some soldiers and began shooting downtown.

20 — Spent the day waiting for trouble and Carranzistas, and neither arrived.

21 — Irving went out to Cubo for the day — a bunch of natives headed by a couple of Camarena's brothers "took the town" [Guanajuato] in the evening. It consisted of shooting into the air and shouting.

23 — Irving rode out to Cubo in the morning. At noon there was a holdup of burro men on the hill back of Pastita [where they were staying in Guanajuato] by five men with rifles. The shots disturbed our luncheon. I worried all afternoon about Irving coming to town for fear he'd meet the bandits but he arrived safely at 6.

24 — The first bunch (a few) of Carranzista troops arrived this evening.

25 — [Sunday] Irving decided to take the boys to the moving pictures and about 4 o'clock we heard all the church bells ringing and learned that about 2,000 or 3,000 Carranzista soldiers had come to town, so he didn't do it and we played auction [bridge] instead.

26 — A bunch of soldiers is quartered in the street here in front of the house and they spent the afternoon shooting at bottles and we didn't enjoy it — fearing stray bullets.

27 — Mrs. Gilmore and I decided we'd like to go downtown to buy some candy and see the soldiers. Irving went with us and we saw plenty! Such a dirty town! Also the army is commandeering all the food supply. We were much delayed on the tramway by flatcars hauling corn.

28 — Irving planned to go to Cubo but was kept in town by a decree declaring all the money we've been using [probably Villa paper money] no good. Such a mess! General Obregon came to town in the afternoon and left with many of the soldiers in the evening.

29 — Most of the Carranzista soldiers have left Guanajuato. There is a battle on between Silao and Leon.

1915 - May

2 — Our guard of soldiers have returned to camp in the street in front of the house [at the Guanajuato Power Plant].

8 — [Now back at Cubo] A good deal of excitement in Guanajuato over the arrival of more Carranzistas and outposts all about. None have yet come to Cubo however.

11 — We were surprised and not pleased to have twenty Carranzista cavalry land on us about noon. They came for horses but didn't take them because of Irving's *salvo conducto* [safe conduct] signed by General Obregon. But they stayed three hours and we felt nervous while they were here.

13 — Soldiers visited us again — the same ones, only a major came with them and they were more disciplined. They were out scouting and only here a little while.

17 — Peregrina mine was robbed last night of precipitates [mine product ready for shipment to the smelter]. . . . Irving seems to think the Cubo Company may have to shut down soon, due to lack of supplies.

As Villa tried desperately to hold on against mounting pressure from Obregón in the "valley" below Guanajuato, the Herrs went to the Endweisses in town on May 28 "to visit for a few days." Luella reports:

1915 - June

1 — [In Guanajuato] Mr. Endweiss came home at noon and said very emphatically that we were to *stay* at home. The Villistas took Silao. At 10 P.M. the Carranzistas all rode by the house where we were staying. Special cars — flatcars — bundles, etc. Evacuating, we thought.

2 — Having watched the Carranzistas evacuate the town at 10 P.M. (as we thought) we saw them all return early this morning. They only went up to the Presa [the dam at the upper end of town] to sleep for greater safety. Mrs. Endweiss and I are staying home. Much madness because we wouldn't go to Mrs. Meiklejohn's to a birthday party to be given for me.

3 — The same performance of seeing our friends — the C's — move to the Presa with their bedding in the evening and return in the morning.

4 — Still the Carranzistas do not leave us. Still they dash madly by on the road to the Presa and later madly back again.

5 — A day of thrills and nervous excitement. We spent most of the morning watching Carranzistas ride by as they evacuated the town. The Villistas came in the afternoon and we saw one hundred sixty ride by at 10 P.M.

6 — In the afternoon we watched 1,000 Villistas ride by, leaving Guanajuato. Cubo is full of Villistas — three hundred in the hacienda — glad we weren't there.

7 — All the Villistas had left by morning, more came in the afternoon but went right out again. Rumors of their defeat and victory of the Carranzistas — no one knows what to believe. Lights went out in the Endweiss house in the evening — someone stole the wire. We are all blue and upset.

8 — We learned the Villistas are beaten and retreating on Aguas, and the Carranzistas have Leon. We are pretty blue at the prospect of no way to get out.

Guanajuato was now virtually surrounded by Carranza troops except to the north where Villa's forces still occupied Dolores Hidalgo, a town thirty miles from Guanajuato across the mountains of the continental divide. Railroad access from Guanajuato to the north was controlled by Carranzistas. With flight by train no longer possible, the foreign colony in Guanajuato sensed itself in some peril. They decided to head for Villa territory while there was still time by crossing the mountains on horseback to Dolores Hidalgo, where trains were still running north on the eastern line. Luella notes:

1915 - June

9 — We "made a dash" for Cubo and home at 7:30 A.M. in an endeavor to get out on horseback — which we did except that I rode the mule. Spent the rest of the day unpacking and getting clothes in shape to leave if we can.

10 — Rather downhearted all day because we can't get out. About 6 P.M. Mr. Wallace called up to say they plan to leave after all on Saturday via San Felipe [on the eastern railway, north of Guanajuato and Dolores Hidalgo]. Began packing at once.

11 — Not much sleep last night for me. Irving went to town at 7 A.M. I picked things up, got lunch ready, and got things ready to leave. Irving came home at 3 P.M. to report that we leave for Dolores Hidalgo at 5 A.M. tomorrow.

12 — We got away finally at 6:15 A.M. Lucas and Antonio went with us. We met the Guanajuato crowd beyond Santa Rosa — twenty Americans [on horses or mules] and forty pack animals of baggage. Reached Dolores at 7:30 P.M. *very* tired. Found the town full of Villistas and we had to get our own meals.

[Mother's record here is much too sketchy. I was almost nine by now, and the ride to Dolores Hidalgo was a great adventure. It was an all-day ride, over mountain roads and trails, some thirty miles. The mountains of the Continental Divide were green at this time of year and the air was clean and fresh. Our cavalcade of armed men and the caravan of baggage, including trunks, was an impressive sight winding over the mountains. John and I, each on a horse, enjoyed the thrill of the excitement. As we came down out of the mountains late in the day we could see Dolores lying deep in the valley, the pinks and blues and yellows of the calcined houses blending in the late afternoon light — and we also saw a patch of dust moving toward us up the slope. They were coming to meet us. They were armed also. It seems that the Villa commander headquartered in Dolores Hidalgo had sent his scouts to see what ammunition train might be threatening his position. We were escorted into Dolores by his men, and our people were given passes to proceed. Presumably because of uncertainties on the eastern railroad line, our route from San Luis Potosí took us west on a branch line to Aguascalientes and the western railroad line to Ciudad Juárez and El Paso. Here Villa was still in control and we found that Villa himself was in Aguas. Our men were able to talk with him in the freight car he had preempted for his office, and he was happy to grant us safe conduct to board the train for the north and so reach the border.]

In retrospect John adds color as he tells of seeing Pancho Villa:

It was mid-morning of a hot day in June 1915 that my father took me and my younger brother by the hand and led us into the railroad yards of

Aguas Calientes to peer into the open door of a boxcar to see this Titan, who to many was a devil, but to many more was a saint. He was seated at a large desk set up in the middle of the car, his sombrero pushed back on his head, his black hair and bushy eyebrows setting off a pair of piercing black eyes which flashed constantly at the men about him. His name was Francisco (Pancho) Villa.*

At the age of ten, John was obviously impressed.
As Luella tells it in her diary:

1915 - June

13 — Busy getting meals for the crowd and unpacking lunch baskets. Mr. Wallace and Mr. Meiklejohn had an unpleasant experience with General Natera, trying to get passports. We left by train for San Luis Potosí at 4 P.M. Reached there at 10:30. Also full of Villistas and we had some difficulty in getting rooms.

14 — Left for Aguas by train at 9 A.M. We were held up from 11 till 3 waiting for a burned bridge (ten feet long!) to be rebuilt. We were held all night at Salinas as the engine had no fuel. Three troop trains of Manuel Chao ahead of us. The most wretchedly uncomfortable night I ever spent.

15 — Reached Aguas — thick with dust and Villistas — at 10:30 A.M. We found a hotel near the station which was closed, but opened for us and we got our meals. I felt completely done up. We left on a Pullman for Juarez at 11 P.M.

16 — Hot and dusty and everyone is tired. An improvement over our previous traveling but still bad enough. We had lunch from the buffet which cost — for the Herrs — eighty pesos!

17 — Another hotter and dustier day, but always nearing the U.S. and finally reached there at 7:30 to our great relief and delight. All came to the Paso del Norte [Hotel in El Paso].

After a series of encounters that began with a severe engagement at

---

*John W. Herr, "¡Qué Hombre!" submitted to The [Cincinnati] Literary Club, October 1947.

Celaya and ranged up and down the central valley (including forays over the mountains around the city of Guanajuato), the superior generalship of Obregón ultimately prevailed, and in July Villa was forced back to Chihuahua, badly beaten. In November he made one last effort to regain a foothold in Sonora, but his men were defeated at Agua Prieta and again at Hermosillo, where his few remaining troops were virtually wiped out. On December 24, 1915, Villa left Chihuahua for the surrounding hills where he was reduced to hit-and-run tactics, now a Mexican "bandit." Zapata had once more retreated south.

As early as June 11, 1915, after the battles around Celaya, Carranza, from his safe retreat in Veracruz, had claimed control of major parts of the country. On October 19, 1915, the United States finally recognized him as de facto president of Mexico.

CHAPTER 7

Carranza

After recognition by the United States on October 19,
1915, Carranza toured Mexico, accepting plaudits in
the areas where his men had prevailed. There was no
effective government. Mexico City was seething with
dissatisfaction. Services were disrupted. Elsewhere in
the country things were just as bad. Crops were short,
food was scarce, transportation was uncertain, authority was lacking. Bands of disgruntled revolutionaries
with no real leadership roamed the hills looting and
marauding. In Chihuahua, Villa found more men and
harassed the Carranzistas with guerrilla tactics.

Meanwhile, back in Massachusetts, information on
conditions in Mexico was received by the Herrs indirectly. A few days before Carranza was recognized by
the United States, H. Vincent Wallace, the English
mine manager who had helped the Herrs escape to
Veracruz in 1914, wrote Irving from New York to
report on the situation in Mexico as seen by another
of the Guanajuato managers who had just left the
country. By this time Villa was licking his wounds in
Chihuahua, and Obregón was largely in control on
behalf of Carranza. Wallace's letter:

[October 15, 1915] I suppose you know that Endweis
came out to have a confab with Reid and the Directors
of the Guanajuato Development Company, and . . . I
had an opportunity of discussing the situation as far as
Endweis was able to size it up from his travels from

Guanajuato, via San Luis Potosi, Monterrey, Tampico, Vera Cruz and Mexico D.F. The matter stewed down to a jelly is that he does not consider the outlook for an early settlement as in any way bright. While Carranza is virtually recognized, he is short of rolling stock, especially engines, and Endweis had it on very good authority that, although they had recently borrowed twenty-seven new engines from the Isthmus road, ten only are now serviceable. Worse conditions of the pulling force obtain in other parts of the republic, and when he left, the expectation was that only about 10 percent of the trains would be running for sixty days, and within four months they expected a complete shutdown of train service throughout the republic.

Therefore, how can Carranza work the miracles that are necessary to:

1st — Quickly and efficiently move troops to disturbed areas.

2nd — Transport food supplies to famine stricken areas. . . . Although he says there is no lack of food anywhere, he knows to the contrary. In Guanajuato Hayes wired about ten days ago that all the companies had been called upon to subscribe towards "soup kitchens." How to make soup without the material is the question.

3rd — How can Carranza, in the face of a non-rainy season, without seed grain, and with a disheartened and suspicious people, suddenly plant, grow, and harvest crops to avert the dire consequences of his jellyfish acts in the past?

4th — Establish a properly guaranteed currency that will tend to give the mass of people a chance. And furthermore, what has he got left to export to tend to equalize the exchange?

Joe Macdonald almost got article 33, but by supplying Davis the Greek with a lot of cash, and filling up the powers that were (a General Espinosa, et al.) they decided that the order could be withdrawn — but it was actually signed! [Translation: Joe McDonald, one of the American managers from Guanajuato, was threatened with death, but bribed his way out of it.]

After ample discussion it is the decision of the Guanajuato Development Company and also G. Consolidated to not endeavor to get more supplies in for a couple of months, and I was given to understand yesterday that they did not figure on starting up for three or four months at the *soonest*. I was up with the Phelps Dodge crowd yesterday and Douglas and Cleveland Dodge both told me they had shut down the Nacosari plant last Wednesday, and didn't have any idea when they would start up again. . . .

I feel as you do in regard to Mexico, and certainly don't want to have to go back in a hurry, or at the first imaginary indication that everything is lovely. Endweis says the suffering is dreadful in Guanajuato even, and that hundreds of the poor and those who were moderately well off are simply starving to death, and it's a good deal worse in Mexico City. Tortillas are selling at *three* for the peso. Eggs are the same. What do you know about that!

A bunch got into Tajo, tied up the three watchmen, and got into the almacen, where we had removed the fourteen inch battery belts, took two hundred seventy feet of that, all the filter twine, a gross of files (for breaking jail I suppose) and two small motors. They are still chasing the thieves!!

H. Vincent Wallace

An officer of the Cubo Company in the Chicago office was not so well informed. In November he wrote to Irving:

[November 11, 1915] Since your letter came Carranza has been recognized and it looks as though he would succeed in straightening affairs out so that Mexico will be a place where people can live. Mr. Hollis thinks that we ought to be able to resume operations in a month or two.

Another letter from Wallace (in New York):

[December 3, 1915] I gather that the situation in Mexico is clearing up a little bit but am opposed to any sudden rush of blood to the head on the idea that everything is lovely down there.

I hear from the American Smelting and Refining Company that they believe that somewhere about the first of the year they may be able to open up the Monterrey smelter *provided* that they furnish engines, rolling stock and guards for their trains which carry in the necessary supplies to run the smelter. Several companies are rushing in or trying to get in machinery and metallurgical supplies. For my part I believe the much more necessary supply to send in would be corn or beans, because without these articles it would be impossible to get manpower out of our workmen.

With Villa supposedly no longer a military force and Carranza now recognized as president by the United States, Irving returned once more to Guanajuato in January 1916, to find that indeed there was no effective government in Mexico. From Guanajuato he wrote to Luella in the States:

[January 9, 1916] I finally reached Guanajuato yesterday morning after a — of a trip. I certainly wish I was back in Cambridge [Mass.], job or no job. The people in Guanajuato are very pessimistic, more so than ever. The hills are full of bandits and I hate the idea of going out to Cubo, which I will have to do. . . . We had a very good trip from Nuevo Laredo as far down as Gonzales, which is a few stations this side of Queretaro on the National line. We got off the train at Gonzales instead of going on to Queretaro because we learned that Carranza was at the latter place, and that all the hotels were crowded. As there was no telling how long we might have to stop in Queretaro waiting for a northbound train to Guanajuato, with no place to stop at, we decided to take a little branch line that starts from Gonzales and runs over to Celaya and thence on to Acambaro. We reached Gonzales about half past six at night having been told that there was a hotel right at the station, at which we might stop. We found the hotel was one for railroad employees and was entirely full, so we had to spend the night sitting up in a restaurant. Our train to Celaya left at four A.M. and we were well-nigh frozen when we got on it. It was only eighteen kilometers across to Celaya, which we reached at five o'clock. There we got into a rickety broken-down coach and were driven uptown to a dirty hotel and went to bed. We got four hours sleep from six until ten and then woke up. We spent the day trying to find out when we would be able to get a train up to Irapuato, but nobody knew when the train coming from Mexico City would pass Celaya, or in fact whether any train was coming at all. At any rate we went down to the station at six in the evening, and waited until midnight, and then with the aid of a little grease we were taken up to Irapuato on a caboose which was carrying some military men. We reached Irapuato at one in the morning and it was a pathetic sight. The worst-looking bunch of ragged peons I ever want to see. We had to stand out in the open until five o'clock watching our grips, as the restaurant was closed up, and the interior of the station was already full with a crowd that we did not care to associate with. So we nearly froze again.

At five o'clock the train from Mexico City rolled in — nothing but a bunch of freight cars, full of humanity inside and out, and with one third-class coach on the rear. Then the restaurant opened up and we took our baggage in there. I nearly fell over when I saw Dr. Hislop and his wife. [Dr. Hislop was a Canadian dentist who served the foreign colony in Guanajuato.] She looked more dead than alive. It seems that they had been down to Mexico City to spend Christmas, and were just getting back. They were disgusted and about worn out, and had lost their trunk into the bargain. At six o'clock the Guanajuato train was due to leave. This consisted of about three freight cars, and one boxcar for passengers made by cutting most of the sides out and leaving only the roof. It had benches on each side and one down the middle. It was a kind of summer observation car, but for this time of year it was cold. The whole business from Gonzales on took the heart right out of me, and I haven't got it back yet.

We had only the four hours sleep from Thursday morning until Saturday morning. . . .

The mozos got back safely from Dolores after we left them there [June 12, 1915, leaving Mexico], con todos y caballos. There are two horses out at Cubo still. Angela and Reyes are both at Cubo. Angela is cook, but Reyes is not working.

On January 10, 1916, a party of Villistas attacked a train en route from Chihuahua City to Cusihuiriáchic in the western part of the state. Seventeen American engineers and miners whom Hollis had sent out to reopen the Cusi mine were lined up and shot — an event that became notorious as the Santa Isabel massacre. The United States had recognized Villa's enemy Carranza, and gringos were now fair game. Devastated by news of the massacre, Hollis ordered the American employees of the Cubo Company out of Mexico once more.

[January 16, 1916 — to Luella from Cubo] This is Sunday morning and I have been spending the bulk of the morning having a housecleaning in the office; throwing away useless mail, sorting out magazines, and cleaning up generally. The office has been left untouched by the hand of man apparently since last June, and there was a sad mixture of dirt, papers, etc. . . .

I have just received a telegram from Hollis telling me to draw immediately on Chicago for funds. What do you think of that? So no more for the present.

One day later Irving tried to reassure Luella, not with complete success:

[January 17, 1916 — from Guanajuato] It just this minute dawned on me that this is my birthday, and that I am now thirty-nine years old. I certainly forgot all about it on account of other worries. I am in town again. I came in rather a hurry yesterday afternoon, on account of a telegram I received from Hollis. He wanted me to draw on Chicago for funds and as I had no need for funds it quite took me off my feet. I have sent him several wires since receiving his and received another from him this morning which eased my mind somewhat. If this sort of thing is to continue indefinitely I certainly am sorry I did not resign my position when we reached the States last June. It all makes me sick and mad. . . .

Every thing is quiet here in Guanajuato. General Carranza was to have reached here today or tomorrow, but after getting as far as Celaya has gone back to Queretaro. So his trip here is postponed. . . .

While I was on the train between Chicago and Boston, it occurred to me to request the Cubo Company to take out $10,000 insurance on my life for the year 1916. I am sorry now that I let the matter pass and did not mention it. It might possibly be a very useful asset to you. Let us hope not however, and really I believe my health is going to continue good. . . .

Dearest this is a most unsatisfactory letter, but I know you will realize why. It may never reach you, although I believe the mails are going through somewhat regularly. . . .

In February 1916, Irving returned to the United States, where he would remain for the next four years. On his return he was interviewed by Luella's brother Laurence Winship, who was now on the staff of the *Boston Globe*:

February 25, 1916 — Irving Herr of Cambridge, a mining engineer who went into Mexico only a few days before the party of 17 miners who were massacred in Chihuahua January 10, came back to Boston yesterday with impressions which make the prospect of tranquility in the troubled Republic seem to him more remote than ever.

"Reforms" weird and incongruous in a bandit-ridden country; a loosely organized Government and a highly organized laboring class; starvation so tragic that it is called a "disease"; currency so debased that a bean crop sorely needed to feed Mexicans is shipped to Havana in return for gold — these were among the observations which left him wondering in what direction the salvation of the people lies.

Mr. Herr, a Harvard graduate, has been in Mexico much of the time since he first went there in 1901. Several times he has made hasty exits with his family when crises threatened. This time he went to Mexico alone, soon after Christmas, to resume operations at a mine near the city of Guanajuato.

— *No Superficial View* —

He went into Mexico from Laredo, Texas; went to his mine; was soon recalled, and returned by the way of Vera Cruz, sailing to New York.

So that his acquaintance with the country is not superficial; but he hesitated to give definite judgments or to make predictions when talking to a Globe reporter last night. "One man's guess is as good as another's," was his explanation. He made "merely observations," as follows:

"On the surface conditions seemed improved. Trains ran on schedule. There were fewer soldiers in the cities. But it was not long before the seething undercurrent of discontent became apparent — there was something stirring which showed things were hot under the surface.

"My first tangible evidence of this came with the knowledge that the working class was organized in a way formerly undreamed of in Mexico.

The laborers all over the country had joined in organization which you might translate as 'world workers.' They demanded more money, for one thing, and the reason was obvious.

—A "Dollar" Worth 4 Cents —

"That reason was the debased currency, the problem which men I met in Mexico regarded as the most serious of all today. A Carranza peso (dollar) is worth about four cents in gold now. A peon earning two pesos a day found that wage would buy him only a small fraction of the amount of meal it would buy a couple of years ago.

"The Carranza money was printed in Mexico and it has been counterfeited and counterfeited, I was told. Now the Government has its vaults full of new notes printed in the United States, but the Government and every one else seems at a loss to know how this new currency can be put out and how it can be secured.

"This currency situation is the fundamental point at issue in the general strike of every laborer in Mexico which was scheduled when I left Vera Cruz to come off February 23, I was told; but which has been averted, temporarily at least, the dispatches say.

"The thoroughness with which the labor organizations have developed cropped out in the most unexpected places. The proprietress of a small hotel in Vera Cruz who used occasionally to attend personally to the cooking for her guests told me that she was sorry, but she was not allowed to go in her kitchen now. 'A rule of bakers' organization forbade it.

— Education by Edict —

"And so, it was told me, the Government is facing the situation with most unusual innovations. Education is a great thing in the movement. Everybody is 'being educated.' Schools are held at all hours in some cities, and in Vera Cruz a decree went out that every grown inhabitant must learn to read or write within the specified period under penalty of imprisonment.

"The sympathies of many in high authority were for not obeying the decree, Socialistic, I was informed. While I was in Vera Cruz the news came that they had started a feminist movement in Yucatan. One thing the Carranza Government has made it hard to do is to get a drink of anything but beer.

"It was in Vera Cruz that the transportation problem loomed most serious. Only a very few freight cars are running up to Mexico City and the docks are piled high with supplies. Joining the waiting list for a freight car was like joining the waiting list of a club — and the chances of election were not absolutely certain and just, I was told.

"The equipment of that road is in deplorable shape. We ran down from Mexico City through the night without a headlight, and there is no semblance of a signal system working now. But the roads were apparently undisturbed by the bandits.

"These bodies of men live off the scanty crops of the country districts and keep away from the cities. It is the isolated haciendas that they have attacked. They camp in large bands often — hundreds of deserters or men tired with four years' fighting under Carranza or Villa — Zapata discipline — just far enough away from cities to be out of reach of the garrisons.

— *Starvation "Stomach Disease"* —

"It is poor Mexicans more than Americans who suffer at their hands. I didn't see the 'starvation' much; I was only told of it. An old acquaintance in Vera Cruz told me that [the] 'stomach disease' so many died of was simply starvation.

"And the steamer I came out on carried a hold full of frijoles (beans) for Havana. They needed the gold in payment in Mexico.

"Going down to Mexico I heard great things of the 'new era of prosperity' in Mexico. Once inside I found all the business men pessimistic. As a man from the States who went with me said: 'Why, everybody knows things are better in Mexico except these Americans who are down here.'

"And in Mexico I everywhere heard that nothing could change things except intervention."

"Well," said Mr. Herr's listener, "something will have to happen pretty soon, one way or the other."

"Yes — something has been just going to happen for four years," he agreed or disagreed.

His last was a remark of wonderment and appreciation — "How did Porfirio Diaz rule the country for 20 or 30 years? Ten years ago no one knew there were any such people in Mexico as we've heard from since. And old Huerta wasn't such a poor —, well, perhaps some people in the States are beginning to think that assassination — " Again he left his sentence unfinished.

How long Carranza will continue to be upheld by his "supporters" is regarded as uncertain, he intimated.

How long anything will remain as it is in Mexico — except uncertainty — is uncertain, in Mr. Herr's guarded opinion.

The situation at the mine in January 1916 was outlined by Irving in a letter to an associate after his return to the United States. He wrote:

[August 18, 1916][1] I returned to Guanajuato in January of this year taking several men with me. . . . You probably know that we have had a lease on your old Providencia Mill since March 1915, but so far have never been able to start running it. When I went back to Guanajuato this year it was with the intention of starting up the mill. The tramway from Villalpando [the Cubo mine shaft] to the mill was almost completed; this we had done in 1915, and I was hoping things would settle down and that we could have a profitable run, for we have the ore. But soon after my return came the Santa Isabel massacre west of Chihuahua, when seventeen Americans were taken from a train and murdered. These were all Mr. Hollis' men who were returning to open up the Cusi Mine. When this happened Mr. Hollis immediately wired me to close up everything and come back to the States, as he did not propose to keep any men in Mexico after that occurrence. Between you and me I was quite ready to come, for things were decidedly nasty in Guanajuato, what between the I.W.W., lack of food, bandits and one thing and another.

On March 9, 1916, Villa raided the U.S. border town of Columbus, New Mexico, looting and departing with U.S. cavalry horses and mules. General Pershing's punitive expedition pursued Villa for eleven months (to February 5, 1917) across the northern wastelands of Chihuahua and Sonora, but never found him.

Shortly after Villa raided Columbus, New Mexico, Irving wrote Luella from Orleans, in northern California, where he had relocated:

> [March 22, 1916] According to the last paper I saw Mr. Villa was surrounded on three sides by Carranzistas and on the fourth by U.S. troops. I hope he does not get away but I would be willing to bet that he escapes through the Carranza troops. I can't imagine the Mexicans co-operating with American troops.

After touring the country for six months following recognition by the United States, Carranza finally arrived in Mexico City to assume the duties of his office on April 14, 1916, where he was met with strikes by electrical workers and street railway men in May. When these were followed by a general strike in the Federal District, he resorted to death penalties to control the situation. During his travels through the country he had left behind him a trail of appointees in state offices who were dedicated to the proposition that self-enrichment was the name of the game. In Guanajuato the results were devastating. The Cubo Company's cashier, a Mexican by the name of Atenedoro Tinajero, reported in detail to his former employer, Irving (in Spanish, of course) as follows:

> [May 15, 1916] Don Carlos [who was in charge at Cubo after Irving returned to the United States in February] left here on April 15, and gave me orders to look after the Company's affairs, but he told me this after he had come to the city. If I had known sooner perhaps I would not have accepted because now it is very dangerous to live outside of Guanajuato, and here too it is dangerous because there is typhoid fever.
>
> After you left, Don Carlos boarded up some of the entrances to the mines at Villalpando and La Loca, but the workmen continued to steal

ore, and at that time there wasn't the hunger that there is now. I asked Don Carlos if all of the openings they were using to rob had been sealed and he said he had closed all he could but he wasn't sure. It is true that he closed many entrances to the mine but it is also sure that some are still open and they are continuing to steal plenty of ore. I have advised Mr. Hollis and suggested that a better way would be to open the mine to these men and let them work on "shares" because this way we could get half, but the way it is now they are taking it all and the Company gets nothing. . . . We should give them only a few drills so that they cannot break too much ore, since they will naturally go for the richest.

We cannot keep rich ore in the office because the soldiers will come and take it, so that as soon as a little is collected it would be good to send it to Mr. Furness [a broker in Guanajuato].

There are no guarantees here now, because there are few soldiers and they say they are chasing bandits, of which there are many around Guanajuato. All the mines that are shut down are being robbed even to the machinery; they are taking anything they can carry saying they are hungry, and as for being hungry that is certainly true.

I requisition Company money from Mr. Furness, but since there are not many five-peso bills, they give me tens and the watchmen can't use these because the corn merchants don't want tens, but only fives. They don't deny me funds, but they give it to me this way and I have to pay a premium to get change [of the tens], and the exchange houses are charging 15 percent and sometimes more.

[May 18, 1916] Since you were here in January and left me an accounting of the checks you used, I have been unable to keep any records because Don Carlos couldn't explain anything, absolutely nothing. . . .

It would be well for you to come back immediately. The Americans who are here in Guanajuato seem to be well, and I am not aware that they want to leave the country.

I am ready to sleep and rest for a while, because shortly after you left in June last year Mr. Smith [who was left in charge after Irving's departure in 1915] became ill and stayed in Guanajuato and that is where you found him in January, while I have stayed here in Cubo nervous and frightened almost every night, and I am a little tired.

Don't forget the recommendations I made in my last letter and please advise.

[May 18, 1916, second letter] Last night buscones [high-graders, or rich-ore takers — usually thieves] began to enter the mine. They were thirty-four. During the day today ninety-four entered.

Meanwhile, the governor of the State of Guanajuato, resident in the city of Guanajuato, ordered the Cubo mine to be reopened, allowing miners who were out of work to go in and bring out what ore they could. Men were brought in from other mines as well over Tinajero's protest that the opening should be limited to the men from Cubo. He continued to send reports, including transcripts of ore values taken from the mine. He pled for help:

[May 25, 1916] Our lawyer has been afraid to see the Governor, so I personally went to see him. . . . My purpose in urging that only our Cubo people work in the mine was to prevent destruction of the mine and to keep order there, because these people see an order from the Government to operate the mines that are closed and will obey no one. The Governor said things should continue as they are. I have asked Mr. Hollis to send someone as soon as possible to look after things.

[July 30, 1916] Since July 1 we have been ordered to pay the equivalent of five pesos to one peso over the wages we were paying on January 1, 1914, so that now a hand driller costs 15 pesos no less, a peon in the mine 5 pesos, outside of the mine 3.75, watchmen 45 pesos a week, and so forth. I should be getting 180 pesos a week but seeing that the payroll is very large I am taking only 150 pesos, the minimum necessary to buy food, except that the first week I took the full rate so that in case they should audit the payroll they would see that everyone received the equivalent, but since then I have taken only 150.

There is much typhus here in Guanajuato and many people have died.[2]

The first of July the hacienda was broken into and much ore of good value was stolen. I will give more details later.

[August 7, 1916] There is a buyer of ore in Cubo who sells to a well-known house and it is obviously good business because he is paying the authorities 600 pesos a month for a license. It is clear that he is buying what is stolen from the Villalpando mine and he is financed by some of the employees — I will not name them now because when I tell you you won't believe it. When you come we will go into details.

Regarding the house of Furness who handles our business, I have to be there whenever any ore comes in from Cubo, and again to see what is being sent to Cubo such as dynamite, fuses, candles and so forth, and I can see that one of their employees doesn't like it. But he says nothing to me, nor I to him. I do my business and leave, but of course I know what the trouble is, and I'll tell you more when you come.

Ore that was set aside at Cubo in July [on the orders of the Governor] was shipped immediately to a warehouse in Guanajuato, and I agreed to this so that it would not be stolen in Cubo. The ore was sampled and assayed but I did not see the operations. They give me the values and that is all I know. I assume they are following orders from the Chicago office, but I don't know this.

Yesterday ore began arriving in town in small bundles, carried by women from the mines as they would carry children in their arms. The seals placed in the tunnel at La Doctora [a Cubo property] have been broken open and they are stealing ore from there also.

Last week Don Felipe, in charge at Cubo, and I don't know who put him in charge, paid me only 75 pesos. I said nothing and thought it better to tell you. I don't think it is just, but if Mr. Hollis ordered it so, then *"está bien."*

Do not delay your return for long.

[August 10, 1916] We have an obligation to provide corn for those who work in the mine, but it is very hard to find. It is true that carloads of corn do arrive, but this is not for sale. Today we went to the man who sells corn but he wouldn't sell us four bags to send to Cubo, and out there there is nothing to eat. Tomorrow we will send some flour. In Cubo a measure of corn is worth 8.50 pesos, the same that used to cost 20 centavos. Charcoal is 50 cents a kilo, wheat 2.30 a kilo, low-grade meat 3.00 a kilo. The price of lard has just gone down to 8.50 a kilo. A turkey brings 10, 12, 15, and up to 25 pesos. Chickens 5 to 7 pesos, and so it goes.

The typhus gets worse each day in spite of hard work and all efforts of the police and the health authorities. Many have died and it is the same in Silao, Leon and other parts. But here it has rained a lot and the corn seedings are very good. I expect all this will pass, and I hope you will be back "pronto."

[August 18, 1916] Much ore continues to come into town in small bags and in baskets, and it seems to be impossible to stop the stealing. We have many watchmen now and nine soldiers on duty but the ore still comes out of the mine.

If work should cease at the mine I would like to keep busy at something, because I have nothing to live on. Perhaps that can be arranged with Mr. Hollis. I hope you can arrange it.

In August 1916, Irving acknowledged Tinajero's letters and explained that he was no longer working for the Cubo Company. He asked Tinajero to find some correspondence that he needed for reference, and which he believed was "in the room next to our living room in Cubo." On September 2, Luella received a letter from their faithful cook, Angela, who was looking after the family's possessions at Cubo (in Spanish, of course):

Señorita — Last night Don Felipe got angry and ran me out. He said the street was mine and if I didn't get out he would have the soldiers take me out. I had done nothing wrong except that I did not want to give him the key to the rooms upstairs [the Herrs' living quarters], for that he got angry. I have stolen nothing. I told him I would not leave until I had delivered the house. As they are paying nothing to Reyes [the kitchen maid] I give her some of my wages so she will not die of hunger.

I do not know if he will get mad again. I will leave, but in that case I will not be responsible for anything missing. Last night I cried a lot. I have been looking after the house for so long and this man runs me out. I beg of you, do me the favor of coming back "pronto" so I can deliver the house. No one has told me that I should get out of the house, everyone has been very good with me except this man. I have conducted myself well, Atenedoro [Tinajero] will vouch for that. I am only waiting for an American to turn the house over to, or you can tell me what I should do. I don't know whether Señor Jalis [Hollis] has said I should leave. I don't know.

Only because I did not want to give him the key to the rooms upstairs, that was the only reason and that is the truth. I keep them locked all the time so that nothing will be lost.

I cook meals for Don Felipe and his son, but I am not content. I am very unhappy. Come back quickly.

> A Dios Señorita,
> *Angela G.*

[Don Felipe, whom we came to know later, was a Mexican Indian of indeterminate age, and you could never be quite sure which side he was on, but I suspect he was acting at Tinajero's request to look for the correspondence that Dad had requested.]

On September 2, Irving wrote to Mr. Hollis in Chicago:

I have just received a letter from our old cook at Cubo, Angela Gonzalez, in which it appears that she is having more than her share of trouble due to the fact that to the best of her ability she is looking out for the goods belonging to me which are still at Cubo in our living quarters. It seems that the Mexican, Felipe Somebody, who is in charge at Cubo, threatened and as near as I can understand her letter did actually run her out onto the street, because she refused to unlock the rooms where our goods are.

Angela is one of the Mexicans who are white in everything but color and is worth standing by, and I shall appreciate it as a personal favor if you can in some way intimate to the man in charge at Cubo that she should be unmolested and respected.

Angela has no home around Cubo to which she can go, as her home is near Mexico City, and she is remaining at Cubo partly through a sense of duty, and presumably partly because she is afraid to go back to their former home. She is trustworthy in every respect and an excellent cook, and worth protecting.

On September 5 a letter went out from Chicago (copy to Irving) which gave instructions that Angela was to be let alone, as she was looking after Mr. Herr's things.

Later in 1916, Irving clarified these events, writing from the United States to his old friend H. Vincent Wallace:

[August 18, 1916] I wonder whether you have heard about all the happenings at Cubo during the past few months. About the first of May our good and honorable Governor of the State of Guanajuato learned from his loyal henchman, the Jefe of Cubo, that there was a small-sized bonanza in the north end of the Villalpando mine [also Cubo property]. It did not take him long to devise ways and means for transferring same from its quiet resting place in the mine to his strongbox in Guanajuato. He simply decreed that the mine could no longer remain shut down, but would be worked a fuerza [willy nilly], and opened the mine to buscones. In order that the poor buscones should not be maltreated by the conscienceless owners of the mine, he further decreed that the work should be supervised, and the division of the ore made by the Honorable Jefe of Cubo. You can imagine the rest and how much of the rich ore was turned over to the Company.

They say that for a time our mine was a free-for-all cross country steeplechase, and about four hundred hungry buscones crowded into the north end and started harvesting the crop. It must have been beautiful, and poor Tinajero lost another ten years' lease of life. I suppose, from what I hear of the grade of ore gotten away with by these robbers, that they easily took a hundred thousand dollars worth of ore, U.S. money. They took out some four hundred tons running between five and fifty kilos silver per ton.

If I could have run the Tajo mill for about a year and gotten 5 percent bonus on the net profits I would be a great deal better off than I am.

Shortly after the hijacking of the "small-sized bonanza" at Cubo, Irving received the following letter from Mr. Hollis:

[July 12, 1916] I am beginning to get affidavits on which to base a claim against the Mexican government for losses, etc., at Cubo, and will you please prepare a statement bearing on the lack of police or troop protection to the property that made it advisable for you to leave last year and made it impossible for you to stay at Cubo this year. What we want particularly is refusal of the Carranza officials (giving names) to furnish adequate police protection and all the facts bearing on the presence of outlaws and bandits in the vicinity of Cubo, and the fact that their presence was known to Carranza officials. . . .

Irving replied:

[July 17, 1916] I find that it is going to be very difficult to make the kind of statement about refusal of Carranza authorities to give police protection, etc., that you desire.

My leaving Guanajuato in June of 1915 and in February of 1916 was not due primarily to refusal of Carranza authorities to afford police protection to the property, as suggested in your letter. Recalling the events that resulted in my leaving Cubo in June 1915 these may be summarized about as follows:

In the early part of April Villa and Obregon began at Celaya the series of battles extending up through Salamanca, Irapuato, and Leon that resulted in Guanajuato being cut off from all railroad connection with other places. Guanajuato changed hands and from being under Villa control was taken over by the Carranzistas. It was abandoned again by the Carranzistas and reoccupied for a day or two by Villistas, and at times was without any established government under either side. Our mine was shut down on account of inability to get supplies with which to operate, and the other Guanajuato mines were in almost the same circumstances. They were able to run a little longer than Cubo on account of being better supplied, and also by making a pool of supplies between them.

The immediate cause of my leaving Cubo about this time, probably about the 12th of June, was a telegram from you instructing me to bring the staff and return to the United States. If I remember correctly the probable cause of your sending this telegram was that I had advised this in order to reduce the mine payroll, as we were carrying several high-priced men who were paid in U.S. currency and were not doing any work on the property. In addition to this reason there was the additional one that President Wilson had just issued an ultimatum to the Revolutionary leaders in Mexico to the effect that unless they got together in two months he proposed to take some drastic measures.

It is true that about this time, that is in May and June of 1915, we were unable to get adequate police protection, but I am unable to state that this was refused us. Rather the conditions were such that the Carranzistas were unable to furnish such protection, being rather in need of more protection themselves against the Villistas who were on all sides of Guanajuato. The only instance that I can cite was that at one time sometime in May I called at the Governor's Palace in Guanajuato and requested a garrison for Cubo. This request was made to a Mayor Peralto, Jefe del Estado Mayor del Gobernador. That is he was the Governor's Chief of Staff, and such matters came under his direction. He was very agreeable, and promised to send a small garrison to Cubo. But the garrison never put in an appearance.

My leaving Guanajuato in February of 1916 was in accordance with telegraphic instructions from you sent me from El Paso at the time of the Santa Isabel massacre. It is also true that at this time conditions in Guanajuato were such that I did not believe it wise to attempt to resume operations at Cubo. These conditions were about at follows:

There was a great shortage of food, especially corn for the laboring class, and the indications all were that this shortage would soon become acute. There was also in existence a railroad traffic condition that made it impossible to get any local supplies such as lumber and timber, of which we were in urgent need for construction purposes. No freight of any kind was being handled on the railroads, and there was no prospect of any freight service being initiated in the near future. In addition to these two reasons there was a very unsatisfactory labor situation due to the establishment of labor unions throughout the district, not properly organized and incapable of producing anything but trouble for the mining companies. There was also the general public opinion that the Carranza government could not survive more than a few months at best. These considerations in view of the fact that to resume operations at Cubo would necessitate at least two months of preliminary work, with the prospect that by the time this work was finished and the mill ready to run, conditions would have become so bad that running would be impossible, determined me to advise not making the attempt.

At this time reports of bandits were current on all sides, and it was known that a large band was operating between Guanajuato and Leon, and another between Guanajuato and San Luis Potosi. This latter one kept the telephone line of the Guanajuato Power and Electric Company cut between Guanajuato and San Luis Potosi. All attempts on the part of the Power Company to have these bandits done away with were unsuccessful.

Personally I made no requests of the Carranza government for any police protection at this time, because I knew from experience of the other companies in Guanajuato that it would be a waste of time to do so. Learning that the Peregrina M. & M. Company had secured the right from the State government to install a number of armed guards at its own expense at Peregrina to protect its property, I went to the Jefe de Armas in Guanajuato and made a similar request for Cubo. I asked for authority to arm ten of my watchmen at my own expense for the purpose of protecting Cubo against bandit raids, and the mines against high-graders. This authority was granted me in the form of a written statement signed by the Jefe de Armas. But on afterward reading over the authorization carefully I found that it also stated that these ten watchmen could at any time be called upon by the constituted government for use by it. This made it valueless to me because none of the Cubo workmen, who feared nothing more than to be taken into the army, would consent to act as an armed guard under these conditions.

This happened at about the time I was preparing to leave Guanajuato for the United States, and I did nothing further in the matter.

Shortly before the end of December 1915 there was an actual raid on Cubo by bandits, and these were driven out by some of the citizens of Cubo. After this raid the Jefe Politico of Cubo, who is mayor of the town, and the direct representative of the Carranza government appointed by the Governor, came at night to the mine hacienda to sleep because he felt himself safer inside the walls of our mine enclosure than outside in the town. During February 1916 while I was at Cubo he came each night to the hacienda to sleep. The citizens of Cubo were living in constant dread of another raid during this time, and there was no relief afforded in the way of troop protection.

Hollis prepared a legal demand for compensation from the Mexican government for the losses suffered by the Cubo company, using as part of his evidence an affidavit of Irving's that evaluated the condition of the mine when he left. He appealed to the U.S. government to press his claim. It does not appear that the Cubo company ever recovered any money, but Hollis was able to write to Irving:

[September 13, 1916] For your information I will state that by persistent following up of the case, I succeeded in having our Government investigate the charge I made against the governor and his brother, the military commander, with the result that this investigation corroborated all my charges, and, confidentially, I can state that the Carranza government has been forced to fire both the governor and his brother for their actions in the Cubo matter.

Irving's Mexican adventures continued to follow him after his departure. In September 1916, he received a copy of the following billet-doux from the U.S. Deputy Commissioner of Internal Revenue, directed to the Collector at Chicago, Illinois, referring to him:

Please report taxpayer, of Guanajuato, Mexico, for assessment of a tax of $8.78 for 1914, in accordance with the audit made in this office.

In a note on his return taxpayer states that $1,000 claimed as a deduction on account of losses represents the estimated value of silverware, rugs, linen, house furnishings, and other valuables stolen between Guanajuato and Vera Cruz while fleeing from Mexico during American occupation in 1914. This claim has been disallowed as representing a personal loss.

Again in September Irving received the following from the Mexico City office of the Canadian Bank of Commerce, which sheds some light on the monetary situation eleven months after Carranza was recognized by the United States. The letter:

[September 18, 1916] In February last we advised you that we were liquidating our deposit business and requested you to give us instructions regarding the disposal of your balance with us. Shortly afterwards, it was announced through the newspapers that the Government was about to issue a decree fixing the rates at which obligations contracted prior to the time the Government paper came into forced circulation would have to be liquidated and in justice to our clients we decided to await the issuance of the decree before pressing withdrawal of funds by depositors.

The decree in question has now been issued under the date of 15th September 1916, and in terms of same, deposits made prior to 15 April 1913 have to be repaid in current paper money at five times the amount of the deposit, those made between the above date and 10th September 1914 at four times the amount, and those since the latter date at par.

We consider the above rates equitable and as the balance at your credit represents deposits made between 15th April 1913 and 10 September 1914, we must ask you to arrange for its removal on the basis stipulated, i.e., four times the amount in Government money or convert it into New York exchange or an account in United States currency or Mexican Gold. The exchange rate at this date being 3.25, the rate for conversion of your actual balance into American money would be 13 cents, or into Mexican Gold, 26 cents per peso.

The above offer is subject to your immediate acceptance.

The conversion formula would read like this: 1 paper peso = 3.25 cents U.S. × 4 to 1 payoff = 13 cents U.S. per peso deposit. However, for the Herr family there was not much at risk. Five weeks later the Canadian Bank of Commerce forwarded to Irving a draft on New York for $5.50, the conversion value of 42.31 pesos, the balance in his account. This would at least help to pay the grave deficiency in his United States income tax.

It would be some time before the family again returned to their life in Mexico.

Notes

1. To Carter Norris, Mexico, Missouri.

2. The British embassy in Mexico City reported in February 1917 that the typhus epidemic in Guanajuato pushed the death rate up to 300 per 1,000, meaning presumably that 30 percent of the population had died. It said the population of the city had fallen from 35,000 in 1910 to 13,000 in 1917 (Knight, *Mexican Revolution*, 2:420). These figures show how serious the epidemic was

considered to be, but they should not be taken at face value. The 1921 census gives a population of 32,915 for Guanajuato City. The recorded population of Guanajuato State decreased from 1,081,651 in 1910 to 860,364 in 1921, a decline of 20 percent. See Mexico, Dirección General de Estadística, *División territorial de los Estados Unidos Mexicanos* (Mexico: Impr. de la Secretaría de Fomento, n.d.), includes the census of 1910; and Mexico, Departamento de Estadística Nacional, *Resumen del censo general de habitantes de 30 de noviembre de 1921* (Mexico: Talleres Gráficos de la Nación, 1928).

CHAPTER 8

Interlude

After their "escape" from Mexico via Dolores Hidalgo in June 1915, the Herr family took a short vacation at a summer resort in Montague, Michigan, on the shores of the lake — recovering from the trials of revolutionary surroundings. From there they set up housekeeping, renting one-half of a two-family house in Cambridge, Massachusetts, where the boys could go to school while Irving bided his time. He was already thinking that the life of a mining engineer was hardly suitable for raising a family, and certainly difficult for the mother of a family. After his next exposure to Mexico in January and February 1916, he became convinced and began seriously to consider other alternatives.

In the spring of 1916 while his family remained in Cambridge, Irving explored mining properties in California and Arizona for his Chicago employer, but gave serious thought to farming and explored the field thoroughly. On July 13, 1916, he wrote to his friend Wallace: "I would like to get into some other business, not mining, where I could settle down permanently in a civilized community. It does not seem a very easy thing to do and so far I have made no progress. . . . I have decided positively to let farming alone."

After extensive advertising and correspondence in the summer of 1916, which yielded nothing, Irving finally accepted an offer to take charge of a graphite concentrating plant in Alabama, and on September 19 he began work with the Crucible Flake Graphite Company in Ashland, Alabama, leaving his family still in Cambridge.

His description of this adventure is illuminating. Writing to one of his college classmates in January 1917, on a Graphite Company letterhead with the caption "Irving Herr, Gen. Supt.," he said:

> I have to date had four months of Graphiting and that length of time has been sufficient to prove to me that I do not like it. In the fifteen years since we all walked out from the doors of our Alma Mater with the little sheepskins fondly tucked under our arms, and thinking how much more we knew than the vulgar mob, I have been in several parts of the world and have tackled a number of propositions. But this one takes the cake.
>
> I wonder whether you have been much in the South — they call it the Sunny South. It is a misnomer. So far this month we have had twenty-one days of either rain or clouds — mostly rain. Do you know anything about Southern labor? We have it here, and all I have to say is, give me a crew of Mexican peons, just ordinary ones, and I can show these Southern laborers cards and spades.

In February 1917 he resigned, and on March 8, he wrote to his friend Gerald Rives, the Cubo Company's forwarding agent in El Paso:

> My experience in Alabama was not exactly pleasant and I am very glad I resigned and am out of it, while at the same time I am also glad that I spent the months I did down there and gained the experience.
>
> So I am again a person of leisure, which put into less attractive language is to say — I am looking for a job. What a pity the Mexican Revolution came along and spoiled everything, for at Cubo I was certainly it, and had a very enjoyable position.

However, through acquaintances of long standing, Irving was at last persuaded to accept a position with the Oneida Community Ltd. in New York State at meager pay (a starting salary that would probably have been turned down by a new college graduate), based on the premise that advancement would be forthcoming. In the meantime he would have to draw on his savings to maintain his family.

In August 1917 the Cubo Company office in Chicago once more offered him his former position in Mexico at an increase over his previous salary plus the usual perquisites of housing, utilities, household help, and transportation, which would have greatly improved their financial condition. But Irving first checked on conditions south of the border.

Earlier, Gerald Rives had reported the following from El Paso:

> [March 13, 1917] During the past month or six weeks a great many of the Guanajuato men have been here. . . . but I do not believe the companies will begin operations until some guarantees are given from this side of the river, and another thing labor must now be paid in gold or silver coin and all kinds of supplies are high, especially cyanide which is selling for about $1.00 to $1.25 per running pound regardless of strength contained. . . .
>
> Hollis was in a few days ago on his way West, as usual with any number of questions about news of Guanajuato, and stated he would under no conditions open Cusi [the mine in Chihuahua] again until he had some assurances that property could be operated without danger of life.

In reply to a request from Irving, Wallace wired from Los Angeles as follows:

> [August 15, 1917] Mexican conditions generally improved — continuance doubtful — Operations dependent political economic labor and crops — Consider only method assure corn and supplies owning private freight trains — Difficult find locomotives cars or repair material — Strikes — Rains Silao valley late more than quarter normal crop doubtful — Strikes Potosi Monterrey Tampico — Anticipate increasing wages — Regards.

So he refused the Cubo Company offer and decided to await the promised advancement at the Oneida Company. In 1918 they sent him on an extended trip to South America to utilize his Spanish in an attempt to open up the territory for Oneida Community silverplated ware, where he made stops in Brazil, Argentina, and Chile. Later he loved to tell stories of the trip, but as a business venture it was not a success, though not because of him. Because European, especially German, suppliers had been eliminated by World War I, Irving collected many orders, promising prompt delivery. On returning to Oneida he discovered that the company had made no shipments. He was furious, not only because of the loss of his customers, but because he felt his own word and honor had been impugned.

Our sojourn in the United States was a new experience for brother John and me, but at ages eleven and nine we accepted our new surroundings readily enough. School was another matter. I recall being sent to public school for the first time when I was nine. After cursory tests they placed both John and me in the sixth grade — all because of Mother's daily lessons on the porch at Cubo — and I can remember that I was terrified, mostly, I guess, because of the older children. One day I came home and told Mother that I couldn't possibly keep up because I was supposed to know decimals and we hadn't had decimals. Mother said, "Well, you know fractions, don't you? And decimals are the same as fractions." But I failed to see the similarity, and they finally took pity on me and moved me back to the fifth grade.

As we grew older our memories improved. But there really was not that much to remember. For four years we went to school in the States like any other American boys. The war was bad, and I remember the horror of the daily news with graphic stories of the miseries on the western front, men living in a sea of mud in the trenches and going "over the top" to meet sure death from machine-gun fire, men crawling on their bellies under barbed-wire entanglements to capture Germans in their steel helmets with the vicious points on top. Sugar, when we could get it, came in oversized crystals, multicolored because it was not fully refined. We used oleomargarine instead of butter (later there were little color capsules that came with the oleo so you could make it look like butter if you wished), and everyone grew their own vegetables.

One winter the snow in upper New York State was so deep that we dug tunnels in the snowbanks and carved out rooms beyond, like igloos under the snow. We skied down small hills on barrel staves or anything else that we could find. And because it was the thing to do I laid out my own trap line along a creek bed through the fields, hoping to catch a muskrat. They said the furs were valuable, but I never caught one, which was lucky, because I would never have been able to skin it. I would get up at six in the morning to tend the traps and be home for breakfast in time to get off for school with the rest.

One morning in November as I was coming in from the trap line (it was

November 11) I heard the assembly bell ringing and ringing. And ringing! There would be no school. The Allies and the Germans had declared an "armistice," whatever that was. But what it really meant was that the war was over! We were as excited as any of the mothers and fathers and wives and children of those overseas. There was to be a big celebration and a parade in the city some four miles away. We rode to town on our bikes to join in, and it was quite a parade with Elks and Odd Fellows, policemen, firemen, fire engines, and bands. Somewhere I found a giant whistle, four inches long, and I rode on the bumper of one of the fire engines blowing the whistle all the way.

While we were growing up in the States, Mr. Hollis in Chicago was struggling to get the Cubo mine back in successful operation. Correspondence of 1918 and 1919 in the Cubo archives gives a taste of the difficulties he had.[1] Revolutionary activity around Guanajuato had ended, but it had left the mining business disrupted. Mexican red tape could be infuriating. A much-needed shipment of explosives was held up at the border awaiting the signature of a colonel in Mexico City. When the mine's attorney was unable to dislodge the permit, even with daily visits to the presidential residence, the Cubo superintendent appealed to the governor of Guanajuato, who broke the jam with a wire to the Mexican consul in Laredo.

The possibility of theft also produced a constant anxiety. The shipments of concentrates from the mill to Aguascalientes for refining were arriving at their destination with much lower assays than when they left, even though they were being shipped in sacks with lead seals. The superintendent suspected crooked work at the Cubo mill, but if he learned the answer, it is not in the correspondence at hand. In August 1919, three men entered the Tajo mill at night apparently with the intention of stealing part of a shipment and were discovered by one of the staff. The robbers fired on the worker and barely missed his head.

Aging equipment and the lack of spare parts dogged operations. Timbers in the mine needed replacing. Some gave way and a thousand-pound slab of rock barely missed killing three men, but timbermen could not be found. The mine's electric locomotive had given up the ghost, or was threatening to do so, and they could not get a new air compressor going because the mechanics "have always been called off for a repair job of some kind that had to be taken care of to keep mine or mill going."[2]

A fundamental problem was that of finding good personnel at all levels.

Skilled workers were hard to come by and keep. In August 1919, Cubo super-intendent R. R. Leslie complained to Hollis: "Carpenters, mechanics, and mill labor are so scarce that it is nearly next to impossible to get anything done." Four months later his successor added: "Owners of many old proper-ties in the Guanajuato district preparing to reopen their mines on account of the high price of silver raised wages, with the result that many of our me-chanics and laborers quit us to accept better positions."[3]

It was also difficult to get foreign personnel for supervisory positions. The Cubo company was offering 10 pesos a day, but this was not competitive. Their Mexico City agent advised them that mine foremen, men with mining degrees, were getting $200 to $250 U.S. per month, and shift bosses from $150 to $200.[4]

The mill superintendent was a most critical position because the company was in the process of modernizing the Tajo mill they had acquired during Irving's last year. They were introducing steel balls to replace "pebbles" (hard stones) for grinding ore in the tubes of the mill, and the cyanide pro-cess to replace flotation. The steel balls were introduced with success, but cyanide proved a poison in more ways than one. L. F. Carrouché had been hired after Irving's departure as superintendent of the Tajo Mill. When Leslie arrived as general superintendent, Carrouché rubbed him the wrong way. Leslie denied him a raise, and in November 1918 Carrouché threatened to quit if his salary were not increased to 700 pesos. Leslie conceded to his demand, but when Carrouché's wife became seriously ill and he turned some of his work over to the master mechanic, Leslie accused him of neglecting his job and asked for his resignation. Carrouché had to look for an automobile or four peons to carry his sick wife to Guanajuato, without help from the com-pany.[5] He did not disappear for good, however, as we shall see.

Cubo was left with no one familiar with cyanide, but Chicago's orders were clear to proceed with its introduction. Leslie's search for a cyanide man finally turned up "a metallurgist who came to us well recommended as a flo-tation and cyanide operator." Friberger was to carry out the conversion of the mill to cyanide, but he departed within a couple of months, having quar-reled with the boss. He left a letter that described the mill as being in terrible shape, and the machinery as being operated in destructive ways. Leslie was gone by now, and his successor, F. H. Lerchen, on the spot with Hollis, gave his own version: Friberger "ran up against trouble with the mill men, most of whom went on strike and left, and with new, green crews he lost control, absolutely, of the men and could not get tonnage through the mill or satisfactory recovery. He finally threw up his hands, and his job, admitted his defeat, and departed, leaving the men badly disorganized and the crushing part of the mill nearly a complete wreck."[6]

Whoever was at fault, the conversion to cyanide had not yet been accomplished by the end of 1919, and production was down to a third of the level at which Carrouché had left it. Lerchen blamed the delays on petty strikes and other labor troubles,[7] but Hollis by now knew that the main problem was in the quality of the men in charge of the mine. The irascible natures of Leslie and Lerchen had brought about the departure of two mill superintendents and no doubt contributed to the difficulties with the workmen. Drawing on his experience with them, Hollis would a few months later advise a prospective new mine supervisor: "No one wants to tackle this job unless he would be interested in the work and have the very greatest patience. Much can be made of a Mexican if they are treated patiently, fairly, and kindly, but nothing can be accomplished by rough work."[8] He had tried three men as general superintendent in two years since Irving had turned down his offer, and Hollis needed to find someone who could bring stability to the situation. Hollis wrote Irving again at the end of 1919 to invite him to take over the Cubo mine.

Still smarting from his experience with the Oneida Company, Dad was prepared this time to consider seriously returning to Guanajuato. Although she had made the best of it and had her friends in Mexico, Mother much preferred the good old United States of America. At least here you could drink the water without first boiling and filtering it, and you could get to town without riding a horse. She was not athletic. But she finally agreed that if Angela would come back and cook for her, she would try it again. So they wrote to Angela at her home near Mexico City. When the answer came it was four pages of closely written hand in excellent Spanish. For three and a half pages Angela explained in great detail all the reasons why she could not possibly leave home — but she said in the last line, "*si Usted manda, voy*." If you say so, I will come. Early in 1920 we went back to the scenes of our childhood.

Everything was much smaller. The garden paths were not as wide as I remembered them and the hacienda nowhere near as vast. The long hike up the steep river trail to the mill was only a short walk, not very steep.

Notes

1. The following information comes from two loose leaf binders in the Cubo archives. One is labeled "Cartas A-Z, September 1 [1903? illegible], Marzo [1905? illegible]," but its contents are letters of later date (cited as AZ). The other labeled "General Correspondence" has letters ca. 1915 to 1929 (cited as GC).

2. These two paragraphs come from the letters of F. H. Lerchen to R. R. Leslie in April and of Leslie and Lerchen to Hollis in August and September 1919 (AZ).

3. Leslie, August 9, and Lerchen, December 18, 1919 (AZ).

4. O. Gisholt to G. R. M. Campbell, "The Technical and Clerical Employment Agency," September 8, and reply September 10, 1919 (GC).

5. Letters of Carrouché, Leslie, and Lerchen, March 28 to April 10, 1919, and Carrouché, November 8, 1919 (GC). Cubo Ledger (1919–25) shows Carrouché's salary for January 1919: 700 pesos.

6. Friberger to Lerchen, September 29, Lerchen to Hollis, November 11, 1919 (AZ).

7. Lerchen to Hollis, December 18, 1919 (AZ).

8. Hollis to J. P. MacFadden, Supt., Sandon, B.C., June 11, 1920 (GC).

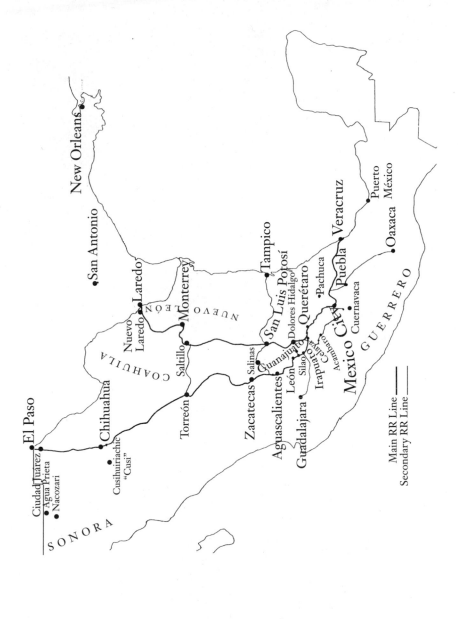

Mexican Railroads,
1910–1930

Irving in the twenties, cradling his pipe

Luella on Alazán, ca. 1923
"My old horse, the Alazán,
is so lively you'd never
know him."

Luella's household help, 1920
Concepción on left,
Angela second from right

Francisco (Pancho) Medina,
Jefe de Policía *for the mine*
"A certain amount of Spanish
blood mixed with his Indian
heritage lent a sharpness to his
features and a touch of Castilian
pride to his bearing."

Hacienda staff, 1920
Pancho Medina on left, Pánfilo second
from left, Froylan second from right

The Escolta, armed guard of the mine, 1920
Jefe Pancho Medina on right

*H. L. Hollis, President of the Cubo Mining and Milling
Company, brings his family to visit Cubo, May 1921.*
Robert, Luella, Mrs. Hollis, Mr. Hollis, Clara Hollis, Irving

*Irving and Luella confer with government
soldiers on the road to Cubo, ca. 1920*
Irving in center, facing away,
Luella on right with tall hat

The Cubo Panteón (cemetery)
"If rented only for a specified term the grave will be
opened at the end of the term and the bones removed
to make room for another paying customer."

The 1960 monument to the seven union
organizers murdered on April 22, 1937,
outside the wall of the Cubo hacienda

CHAPTER 9

The Mining Business

It would be of interest here to look at the situation facing mining engineers in the early 1900s, particularly those like Irving who had been displaced by revolutionary activity. The engineer was in a sense a floater, with no permanent location. By the time he left Mexico in 1916, Irving had worked in four countries: the United States in California and Nevada, Mexico at El Cubo, and briefly in Costa Rica and Nicaragua. Having tried to establish himself as an engineer again in the United States, and after the trials and frustrations meted out to him and Luella by his choice of profession, he thought seriously of getting into another business. In fact, after more disappointments, he ended up taking a job with Oneida Community, as we have seen. His experiences provide a good primer on the mining business. How was it practiced in the United States, and how did it differ when the mine was abroad? One may not be able to generalize broadly from Irving's experiences, but his case does help one understand better the American role in Mexico.

One can recall that the New Calico Mine in Stent, California, that turned out to be a swindle had been bought by Harry Selfridge, founder of the London department store. Selfridge was an example of the persons who put up the venture capital to buy a mine and get it going, the men at the top of the mining business, the mine owners. The owner could be a large organization like the United Mexican Company of

England that had owned the Cubo mine and a number of other mines in Guanajuato at the end of the nineteenth century and then slowly sold them off.[1] But Irving's experiences show that frequently the owner was an individual who was an important entrepreneur in a different field. The owner of the Cubo mine was the Potter Palmer Estate, well known for the Palmer House hotel in Chicago. In March and April of 1916, when Irving was barely home from his last attempt to reopen El Cubo, he went to evaluate a major gravel deposit on the Klamath River near Orleans in northern California. He searched it for signs of platinum or gold that would make it worth working. Writing from San Francisco after a month on the site, Irving sent the potential buyer a final report to the effect that he found little evidence of mineral deposits, but that the gravel might be exploitable. The addressee was Mr. W. D. Baldwin of New York, president of the Otis Elevator Company.[2]

Mining was an investment that men of wealth were ready to explore, hoping that they might make some money on the side. They did not, however, associate the mine with their major enterprise, or run it as personal property. In the cases revealed in Irving's correspondence, they set up a separate company for each mine. The Cubo mine was owned and operated by the Cubo Mining and Milling Company, whose address was 1025 Peoples Gas Building, Chicago. The Peregrina mine belonged to the Guanajuato Development Company, 27 William Street, New York. The Nueva Luz Mine of Guanajuato was part of the Mineral Development Company.[3] The single mine company was not unique to silver and gold mining. In Ashland, Alabama, Irving worked for the Crucible Flake Graphite Company, whose home address was 50 Broad Street, New York City. These companies had boards of directors, but one cannot conceive that the owners, men or entities of major stature, had directors who challenged them. The company structure was a legal convenience.

The Chicago address of the Cubo Mining and Milling Company was the same as the office of H. L. Hollis, Mining Engineer and Metallurgist. With this person we come to the key individual in a mining enterprise, the consulting engineer. He was a trained mining engineer who had worked himself into a position of managing other people's investments in mining. Hollis had been born in Boston in 1866 and had received a degree in mechanical engineering from Columbia University in 1885. In 1914 he described his professional work since 1889 as "examination and management of mining properties, and consultation work in connection with development and operation of mines and metallurgical plants." He was then president of the Cubo Mining and Milling Company, which he ran for the Palmer estate, managing director of the Cusi Mining Company and the Elko Mining Company, and consulting engineer for four other mining companies. In 1922 he became the managing director of the Palmer estate.[4] Hollis was the man who employed Irving on most of his jobs and to whom Irving reported. In 1907, Irving sampled the Cusi Mine near Chihuahua for him, and Hollis hired the men who were shot on the way to that mine in the Santa Isabel massacre in 1916. Hollis was not the agent of a particular investor, but operated indiscriminately as manager of different mining companies for their owners. He had a well-staffed office to handle his affairs.

The major axis of communication in the American mining business thus ran between the engineer, who was superintendent of the mine on the spot, and the consulting engineer at a major city in the United States, who acted as the home office for the company. Instructions and authorizations went from the consulting engineer to the mine, and financial and other reports went the other way. The mining engineer counted on the home office to answer questions and provide information not available in the field. For the enterprise to be successful, the relationship between the two men had to be one of confidence and trust. Yet they maintained a certain formality. The letters between Irving and Hollis were addressed "Dear Mr. Hollis" and "Dear Mr. Herr" even as late as 1931, when they had been working together thirty years. Of course, relations were not always cordial. If the mine were not developing as expected, the consulting engineer would try to shift the blame to the local man in charge.

In addition to the undertaking at hand for which the mining engineer was hired, he was expected to perform another service for his superior. In 1916, after Irving left Cubo, Hollis sent him to investigate different properties in California and Arizona. While he was so engaged, Hollis asked him to "keep on the lookout for silver mines or prospects." Nothing turned up then, but Irving kept his eyes and ears open for Hollis. In 1931 he wrote Hollis from Mexico City that he had learned of a silver and gold mining prospect in the state of Durango that might interest Hollis. Irving added, "In case it turned out to be a real property and you took it over for the Palmer Corp. or other interests, I would expect to be considered financially to some extent, along the usual lines."[5] The mining engineer, in other words, was also a scout for his employer, and would be rewarded if his tip led to investment.

The consulting engineer and the mining engineer sought to keep their relationship on a businesslike, contractual level. When Irving discovered the scam at Stent, saving Hollis money, Hollis was under no obligation to continue his employment. Nevertheless, in the case of the Mexican Revolution, Hollis did feel a duty to compensate him for the loss of his job in Cubo, or maybe he felt it was in the owner's interest to do so. Irving described Hollis's concept of generosity to his friend Wallace:

> [July 13, 1916] While I was in Chicago reporting on my work in Kingman, Mr. Hollis told me in his best office style that the Cubo Company would continue to carry me on the payroll at half salary, pending the possibility of my return to Guanajuato. Thereupon I told him that I did not believe I cared to accept it. Then he very quickly and incisively came back with the remark that that was the best the Company could do. Whereupon I explained that he had misunderstood my meaning, which was that I did not care to accept anything at all. I never saw a man look more surprised than he did. I told him that with conditions as they now are in Mexico, I did not feel like being bound to return there, which my accepting salary would mean, and for that reason, my wife and I had decided that we could not longer accept the small stipend. I am afraid that Mr. Hollis is not quite so friendly with me now as a result, at least that is how I have sized up the situation, although I can't see why he should be peeved, because I am not taking the Cubo money. Maybe it is all imagination on my part.

Irving told his story to another Guanajuato refugee, Carter Norris, who had run the Tajo mine near Cubo. On September 16, 1916, Norris replied, "I think you did the right thing in not accepting the retainer from Mr. Hollis, for that would put you under obligations to return when he considered it safe, and I am afraid that Mexico will be no place for a married man for a long time to come, and not any too safe for a single one either, for that matter." A retainer was an accepted arrangement, but after what Irving and Luella had been through, their independence meant more to them than the assured income, even though Irving had no employment prospects at the moment.

At the local level, the engineer as superintendent had to deal with the labor of the mine. Success of an enterprise depended on an effective work crew, as the experience of Cubo in Irving's absence demonstrated. Irving felt closer to his men than was usual. He had respect and even affection for his Mexican workmen, as he revealed in his response to a request from Hollis to inform Bennett R. Bates, the man who was due to take his place at Cubo, of the names of the employees he considered the most reliable. Irving responded:

> [September 2, 1916] Tinajero writes me that almost all the old employees are either dead or have moved away to various other parts of the Republic, some even having gone to Cuba. However I will name a few of those that I remember.
>
> Stable mozo, either Brijido or Lucas who are both good men. Gatekeeper, Concepcion, last name also forgotten, but is an old employee and faithful. Mozo to Guanajuato was Antonio, who is a good old scout. Panfilo was gardener and is also dependable. . . . For contractor Dionisio Paz, one of the faithful and in Villalpando you should find Eusebio Morales. I always trusted Eusebio and believe he is to be depended upon. . . .
>
> During the last two years I did not come into as close contact with the contractors in the mine as formerly. The mine Superintendent gave out most of the contracts, and I cannot recall the names of the men, but the mine books should show them all. Most of our men were a rather decent sort. Any of these old employees can tell you of other good men.
>
> But look out for any of the Argote tribe of Villalpando. They are a bad outfit. Old Argote lives in Guanajuato and sells stolen ore which his son who lives in Villalpando steals.

Irving had counted on his staff to defend the mine against the bandits and marauding revolutionaries, and his Mexican miners had responded with loyalty and respect.

The engineers who had fled the Guanajuato mines were finding it difficult to relocate satisfactorily, and they became a kind of fraternity, whose members looked out for each other's welfare. Carter Norris seemed the most fortunate. He had become general manager of the Callaway County Coal

Company in Missouri, a small enterprise with thirty employees. "I am well located here," he wrote on September 15, "and it looks like a permanent thing, but 'quien sabe' where I'll be a few years hence," adding: "I often think of the good old days in Guanajuato, and the many pleasant evenings spent at your house, with fine eats, music, etc." Wallace also missed the old days. He was running a low-grade mine near Helena, Montana, "where a blanket of snow covers the land from late September to April."[6]

Wallace made Irving envious because he had a car, and Irving dreamed of buying a Dodge, but he realized he was "too poor for such luxuries."[7] The experience with graphite that left him again without a job where he could have a home for Luella and the boys made him the most bitter of the three. He wrote to Wallace on resigning from the Ashland mine:

> [March 6, 1917] And thus endeth the next chapter in the life of a Mining Engineer, and may the good Lord someday rest their souls. They certainly have a — of a time on this earth, and maybe in the next one all they will have to do will be to placer mine on the golden streets of Gabriel-land. . . .
>
> I am thoroughly at outs with the mining profession and can see no future in it, and that is the truth. It seems to me about the most unsatisfactory kind of business, possibly excepting the traveling salesman, ever invented for the worriment of man. And I have an idea that you will agree with me on this point.

These men were close friends. Between Irving and Wallace the letters were addressed to "My dear Irving" and "Dear Jim." Norris called Irving "My dear Herr." Norris suggested to Irving he look into the job prospects in the Joplin district of Missouri. Wallace had landed his place in Montana from the recommendation of another Guanajuato miner, Dave Meiklejohn, and he proposed Irving to his people for the inspection of a mine at Oatman, Arizona. In return he asked Irving if he was enough of a placer expert to get someone to buy a placer mine on his say-so. Irving denied that he was "a placer or any other kind of expert," but he offered to approach potential buyers in Boston through a close friend, if Wallace could send him detailed information, although "you do not need to tell me where it is or the name of it." Later he added, "I happen to know of a little group in Boston who are looking for things. . . . If you should know of any promising property that would bear an examination let me know. These people here seem really anxious to spend some money."[8] Unfortunately, nothing came of this prospect.

Another person who addressed Irving as "My dear Herr" was Gerald Rives of El Paso, Texas. He had been in Cubo with Irving in 1904 as the bookkeeper and was now the forwarding agent for the Cubo Company and was closely involved with American mining in Mexico. In June 1916, Rives mailed Irving a form letter with the letterhead "Committee of One Hundred of American Refugees from Mexico." It announced the formation of the committee so titled with the purpose of bringing before the public the seriousness of the situation south of the border. ("Committees of one hundred" for religious, antivice, political reform, and other good causes had been founded since the 1880s.) Appeals to Washington, Rives's letter said, are referred to the State Department and buried, while senators and representatives "believe there are other matters more important to their political success than our troubles in Mexico." The committee would "submit to the American people the question of whether we shall receive the respect and protection we deserve in advancing our commerce in Latin America in competition with England, Germany, and France; as to whether the name *American* shall be borne with honor or disgrace." The immediate plans were to appeal to the Republican convention in Chicago for a platform advocating "protection for Americans at home and abroad." The letter asked Irving to become a member of the committee and support it with a contribution of ten dollars. When Irving turned down the invitation, Rives pressed him further and named sixteen engineers of American mining companies in Mexico who had joined the Committee of One Hundred, along with "many others." He sent Irving a pamphlet he had printed entitled "Wake Up, America."[9] His initiative shows that beyond the intimate fraternity of Guanajuato superintendents there was a larger community of American mining engineers who were prepared to act as a group to publicize their point of view. They were not in touch directly with each other, but a man like Rives, who handled forwarding for many American interests in Mexico, was in a position to bring them together. His motivation came from the ruin of his business caused by the suspension of activities in Mexico of U.S. mining companies.

Irving told Rives that he was counting on the Republican Party to make Wilson's handling of Mexico a strong campaign issue. To Hollis he wrote, "I believe nothing will be done as long as President Wilson is in office, unfortunately, and that meanwhile conditions will get still worse in Mexico."[10] Like Irving, the Committee of One Hundred put its hopes in the election of Charles Evans Hughes: "It is up to us to do everything possible to make it certain." (After Hughes lost, Rives referred to "Woody Wilson" bitterly as "our old and true, true friend."[11]) Those engineers who joined Rives's committee would have been of the same political persuasion, adding to their sense of common identity. Not all in the business agreed, however. Hollis listed himself in *Who's Who in America* as a Democrat until well into the 1920s.

The engineers who had been gathered in Guanajuato shared the knowledge of working with silver and gold as their product, but in 1916 Irving investigated the potential of a platinum placer mine in northern California and a copper mine in Arizona, and ended the year managing a graphite mill in Alabama. Carter Norris was running a strip coal mine in Missouri, where the major machine consisted of a revolving steam shovel. Mining engineers had been trained, and had later gathered experience, in the development and managing of mines. The stories of these men reveal that within their field the mining engineer was versatile, not tied to one kind of technology or product in the pursuit of his career.

After Irving's break with Hollis, he asked Rives to keep an eye out for openings for him. Rives referred him to the president of the Rio Plata Mining Company of New York City, whose manager of their Chihuahua interests had recently drowned. Irving had just taken his job in Alabama when the letter arrived and he was not interested. A few months later Rives announced to Irving that he had recommended him for a position as adviser and consulting engineer to the Bureau of Mines of the government of China, whose duties would be to develop the mining industry in that country. Irving had just sent in his resignation from Graphite and so he wrote of his interest to the person who announced the position.[12] There is nothing more in Irving's correspondence on this feeler, but it provides evidence of another important feature of the career of the mining engineer. He was willing to go where there was employment, even if it were China (and China at this time was in the throes of postrevolutionary instability). Wallace was an Englishman, but he was now in Montana, and wrote in August 1916 that he was headed for Brazil for three months. Unlike a member of the diplomatic corps or a missionary who had prepared himself for work abroad, for the American mining engineer a job outside the United States was an accidental rather than an essential part of the career. That all of Irving's jobs abroad were in Spanish-speaking countries in Latin America can be largely attributed to the choice of investments of the men who turned to Hollis for management.

The wife of the mining engineer lacked the challenge and satisfaction of a professional job. But Luella's concern was to keep the family together. When the Mexican Revolution led to the Herr family's return to Cambridge, where Luella's parents now lived and next door to where she grew up, it meant that Irving was away from his family for long stretches to inspect prospects or to begin a new job. Luella longed for a quiet home in an urban community in the United States, but whenever conditions permitted, she took the boys and joined Irving at his mine, even if it meant rugged conditions without decent schools. If the mine were abroad, the engineer and his family might have to learn another language, but the ultimate desire was to have the family together. When Irving was on his way back to Cubo, Luella wrote him from their home near Oneida:

> [January 1, 1920] This whole thing seems utterly unreal to me. I can't seem to realize that you are actually back in the mining game—have left the Oneida Community Limited for good and are en route to Guanajuato. . . . I'll confess to you what I'll breathe to no one else—that I have a little dread of getting back into that land of apprehension. All this talk I've been getting off over being eager to go has been for outside consumption. I don't want *anyone* to worry about us or think us wild and reckless—hence my insistence on its security—and my eagerness is over getting away from the OCL and my delight in having you once again hold a place in the world that is worthy of you. My impatience to return to Guanajuato (which is now very real) is to be with you again—to be all together as a family in a place where you are happy in your work and can feel that you have an opportunity to show what you are really capable of.

Indeed, the Herr family found a more satisfactory life in Cubo than at any mine site in the United States.

Notes

1. Percy F. Martin, *Mexican Treasure House (Guanajuato)* (New York: Cheltenham Press, 1906), 214–15.

2. Irving to Baldwin, April 24, 1916. Baldwin wrote to Irving on the letterhead "Otis Elevator Company, New York, Office of the President" (March 3, 1916).

3. Letterhead of Guanajuato Development Co. to Irving, December 11, 1915; and of Mineral Development Company used by Irving to Luella, written from Wallace's house, where he was staying (January 17, 1916). The stationery does not identify a United States address for the company.

4. *Who's Who in America*, vol. 8, 1914–15. From 1922 to 1946 he was managing director of the Palmer estate (see his obituary in the *Chicago Daily Tribune*, November 21, 1958). By 1924 he was president of the Palmer Corporation and by 1930 vice-president of the Palmer House Company (*Who's Who in America*, vols. 13, 16, 1924–25, 1930–31).

5. Irving to Hollis, June 8 and 11, 1931.

6. Norris to Irving, September 15, 1916, and Wallace to Irving, March 26, 1917.

7. Irving to Wallace, July 13, 1916.

8. Irving to Wallace, September 1, 1916; March 6, 1917.

9. Committee of One Hundred to Irving, El Paso, June 5, 1916. Rives was evidently the person behind the committee, for its address was the post office box of his company, Camphuis and Rives. Irving to Rives and Rives to Irving, August 7 and 11, 1916.

10. Irving to Hollis, July 24, 1916.

11. Rives to Irving, March 13, 1917.

12. Rives to Irving, August 11, 1916; January 27, 1917; Irving to Thomas A. Lee, February 12, 1917.

PART II

Aftershocks, 1920–1932

CHAPTER 10

Back to the Mine

While we were away a new constitution for Mexico was proclaimed at Querétaro on January 31, 1917, and a formal election was arranged for on March 11, in which Carranza was duly elected. The Constitution of 1917 — which has remained the fundamental law of Mexico to the present day — was one of the most radical in the world at its time. Reversing the policies of the Porfiriato toward the soil, the constitution abolished private property in natural resources, and it specifically reinstated the traditional Spanish and Mexican rule that subsoil rights are the property of the nation. Thus it opened up the possibility of reversal of sales and leases made under Díaz. The constitution also sought to meet the demands of the unions whose strikes had tied up Mexico City and affected the economy of the country. It provided the right to organize unions, bargain collectively, and strike. While all the provisions of the constitution would not be carried out for some time, it provided a basis for ongoing claims. The Guanajuato mines were not immediately affected except for serious labor troubles.

Irving finally returned to mining in Mexico in January 1920. After four years of Carranza, who was supported by U.S. recognition and Pershing's "punitive expedition" against Villa in the north in 1916–17, a measure of peace had been restored and Carranza appointees were responsible for maintaining order. Irving describes what he found on his return in letters to Luella:

[January 26, 1920—from Querétaro] So far on this trip I have very little to complain of. The Pullman was one of those that formerly ran between Mexico City and Vera Cruz on the Queen's Own. I felt sorry for it because it has certainly seen some hard service in the past four years. But it still has wheels on it and rolls along quite smoothly. The service was an improvement over what it was my last trip down. That is to say the washroom had clean towels and soap and a little water. Instead of Mexican porters there were two darkies, nice old fellows, one to tend the grill and the other to look after the beds. Clean sheets were put on the beds. The most noticeable thing about the car was the carpet, which is worn beyond the possibility of words to describe. It is moss grown—is so ravelly that in spots it looks like grass and in others like grass worn down to a hard dirt path.

The first day there was plenty to eat—eggs—steak—soup—bread—tea and coffee. By the second day a leak in the gas reservoir had dissipated all the fuel for cooking and there was nothing doing. I brought some stuff with me which I got at the Sanitary Grocery in Laredo.

As soon as we left Laredo I decided that you must travel in the compartment or stateroom and not in an ordinary berth, because there were some noisy Americans aboard who immediately started drinking beer and drank until one or two of them got half soused and they also got the darky porter drunk. So much for some of our Countrymen. Luckily they got off in Monterrey—to go thence to Tampico. The balance of the trip was quiet and also cold. I had my heavy sweater and it and my spring overcoat proved lifesavers. There is no heat in the car, and it was cold and raw all the way down.

We reached Saltillo Saturday night and there the train stayed all night—because there is a section south of Saltillo where about a month or more ago bandits held up the train and killed a number of passengers. I think this never got into the U.S. papers. So now the train leaves Saltillo at four in the morning preceded by an exploratory train.

We reached Queretaro at eleven last night, three hours late, because some of the engines lost their wind and died on the road. The only train to Silao leaves here at two in the afternoon so I had to spend the night here. I am at the Hotel Internacional which is the best in town and none too good—quite Mexican. But so far I am glad to be back and had all sorts of wuzzy feelings when I got out and walked around this morning—seeing the dear dirty peons, and the burros and tranvias and dirt and sunshine and birds' songs. I really felt strange to say as though I were home again after a long wandering. I even bought a very big, good-for-nothing fire opal for $2.50 Mex. or $1.25 our money. Also bought four very big juicy oranges for 12¢ Mex.

Things seem very peaceful around here. Superficially at least I should say there has been a big improvement during the time we have been away. Same old cargadors. I haven't seen any sort of hostile look. . . .

After four unhappy years away, Irving appreciated Mexico in a new way.

Carranza's government was notoriously corrupt. His appointees were doing little or nothing to fulfill the promises of the new constitution in land distribution, education, and labor conditions. Gradually his strongest supporters began to desert him. Obregón had gone back to his garbanzo farm in Sonora; others began openly to take issue with his administration. As the time approached for new presidential elections in 1920, Carranza proposed to install his selection, Ignacio Bonillas, permitting himself to become an "elder statesman" and continue to pull the strings.

When Irving arrived in Guanajuato the time for the presidential elections was approaching, and dissatisfaction with the Carranza regime was already evident in growing support for Obregón. Irving wrote:

[January 30, 1920] I have been in Guanajuato now for four days, but I am afraid I will not be able to give you a very satisfactory account of things as yet. I spent Tuesday night with the Gilmores [manager of the Guanajuato Power Company] and their place is looking very lovely now, just as it used to in the good old days years ago. But it is about the only place in town that is at all in as good shape as formerly. Frank [Gilmore] seems to be feeling very optimistic about the outlook, and says that during the past three years things have been constantly improving. Guanajuato seems to be fairly quiet, and there is a good deal of work going on, in fact more work than there are workmen to do it. Good labor is very scarce and I think or rather know this is going to be one of our chief difficulties in operating out here at Cubo.

Cubo certainly seems very triste and not like the old days at all. There are a lot of bad people out here, and most of the good ones have gone away. Most the of the things that we left here are still here, and the few pieces of furniture that we left are all intact but a little the worse for wear, which is natural. I have not yet had time to look into the trunks in Guanajuato, but there are two trunks there, and I believe they are intact.

About your coming down here, I am not so sure as I was at first. I do not exactly believe, but I have a suspicion that when the elections come next June or July that something is going to break loose. The opinion in Guanajuato among a number of people is that Obregon intends to be the next President. Naturally all of the Government influence is going to be exerted against him, and while he may be elected by the popular vote, it is quite improbable that he will be declared elected. In that event some people here say that he will fight for it. . . .

It may also turn out that in a few weeks I may change my idea some-what about the looks of things. My whole viewpoint just now may be that I have not yet adjusted myself to the look of things here, after hav-ing been away for three years in more pleasant surroundings.

A more detailed description of the conditions in Mexico on Irving's re-turn in January 1920 is given in a letter he wrote to Christine and Grosvenor Allen, friends at the Oneida Community:

[February 15, 1920] I have been wanting to write you as I knew you would be very interested to hear how I found things Mexican, and how much they were different from what they were when I last left. Maybe you will be surprised when I say that they seem to be indescribably bet-ter. In the first place, when I left here in January 1916 there was little work going on, because some of the companies could not work on ac-count of lack of supplies. Now everyone is working full blast and there is more than enough work to go around. In fact there is a shortage of na-tive labor just now, and if more enterprises are started up in Guanajuato one of our most serious problems will be to get miners enough to go around.

Another thing that impressed me as being decidedly different from 1916 is that now the streets in Guanajuato are being swept twice daily, whereas before they were not swept at all, and there are policemen on them now instead of soldiers. I am not saying anything, mind you, about the quality of these officers of the law, but they are in evidence at any rate. Another very great difference is that now we are paying off the men in real honest-to-God gold pieces instead of the former Carranzista handbills. There is a very acute shortage of small change, which makes business difficult to do. Change sells at a premium of from 10 percent to 15 percent, so instead of paying off exactly what may be due a man, we either make him rustle the change or pay him what we can in even money and let the rest accumulate until in a few weeks we can square the account with a two-and-a-half dollar or five-dollar [i.e., peso] gold piece. Sometimes several workmen are grouped together and paid off jointly. I do not know how long this situation is going to last, but it is quite annoying.

About political conditions in Mexico, you have probably heard that there is an election for President coming off in July, or possibly August. Some say that the present incumbent of the presidential office intends to stick and will not recognize the newly elected one. Quien sabe. The situation is all up in the air at present and nobody can tell what really will happen. The various candidates are Obregon, Gonzales who is at the head of Carranza's army, Bonillas who has been ambassador to Washington, as well as the first mentioned possibility. Some say that there is going to be trouble and another revolution, but I can hardly believe that. During the past week there has been a convention of the governors of eighteen states in the City of Mexico, trying to lay plans that will result in an orderly election [and where, according to our history, they were instructed by Carranza to work against Obregón].

Should the critical time be passed safely, I am looking forward to a very decided boom, and a rapid betterment of conditions all over the country, for we can look forward to four years without political troubles to disturb the course of events. In Guanajuato we are favored with a very good Governor — Federico Montes — who was the father of the gathering of Governors in Mexico City. He seems to be playing the game with the mining companies, and aiding us in every legitimate way. Of course things are not as they were back in 1910 and they never will be again, but there are still a great many of the old-fashioned sort of peons who doff their hat when you come along and treat you with the respect due a titled person. It may not be democratic but it certainly is appealing to one's sense of importance.

Encouraged by these first impressions, Irving decided that Luella and the two boys would come to Mexico and join him, to live at the mine in Cubo. On February 10, she began making preparations for the move. Irving wrote:

[February 15, 1920] I wrote you one letter that expressed grave doubts about your coming down, but I want you to know that for the past week or ten days I have been in a much more cheerful frame of mind. I am not anticipating any trouble of any kind barring petty stealing until election time. And then I hope that there will not be the revolution that a number of people think there is going to be. Somehow I cannot believe that the ones in power are going to be foolish enough to permit the country to be plunged again into a civil war. If the elections do go off peaceably and those that are in abide by the results, I feel sure that there is going to be a great boom in Mexico, and that the present improvement will continue.

As far as having you here is concerned, you can rest assured that you have been here when things were very much worse than they are now. You see there is so much work around Guanajuato now that there is no necessity for being bandits in order to live. There is work for everyone that wants to work. As a result there are no bandits around the hills at all as far as I can find out. . . .

This morning I got a letter from one of my old Mexican mine workmen, Dionisio Paz, written from Pachuca congratulating me on my return to Guanajuato and asking me to give him work here. He was one of my best boys, and I am quite eager to write him and tell him to come back. You see the news of my return here has traveled about quite a bit. In so far as it is possible I am trying to get my old gente back again. That in itself will help to make Cubo more orderly and a better place.

Regarding the effort to get Angela back from the Mexico City area to serve as cook, we have Irving's version of Angela's letter:

[February 27, 1920] You will be glad to know that I finally received a letter from Angela. She says that she will come back to us some time in March, as soon as she winds up her affairs. These consist, as near as I can find out from her letter, in the responsibilities arising from her having sown a number of seeds. She said that she had planted corn, beans, pigs, and chickens. I think it is quite an interesting combination, and I would not be averse to having some of her pig seed. She also says that she is living a very peaceful and happy life and that her brother is averse to her coming back to this dreadful place where she almost died of fright, but as we have asked her, she cannot refuse, etc.

Luella and the two boys arrived back in Cubo on March 8, 1920. Although Irving had reported that there were no bandits around the hills, the boys, then 15 and 13, were each given a .38 caliber Smith and Wesson Police Special revolver and were told to learn how to use them and not to leave the hacienda without them. Also, they were placed under the tutelage of Pancho Medina, chief of the mining company's armed guard, who was to accompany them outside the property and incidentally help them to relearn their Spanish. Of her return "home" Luella reports in her diary:

1920 - March
8 — Left Guanajuato for El Cubo about 10:20 A.M. and arrived at noon. Found the Mexican servants had the place all trimmed up with arches of flowers. Our former home is rather triste but the place is peaceful and sunny.

During March and April life continued as normal at the hacienda in Cubo, with occasional visits to Guanajuato. The boys rode freely over the nearby mountains, always accompanied by Pancho Medina. But the plans of Carranza and his henchmen as to the coming election, as conceived at the convention of governors in February, were going awry. In Sonora, Obregón had declared himself a candidate and campaigned vigorously, and Carranza dismissed army officers and government officials suspected of favoring Obregón. However, support for Obregón grew rapidly, and by May 1920, forces were gathering in rebellion against the Carranza government.

As early as April Luella notes in her diary:

1920 - April

24 — Mexico really seems to be started on another revolution. No one can
tell what it will amount to nor how it will come out. All very quiet
here.

29 — Everyone is more or less upset over this new revolution and there is
a general feeling of uneasiness in the air, but so far everything in the
State and City of Guanajuato is quiet.

1920 - May

6 — Irapuato, Silao and Guanajuato all declared in favor of Obregon so
we are now in rebel territory and hence no train service. No fighting
hereabouts, however.

Seeing his support dissolve, and wasting no time, on May 5, Carranza began preparations to evacuate Mexico City once more for Veracruz. Two days
later fifteen miles of trains were ready to move, carrying the national trea-
sury, dies from the mint and printing presses, furniture from the National
Palace, the national archives, wives, children, and mistresses, among other
valuables. The caravan was intercepted by rebel forces east of the city and
Carranza fled into the mountains on horseback with a few faithful men.
Some days later, in the early morning hours of May 21, 1920, he was ambushed and murdered.

Luella may well have wondered why she had returned. Her diary continues to reflect her concern:

1920 - May

7 — No forces of any sort in Guanajuato and everyone is a bit nervous. A
couple of Carranzista colonels left town at 2 A.M., having first let out
all the prisoners and taken all the horses they could get. They went
out through Peregrina and took horses and arms. Fortunately for us
Cubo escaped.

8 — Still no force in Guanajuato and still everyone is nervous, not being
sure what sort of gente will come to take the town. A force came in at
night, however, and everyone cheered up. Also a train came with
some old mail.

9 — Minda Gilmore called me up to say Obregon and Gonzales are in
Mexico City — Carranza a prisoner, having tried to escape with ten

trains of food, money, and arms — and several of his generals shot. Also trains are running again to Laredo from the City, and from Aguas to Queretaro.

10 — Word came that a bunch a caballo was in the hills and about to descend on Cubo. Much excitement and nervousness. The boys and Angela and I and the patio women [ore sorters] went into the mine but were sent for very soon. Only four men came to the hacienda, took one gun, and departed. The news received about Carranza yesterday is denied. I almost fled to town but thought better of it.

11 — No trains to Guanajuato because the Carranza general in Irapuato took the Irapuato-Guanajuato engine to escape to Guadalajara. Guanajuato has had three governors so far. Nothing seems settled and everyone is still rather uneasy.

12 — Another day of no trains to Guanajuato and of general uneasiness here at Cubo. I sent a suitcase of clothes to Guanajuato in case the boys and I want to make a quick getaway.

13 — Feeling a bit easier. Received a couple of newspapers, which came overland from Irapuato and were sold on the streets of Guanajuato for fifty centavos each. Obregon and Gonzales seem to be behaving themselves very well in the City.

14 — Two trains came to Guanajuato and there are to be two trains from the City through Silao daily. However little U.S. mail, and that old — as Monterrey is still Carranzista. Madrazo is in Guanajuato as Governor — the legally elected man in the last elections — and everyone feels better.

17 — Gonzales has resigned as a candidate for President and that clears the atmosphere considerably.

Irving told much the same story in a letter to Grosvenor Allen at Oneida Community:

[May 24, 1920] Of course you have been following events in Mexico — I refrain from saying revolution-torn Mexico — because this expression has been worn to a frazzle. So far these events have been very satisfactory to me. Most of the mine managers in Guanajuato are still inclined to be pessimistic over the outlook, but for my part it looks like the dawn of a new day. The Chicago Tribune in a recent editorial rather hit the nail on the head in a sense. They say, "Another election has just been pulled off in Mexico and the bullets have all been counted." As a matter of fact very few bullets were fired in this latest turnover. In all my experience in Mexico I have never seen anything like it. City after city, and general after general, simply switched over to the other side without any fighting or disorder or any annoyance whatever.

One afternoon early in May my accountant in Guanajuato called me up on the phone and stated that Guanajuato, Silao, and Irapuato had just gone over to the Obregonistas. I inquired just who had gone over, but he did not know, nor do I to this day. There was really no one to go over. But at any rate from that time on Guanajuato ceased to be governed by the Carranza Government and for a number of days had no government at all. For at least two nights there was no authority whatever in the city, not a soldier nor even a policeman. And it may seem strange to you when I say that not any disorder of any kind resulted. Everything ran along just as usual, except that there was a distinct feeling of uneasiness abroad, due to ignorance of what might happen. For at that time the telegraph lines were all cut or censored so that no news was coming in. I think Boston should take notice of the above [referring to the Boston police strike of September 1919, when then Governor Calvin Coolidge called out the state guard to maintain order].

The few Carranzistas who were in Guanajuato stayed there for a couple of days, and then beat it to the hills one rainy night at about 4 A.M. They collected all the horses they could lay hands on, and about fifty strong came out past one of the mines near us. Here they relieved the veladores [caretakers] of their guns, took all the mine horses, consisting of two, and continued their journey. Luckily for Cubo, we were off the main road to Dolores Hidalgo where they were headed, and so escaped losses and anxiety.

We did not escape entirely, however, for before these gentlemen left Guanajuato, in fact before the turnover when they were still in authority but knew their days were numbered, we received orders from the Presidente Municipal to report immediately all the arms, side arms, etc., both of individuals and belonging to the Company, that we had at the mine. We had to comply with this order and reported about nine Mauser rifles, six Winchester .30-30s and several other miscellaneous firearms. They then stated that they would like us to lend them the Mausers as they were afraid of an uprising in Guanajuato, and wished to be prepared. Gisholt, my accountant and general utility man in town, talked them down to three Mausers, which they said would fill the bill. They promised on their word of honor to return them as soon as the trouble was over. Of course we will never see them again, as they went on the road to Dolores with the horses and other guns they were able to collect.

Then after the Carranzistas had left Guanajuato, and while it was still without a government, we had a visit from about eight soldiers. They came from over the hills, and we knew they were coming before they actually reached the hacienda. I happened to be up at the mill at the time, and on my way back felt that something was in the air. When I arrived at the hacienda I found the shooting towers all manned with my escolta, or armed guard. Frowning rifles were projecting from the loop holes, and the gates were locked. Soon after I got in, four horsemen appeared in the streets of the town, all armed to the teeth. Pancho Medina, the Captain of the Escolta, from his point of vantage at the top of the main gate, called to them to HALT. They did very suddenly, and I believe were somewhat scared or at least nonplussed. It turned out that Pancho recognized the leader as a man he had known slightly at one time in Mexico City. So Pancho and I went out to meet them, and brought them into the hacienda. Then we found out what they wanted, which quite naturally was firearms. The leader said they were Sirob's men and had orders from said gentleman — who by the way is the former Governor of Guanajuato who was responsible for the robbing of our mine — to take our city peacefully or by force as the case might be. Boiled down to brass tacks, can this be done? They wanted three Mauser rifles. I suppose they wanted three because this was the number they saw. We finally persuaded them that one Mauser would be a mighty fine present, and got rid of them by the surrender of one gun. I suppose I was easy not to refuse them entirely, but on the other hand we did not know how many more of them there might be just out of sight, and decided it was worth

the gun to escape a fight possibly, or their return later under more ad-
vantageous circumstances. So now we are shy four of our precious guns,
and have about a dozen left. But I do not expect ever to have to use
them.

While the above was being enacted, Lue and the boys and about half
a hundred women who were sorting ore in the patio made a getaway into
the mine. As usual the Mexican women had counted the soldiers and had
seen not less than two hundred. The same old story.

From the way the present "ins" are taking hold I think there is great
promise for the future, and as I said before I am more optimistic than I
have been for years. They are certainly playing the game so far and are
taking great pains to disturb business as little as possible, are keeping the
trains moving, and best of all seem to be catering to the opinion of the
outside nations. I think this is a very hopeful sign and that they are finally awakening to the fact that Mexico cannot stand alone, nor defy the
public opinion of the world.

On the same day this letter was written, a special session of the Mexican
congress that was convened immediately after Carranza's assassination
named the governor of Sonora, Adolfo de la Huerta, provisional president of
Mexico. De la Huerta arranged for a national election in September. The
victorious candidate was Alvaro Obregón, the man who had defeated Carranza's rivals and then become Carranza's implacable enemy. He assumed
office on November 30, 1920, and a new era in Mexican history began.

The darkest days of the Mexican Revolution can be identified with
Carranza. From the beginning with his "Plan of Guadalupe" in 1913, Carranza's moves left misery and desolation in their wake. In the campaigns
against Villa in 1915, the Carranzistas commandeered all the food supplies in
Guanajuato (and elsewhere no doubt), and tram cars were delayed by "flatcars hauling corn." Later, as we have seen, Carranza's appointee as governor
of the State of Guanajuato helped himself to rich ores in the Cubo mine
while the people around him starved. Nowhere during the early years did the
Carranzistas set up an honest and effective civil administration.

Carranza himself seldom took an active part. Older than most others on
the scene, and skillful in political maneuvers, he arranged for others to take

the major risks and accepted the plaudits when the field was won. Perhaps the best example of his political skill was the placement of a personal representative in Washington, D.C., and the fact that President Wilson and his secretary of state, William Jennings Bryan, were taken in, and finally granted recognition to a spoiler. But of course an idealist would never understand an opportunist.

Irving remained at the Cubo mine for the next twelve years. Although much remained to be done to accomplish the goals of the Mexican Revolution and to stabilize society after ten tumultuous years, the new administration under Obregón restored a measure of stability, and the process of healing was begun. The next ten years were a period of readjustment and social change and were also a part of the revolution, but Irving's optimism that brought the family back to Cubo in 1920 proved to be well founded.

CHAPTER 11

Reminiscences III

In 1920, after the unrest that led to Carranza's exit and ultimately to Obregón's election as president, life in the Guanajuato mining district returned to its normal tenor. Aside from roving bands of displaced revolutionaries — bandits who were not yet ready to give up a predatory life — reasonable order was restored, and relative peace would continue until the approach of the next presidential election, due in 1924. Returning to Mexico in the spring of 1920, John and I were now of high school age and Cubo and Guanajuato offered many new opportunities.

We had an interesting foreign colony, both in Guanajuato and at the mine. The power plant in town (later acquired by the Electric Bond and Share complex) was managed by an American, Mr. Gilmore. He had two children younger than we, and he and his wife Minda were Mother and Dad's favorite bridge partners. His second in command, Mr. Fisher, was also an American who had a son, Carlos, about our age. The DeVoties had a boy and a girl our age, Jean and Frank ("Pancho"), who were our best friends. Mr. DeVotie was with the Dwight-Furness Company, bankers. There was the American doctor and his son, and a number of other mine managers and engineers whom we did not know as well. And Dr. Hislop, the dentist, who added to his meager income by doubling as the British Consul. He was as old as his equipment, but he managed to clean our teeth.

At the mine there was Oliver Steele with his wife and baby daughter, a young man from Texas who was full of beans and had taken a contract with Dad to break the ores out of certain sections of the mine — the drillers worked for him. (Later he bought a ranch in the valley, twenty miles away, to raise hogs, and worked both jobs.) The engineer was an Englishman, Vaughan, who hated to lose and couldn't see the funny side of things, later replaced by an American family (the Moores) with little kids that didn't help us much. And up the river there was Carrouché, the mill manager, a Frenchman from Louisiana. We recall that he had been forced to resign by Dad's predecessor, and his return to Cubo will be narrated anon. He had with him a Mexican wife and a daughter, Josephine, who, alas, was our age. We will come back to her also.

We did not need a program director to work up activities. There was now a tennis court on the old mill floor in the hacienda. Instead of wire netting the sides were enclosed by old mill walls and one thought twice before scrambling for an angle shot across the alley, but it was adequate. The gallery sat atop one of the walls. Every afternoon at four the men would get into their tennis clothes, long white duck pants and a long-sleeved white shirt with a soft collar and a tie, and have at it until six. John and I were included, but it was some years before we could hold our own with the men. They would take their turns at sharing with us as doubles partners. Except in the rainy season (July through September) there was never any question of play or no play, because it never rained and the temperature was always in the seventies or eighties. We were at 6,500 feet above sea level.

Except for our family there were no bridge players at the mine, so we settled on poker and started what we called the Thursday Night Poker Club. (Weekends were usually spent in town.) It was a six- or eight-handed game, the ladies playing with the men and the boys, and Steele kept it lively and made sure that we stuck to the rules. Straight poker, nothing wild, at a quarter a corner and we played for chips. At the end of each month the three highest winners divided the pot.

Sensing the lack of adequate news coverage in Cubo, John and I started a biweekly publication that we called the "Cubo Spark." Somewhere we found an old gelatin duplicator that served as a printing press. Type was set on a discarded typewriter, three columns to the page, and the paper frequently ran to two pages, including jokes and the Editor's Corner. We soon found that seeing one's name in the news was the key to circulation, and the "Cubo Spark" was widely read. It served also to bring out some of the literary talent of our readers, such as "A Cubo Poker Game" by O. W. Steele. The first verse will suffice:

> You may talk of law and Hoyle and obedience to such,
> But when it comes to poker they don't amount to much.
> For all the joys of living that our nights of pleasure claim
> Not one has half the pleasure of a Cubo poker game. . . .

Typical news items (1921):

April 6 – The Cubo mail bag is becoming so heavy that Antonio has requested an assistant. On looking into the matter it was discovered that the congestion was due to the "Pig and Hog" correspondence of O. W. Steele.

May 3 – The Cubo tennis court is in process of having a new surface but the process is much too slow to suit the Cubo tennis players. – The cribbage match between John and O. W. Steele is finished, Mr. Steele winning 50 games to 41.

June 7 – Jesus Gutierrez, the Cubo Co. assayer, is president of the new Cubo baseball nine. They are making a diamond up back of the pantheon and Mr. Herr has purchased first-class equipment for them. . . . On Friday, June 3, Mr. Herr, Mr. Steele, Mr. Vaughan, John, and Bob challenged them to a game and with the aid of four Mexicans defeated the Cubo team 15-9 in a game of six innings.

– On Saturday afternoon, May 28, Mr. & Mrs. Steele and the four Herrs went on an overnight camping trip. It was John's idea. They went to the Cañada de la Iglesia, on the San Isidro ranch. Some on horseback and some on foot, and a mule with two chiquihuites of food, bedding, and raincoats, piloted by three mozos, made quite a procession through the town of Villalpando and over the mountains. They were gone about 26 hours. John had along his .22 rifle and killed eleven frogs, so frog's legs were added to the larder. Insects and all annoying animals were happily not in evidence.

Aug. 27 — Mr. Carrouché was out in the hills again on Sunday, August 7, and the various families here in the hacienda at Cubo have been enjoying venison as a result.

The "Cañada de la Iglesia" was a garden spot in otherwise dreary and often barren mountain sides. As one rode east over mountain trails across the divide for an hour or two to the headwaters of the rivers running to the Atlantic, there was suddenly a break, an escarpment dropping into a canyon some three hundred feet deep heavy with oak and aspen and marked at the bottom with a thin line of bright green where water ran throughout the year, dry season and rainy season. Dropping down a well-worn charcoal burners' trail to the grassy bottom we could follow the stream up or down as far as we liked, but we never reached either its beginning or its end. As we looked up at the side where we had entered, we saw stately towers and turrets rising in the sheer rock walls — hence the name: Canyon of the Church. The other side was also steep, but was covered with trees as though the aspens at the base were reaching higher and higher. This was our picnic spot or camping ground. We went there many times, either for the day or overnight.

Carrouché was quite a character. He had his own establishment at the mill some fifteen minutes walk upriver from the mine, a house that sat on the edge of a precipice overlooking the river with the usual outbuildings for tools and chickens, and a garden tucked in beside the house on the steep walls of the canyon. (At one time the rock base under the front of the house had begun to crack and thick steel cables were drawn tight around the front like a sling and tied to solid concrete anchors on either side to keep the house from falling into the river. In 1960, some forty years later, these cables were still in place and the house was still there.) Opposite the house and across a small tributary canyon stood the mill, an impressive pile of heavy machinery and tanks housed in corrugated sheet metal, three hundred feet wide and dropping almost vertically down the steep side of the mountain to the river bottom. It was capable of processing one hundred tons of ore per day.

The ore was brought in from the mouth of the vertical shaft on the top of the mountain (this is where Dad would ride to when he disappeared up the shaft from the lower levels of the mine), tracked in ore cars to a jumping-off place, dumped down an incline, and picked up in cars again to be taken to the mill. There it passed through giant steel-jawed rock crushers and after crossing a sorting belt was fed into the stamp mills, a series of great triphammers that literally mashed the rock into a pulp. But to make sure that it was fine enough this mass was then put through the ball mills, hollow steel cylinders that revolved half full of steel balls that ground the ore still further as it tumbled among the balls. In the early days selected stones of flinty quartz were used instead of the steel balls, and remnants of these could still be found along the river bed, rounded by the tumbling action until they looked like cobblestones. They were great for building dams or retaining walls when we were in a constructive mood, and occasionally we found cracked flint stones that we used to test our skill at lighting fires with flint and steel.

The pulverized ore was then mixed with a strong solution of potassium cyanide and agitated with compressed air in the Pachuca tanks for hours until virtually all of the silver and gold was dissolved into the solution, which was then filtered out and pumped to the zinc room. Here the loaded cyanide solution was exposed to zinc shavings in the zinc tanks, resulting in a chemical reaction that precipitated the silver and gold out of the solution in the form of a black powder that was accumulated and shipped out as the product of the mill. When I came home from school in the summers Dad would never give me a job because he was sensitive about hiring the "boss's son." But Carrouché offered me a job at the mill, and that was all right, as I was responsible to him. My job was in the zinc room to see that all of the black precipitate went into the sacks for shipment to the smelter, and that none of it went into the pockets or lunch baskets of the men who worked there. There had been some disappearances, and I felt that this was somewhat of a ticklish assignment. As I went home after the last cleanup I was never quite sure who might be walking behind me, or why.*

Also I remember the worries I had about being so closely associated with that cyanide solution. I knew quite well that the smallest amount of cyanide taken in through the mouth would mean a quick death and I doubt that I have ever washed my hands as carefully or as often as I did that summer. The

---

*Cubo archives, Ledger No. 9 (1919–1925), shows a payment July 31, 1925, "Robt. Herr . . Sueldo [salary] . . 80.00 [pesos]."

Mexicans knew this too, and I marveled at the unconcern with which they dipped their hands and arms up to the elbows into the zinc tanks to rinse the shavings and make sure that all of the precipitate went down to the bottom. When they ate their lunch they simply washed their hands under a cold water tap, spread out their lunch and ate their tortillas with their hands. So far as I know no one was ever the worse for it.

After leaving the zinc room the clarified solution was sent back down to the foot of the mill and stored in holding vats for reuse in the Pachuca tanks. These vats were large concrete tanks with the tops at ground level. They were completely unprotected with covers or fencing of any kind. They looked for all the world like square swimming pools and the clear light-green cyanide solution was almost as inviting. We walked close by them without a second thought. The story is told of one of the supervisors who accidentally dropped a gold pocket watch into one of these vats. Before long the watch case would of course be dissolved. He offered a peso to anyone who would retrieve it for him and one of the men standing by dove into the bottom and brought it out. He took the peso, washed his face and hands and went on about his business. Here again I never heard of an accident around these vats. Everyone knew the score.

Carrouché ruled over this domain quietly and effectively. He knew his business, he liked his men, and they liked him. And he was good to us boys. One night when he had a visitor from Guanajuato he invited John and me up for dinner in the evening. Inadvertently, or as I have often thought deliberately, he introduced us to some of the rigors of becoming a man. We ate in a separate little building apart from his household, and the party began with what he called "Habanero" rum. It was horrible stuff but we drank it with the others, and dinner was a gay affair with many tall tales of real and fancied exploits that included pirates in the Mississippi delta and encounters during the Mexican Revolution. And of course the drinking continued, for how long I do not know. I do remember being helped over the mountain trail on the way home (and being very sick en route) — they did not dare take us by the river path, which was pretty steep in places. But Carrouché saw that we got home, and I thought it was a little strange that Mother and Dad never asked how late we had returned. From then on I have always been rather careful how much I have to drink.

Deer hunting was Mr. Carrouché's favorite sport and the mountains toward the Cañada offered considerable game. The deer had their runs between the scanty water courses and he knew where they were. He would send a man or two on foot deep into the hills far beyond these runs to work up toward him and any deer around would move on ahead of them. Unsporting? Perhaps. But Carrouché hunted only with a rifle.

The first time he took me out he gave me a Savage .250-3000 and carried a high-power .22 himself. He provided me with a Mexican guide as well and made sure that I was spotted where the deer were most likely first to appear. He stationed himself over a hill beyond in a broad arroyo that was overgrown with scrub oak and underbrush. My spot was a rocky prominence that overlooked a small stream some two hundred yards below. Sure enough, after half an hour two small deer appeared slowly making their way upstream, nibbling as they went, and stopping now and again to scan the hillside. At first I thought they were goats, seen from that distance, but the guide next to me nudged me and whispered, "Now, Señor." Then I saw the buck's antlers and raised my gun. At the first shot they took off, but I tried two more while they were on the run. I think they were laughing at me. Some two minutes later we heard a single shot from over the hilltop and made our way over to see what had happened. There sat Carrouché on the near side of the arroyo with his gun over his knees, pointing to the bottom where the buck had fallen with a single bullet behind his shoulder. Warned by my shots, Carrouché had been waiting and had picked him off on a dead run through the brush on the far side of the gully. The deer was trussed and carried on the shoulders of the Mexican boys in the party. To them and their families it was more meat than they had had to eat for many a day. We kept only the haunches for ourselves.

Twice a week I would ride to town with Brígido, the *mozo*, for piano lessons. Three hours riding for a one-hour lesson. Mine was a good teacher but very insistent on precise technique, so progress was slow. But I learned a little and always enjoyed it, even the practicing. John and Mr. Steele each had a mandolin and we developed a trio — piano and first and second mandolins. An item in the "Cubo Spark" of June 23 reads:

> The long awaited music for the Cubo trio arrived and the trio is perfecting its rendering of "Dreams at Sunset" and has been requested to

play it at our next dance. It has also learned "Beautiful Ohio," being indebted to Jean DeVotie for the music.

The "dance" was wishful thinking. However, occasionally there were dances on weekends in Guanajuato. It was quite amazing to hear what a Mexican orchestra (probably piano, cornet, one or two guitars, and possibly a French horn and tuba) could do to the dance tunes imported from the United States after World War I. Ingenious, to say the least. Dances were sometimes held in the Casino, a Mexican-American club in downtown Guanajuato, and everyone joined in, young and old. On these occasions there was always a table in a corner of the room with an open bottle of cognac surrounded by tall, thin little liqueur glasses, or *copitas*. It was never crowded in this corner, but periodically the men would wander over and exchange ideas over a *copita* or two. There was no heavy drinking and people did not get drunk. But at this early age I learned that a periodic *copita* of brandy made the music sound better and was especially helpful when it came to be your turn to dance with some of the less attractive girls.

When at a late hour John and I were finally ready to ride back to the mine, we would call the stable to have Brígido get the horses ready.

"But, Señor, he is not here."

"Do you know where he is?"

"No."

"Can you find him?"

"*¿Quién sabe?* Señor, but we will try."

They knew where he was, at the bar across the street, but what they did not know was whether he was sober enough to saddle the horses or even to stay on top of one. So we would walk up through the narrow, dark streets to the stable and find out for ourselves. Sometimes he was and sometimes he wasn't, and there was a time or two when we left him in town to sober up and rode home alone. As I have said before, the horses knew the way.

Other weekends in town were spent visiting the DeVoties, playing tennis as guests of the Gilmores at the power plant, or staying at the Hotel Luna just to be where the action was. The hotel faced on the Jardín de la Unión. This was—and still is—not the usual plaza of a Mexican town, but rather a garden in the middle of the city, as the name implies. It was too small to be a park, yet it was a carefully nurtured spot of dense green shrubs and trees with paths running through it, a covered bandstand in the center, and a flagstone walk or promenade surrounding the garden. Decorative iron benches lined the walkway on either side and the whole was ringed with linden trees carefully clipped and shaped in cylindrical form much like the pistons of an automobile, but much prettier to look at. Here on Saturday night and on Sunday after church there was always a band concert.

The musicians might be miners or bartenders or carpenters during the week, but now they were in uniform (at least from the waist up) and each had an instrument, usually brass or reed, which he played with more than normal skill. The Mexicans love music; they take to a musical instrument like a duck to water, and they play from the heart. Some of their selections from symphonies or grand opera were surprisingly well rendered.

As they tuned up their instruments, people would begin to gather, two or three at a time, and by the time the music started there would be a goodly crowd. The crowd was comprised mainly of the upper classes, but among them also would be some of the better-dressed workmen and their families, who came to hear the music and share in the festivity. In the 1920s the peons with their straw sombreros and serapes would line the sidewalks across the street from the promenade to hear the music and seldom venture across. (Now they too are better dressed and will mingle with the others.) Gradually the older people would find a place on the benches while their sons and daughters walked around the promenade, the girls with bright-colored dresses in the mode of the times circling around in one direction arm in arm, and the young men equally modish walking around the garden in the other direction. As a young man passed the girl of his fancy he would try to catch her eye, while she, of course, pretended not to notice until perhaps the third time around when she would drop her eyes and smile. Courtship in the Latin countries is tedious, to say the least.

We were much bolder. A few years later after I had been away at school I tried my hand at the promenade business. A visiting classmate and I, fresh from the States and courting customs of the North, were enjoying the band concert at the Jardín when we spotted a pair of very attractive señoritas whom we decided we should know better. There was a good crowd and it was no great problem to introduce ourselves. They were sisters, Concha and Carmelita (for Concepción and Carmen — Carmen was my choice), and they would be delighted to go to the Sunday afternoon cinema with us, but first they must ask Papa. Too bad he was not there. We arranged that they would ask him when they got home from the concert, and we would telephone for confirmation. I telephoned and Papa answered. Might I speak to Carmelita?

"And who is this?"

I told him.

"And what did you wish with Carmen?"

I told him that too.

"I am sorry, sir, but Carmen does not know you and she will be away all day."

That ended that experiment.

I saw Carmen later, at one of the dances, I think, and she was as pretty as ever, but no mention was made of our previous encounter and I never took her out. I had learned by then that if you called on a Mexican young lady at her home you were committing yourself to courtship with serious intentions and that all activities would be chaperoned unless you were willing to stand in the street outside her barred window and whisper sweet nothings to the strains of a guitar; and I wanted no part of that.

That is no doubt why the whorehouses in these countries are an accepted way of life. But we never went near them. It was big news, widely circulated, when a shipment of new French girls had arrived in town — so what if they charged higher prices? — yet even such inducements were of no interest. Better leave them to the hot-blooded local boys and avoid the obvious risks involved. Our sex life was nil.

Also facing the Jardín de la Unión was the Teatro Juárez, as unbelievable as it is real. It is unbelievable that a theater of this size and magnificence, in the style of the opera houses of Paris and Rome, should be built in a remote provincial capital such as Guanajuato, and it stands as evidence of the wealth that came from the silver mines in the vicinity and of the pride of its aristocrats. In the 1890s European opera companies made regular stops here, but in our day it was used only on rare occasions. My first recollection of it was before the revolution when we were quite young and went to see a marionette show. We sat in the first-tier boxes that ringed the theater. Each box was entered by a private door from the foyer outside. Above these were two or three more tiers of boxes and balconies overlooking the orchestra, all finished in red and gold with ornate lighting and decorations. Occasionally there was something doing at the Teatro Juárez even after the revolution that would bring us to town again for an overnight stay at the Hotel Luna. Even after the rugged times of the 1910s, Guanajuato had many well-to-do Mexicans — lawyers, engineers, businesspeople — who had money and were the elite.

But being of school age now, and having spent a year and a half allowing my years to catch up with my schooling, it was time to get on with my education. In due course I was put on the train and sent off to New England to take my place as a member of the sophomore class at Loomis Institute. I had scarcely opened a textbook during this year and a half except to bone up for entrance exams. When I went into the tenth grade I had just turned fifteen.

For seven years I lived in two completely separate worlds. One, from September until June, was a world of school and college in the States, entirely apart from family and former associates, and in the surroundings of U.S. culture of the 1920s. John had gone to Exeter and I was on my own. While in school, Mexico was a dream world that only took on reality each year between June and September. And when its turn came, the world up north was equally unreal. It was a different river, flowing in a different direction to a different ocean. The train trip north in September and south in June was the yellow brick road that took me back and forth from the Land of Oz. It took four days, a very necessary time for readjustment and reorientation.

This reorientation took place in gradual stages and in logical order. Coming north there was a day and a half on a Mexican Pullman before we reached the border at El Paso. The train was slow, stopping at least twenty minutes at every station where Mexican vendors crowded around in surroundings that we were quite used to, and puffing its way across the mountains that had been our friends all summer. We were telling them goodbye. On the train there were generally a few Americans not long out of the States who would give us the feel of what to expect up north. We would begin to feel our independence of things back home. At El Paso, usually an overnight stop, things were more bustling but still in the casual tempo peculiar to Texas. Dad had put us in touch with a forwarding agent there to see us through customs and to arrange for tickets beyond, and I remember marveling at the ease and dispatch with which he made the necessary arrangements. Three or four unhurried phone calls while he entertained us in his office and he was ready to take us for a drive and show us to our hotel, the Paso del Norte.

As we left the border and crossed New Mexico and the rolling plains of Kansas the train was much faster. The clicking of the rails was now the fast music of a drum, building us up to the higher speed of life in the United States. In Chicago we were there, and ready now for the mad dash from Union Station to LaSalle Street Station via Parmalee to catch the Twentieth Century Limited with ten minutes to spare. And so back to another year of hard-hitting academic work, organized sports for everyone, and pro- grammed recreation.

Going south was the reverse. Usually John and I traveled together, meet- ing in Boston or Albany to take the train home, and by the time we got on board we were both thoroughly exhausted from the pressures of final exams, storing school things for the summer, and last-minute dates. The trip to Chicago was barely time enough to catch our breath and begin the slow pro- cess of relaxing for vacation. The next day as we rolled on through Topeka on the Golden State Limited we would begin to enjoy it. We liked the luxury of eating in the diner. People were friendly and we found many to talk to, par- ticularly when we rode in the observation car and on the back platform watching the miles and miles of corn and wheat go by. On some of the tighter curves we could look out the side and see the powerful 4-8-4 locomotive pouring on the speed some twenty cars ahead, and almost hear its rushing "Rau-Rau-Rau-Rau," or the "Yah! Yah!" of Kipling's "007" as it threaded its way across the plains at seventy miles an hour, the cars obediently snaking along behind.

We usually had a Pullman section on these trips, and the cross I had to bear was that John, being bigger than I, always claimed the lower berth. (He said it was because he was taller and needed the leg room, but I never really fell for that.) The importance of this, of course, was that the lower berths had windows. In the early morning as you lay in bed you could look out the win- dow and watch the telegraph poles go by. We settled on the basis that when I woke up I could join him in the lower berth and look out the other window, which I did. Looking out the window on the morning before we reached El Paso was always a thrill. We would be coming into Tucumcari or Santa Rosa, New Mexico, and the scenery had changed now from cornfields and wheatfields to sandy desert with sagebrush and yucca palms, and now and then a filmy ball of tumbleweed danced across the scene. I began to feel that we were really coming to the Land of Oz. From then on the journey south brought a growing sense of warmth as we came nearer home.

On the Mexican side the train climbed higher and higher until at the city of Zacatecas it reached an altitude of over eight thousand feet. We reached there in the early morning, and I can still feel the exhilaration of the sharp, clean air and a certain light-headedness that accompanied the first exposure to these altitudes as we got off to stretch our legs. This was the beautiful Mexico that I knew and loved. And so on to Silao and the tributary choo-choo that would take us through the mountain passes to Guanajuato. By this time we were truly reoriented, back in that other world.

To us there was great beauty in Mexico that lay partly in the uncomplicated way of life. In our house in the hacienda we never experienced directly the primitive life of the people who lived in Cubo, but my impression is that they were a happy people who accepted their poverty with fatalism and fortitude. Their miseries were those of any other people — sickness, unworthy sons and daughters, a bad corn crop, a death in the family. Almost everyone had a patch of corn somewhere on the hillside. In May, just before the rainy season, work in the mine nearly came to a stop as the men, one by one, took time out to plow their little fields and plant their corn. There was never any question about this. It was an excused absence. The *milpas* came first.

On the night of someone's saint's day or after a marriage festival there would be a party at some adobe house high up in the town, and as we lay in bed we would hear the sound of voices in harmony accompanied by mandolins and guitars floating down through the night, sometimes until dawn. One of the real joys of being alive is to hear the strains of "Las Mañanitas" coming over the air waves as you lie in bed just at dawn. And of course the flowers, and the birdcages. It was a poor family indeed that did not have its pots of flowers (some always in bloom), and songbirds as well.

Personae Gratae I

A word about some of our Mexican friends.

Angela

Angela González was everything the seraphic name
implies. She was no longer young, and though her face
was wrinkled these were marks of character and charm
rather than age. Her smile was warm, and except when
she was crossed, her eyes were friendly and reflected
an interior serenity. She had never married and had
come from a small town near Mexico City, some two
hundred miles to the south, where her family still
lived. They were above the peon class, probably small
farmers, and Angela had learned to read and write as
well as to say her prayers. She was the Señora's cook.
The oldest member of the household, she had been the
Señora's cook before the revolution. It was she who
guarded the possessions of the manager's family when
they had fled the country. After 1915 she had with some
difficulty found her way to her home, but she was back
now, having been pressured by the Señora's ultimatum
that without Angela she would not return to Cubo.

Her quarters were two small rooms across the
kitchen garden from the manager's house, where she
ruled without authority but effectively over the servant
group of housemaid, kitchen maid, and laundress-
general helper, listening to their problems and keeping
the peace. In her front room was a small shrine embel-
lished with a crucifix, an image of the Virgin Mother,

and flowers from the garden surrounded by pictures of her family in the south. On Sundays she would dress in a fresh skirt and petticoats, don her *rebozo* (head scarf), and make her way to the church in the village, outside the hacienda, to go to Mass. As she came back she would walk by the displays of produce and other household necessities spread out on the small cobblestone plaza in front of the church, stopping to pick up some chili or spices that she fancied for the kitchen. (An ample supply of vegetables was provided by the kitchen garden inside the hacienda.)

It was Angela, too, who saw to it that birdcages were hung on the veranda of the house, one to house a mockingbird that sang its heart out, and another for two canaries, male and female; she also placed potted plants to supplement the flowers in the garden. Other cages and flowerpots were kept outside the kitchen door in the backyard, on the way out to her quarters. And if at times one of the gardeners, or the water boy, or some other yard man, could not be found, he would be in this yard, telling his troubles to Angela and looking for solace or good advice. She was the matriarch of the hired hands.

Concepción

Concepción, better known as "Chona," was probably 99 percent Indian. In her middle years her face was happily wrinkled. She had a friendly smile, and her figure was indeterminate, buried under yards of cloth from head to toe. She was the laundress-general helper who complemented Angela's household staff and had her own room in a dormitory of sorts above Angela's quarters. She felt it a privilege to live in the hacienda, and was equally happy doing the wash or scrubbing floors.

Of her family we knew little and didn't ask. No doubt during the devastating years of revolution prior to 1919 she had suffered much. What men had left her, what sons had ridden off to join the Villistas or Carranzistas and not returned, we did not know. How she had been treated or mistreated by marauding bands we were never told. Chona was happy to be among us and to do her chores.

She was not burdened with abstract philosophies or affairs of state. Each day was its own reward, and on Sundays there was always mass at the little church in town to cure any misgivings.

In September 1923, there occurred an almost total eclipse of the sun in this area. Chona was terrified. The Señora described her as "in the back patio wringing her hands and trembling with fright," but when the sun finally shone once more, she shrugged her shoulders and went back to work.

Chona was a good soul, faithful to her duties.

Pánfilo

Pánfilo had been around a long time. He had probably been a miner in his younger days, working underground and wielding a ten-pound sledge with a short handle while between each blow his compadre turned a length of drill steel set in the hard rock, stopping now and then to flush out the powdered drillings with a dash of mine water. The hole might go five feet into the rock before it was ready for a charge of dynamite. Then on to another.

At the end of the shift, after dynamite and fuses had been set, he would wrap up his lunch dishes, don a cotton shirt and cotton pajama pants over his loincloth, and walk the mile or so through the workings to the mine entrance, where the timekeeper would check him out. If he was lucky he might catch a ride on the electric mule that hauled the ore cars out of the mine. As he left the hacienda he would probably stop at a nearby cantina for twenty or twenty-five centavos' worth of tequila, then make his way up the hillside on a narrow walk to his home — a one-room adobe hut with an outside patio where two or three chickens roamed inside a parapet that was guarded by a dog who was slightly underfed. Atop the parapet several earthen flowerpots sported a variety of blooms, and a birdcage that housed a canary hung by the doorway. Beyond the patio lay a patch of open ground, perhaps twenty-five feet square, that would be his cornfield come the rainy season. He would work six days a week except when it was time to plant the corn, and on Sunday he would go to Mass in the little church in the village. Afterwards he would rest with his family or carouse with what was left of his pay after marketing. He was a good citizen, he took care of his family, and he minded his business.

By 1919 Pánfilo had given up the mine for lighter work. He was still on the mining company payroll, but as a gardener for the manager's house in the hacienda, and as a general handyman. The garden was well kept, and if the Señora needed a helping hand around the house or had an errand to run, Pánfilo would be there with his straw sombrero in his hand and a smile on his face, ready to do her bidding. As long as it was not too complicated. He was aging now, and if the instructions were complex he would say "Sí, Señora" and trot off, but not always in the right direction. Likewise, if he was weeding in the garden there were times when his hands stopped moving and his head would nod under his sombrero. If there was to be ice cream in the manager's house on Sunday, Pánfilo would be called to turn the hand-cranked freezer, and he was known to fall asleep over the handle. But of course this was Sunday, a day of rest.

On the other hand, if Pánfilo was in trouble, if he was in debt or having difficulty in town, he would come to the Señor Gerente or to the Señora and ask for help. Perhaps his dog had run afoul of a neighbor, or he was short of money for the groceries. A word to his neighbor or a small advance would usually suffice. He was a simple man and his needs were simple. He never complained.

Froylan

Froylan Ramírez was Pánfilo's son. A handsome man who was taller than his father, he stood erect and emanated self-assurance. His straw sombrero was a bit more rakish. Yet his work was not demanding. He was the head gardener and did most of the heavy work; he pruned trees, tilled soil, planted the extensive vegetable garden, carried water in tins that hung from a yoke across his shoulders, and cut wood for the many fireplaces.

This was 1920. During the violent years of the Mexican Revolution, Froylan had no doubt been among the revolutionaries, probably allied with Pancho Villa's men, combing the hills, commandeering horses, arms, and ammunition, and holding back the destructive forces of Carranza that threatened the possessions and the women of the law-abiding citizens around the mine, as in other parts of Mexico. He would not have joined the marauders, opportunists who found it easier to attach themselves to the Carranzista hordes and live by pilferage and pillage than to work in the fields or in the mines. For them the countryside provided easy pickings. And men like Froylan would fight to hold them back.

He too had a family and lived on the hillside not far from his father's house, but his would be two or perhaps three rooms, and the dirt floor would be covered with thick *petates*, or straw mats with reds and greens woven in the matting. There would be more furnishings and more space outside, as be-fitted a younger man with greater responsibilities. It is doubtful that Froylan partook of alcohol to any great extent, though he would be likely to join in on a Saturday night when a group was gathered in someone's patio sharing a jug of *pulque* and singing to the accompaniment of one or two guitars and a man-dolin. Marijuana, no. He would not weaken his will nor his ability to provide.

Froylan preferred outdoor work to working underground in the mine. Yet he would have been an excellent miner — one of the few who could take on responsibility and become a contractor, arranging with the mine manager to cover the necessary work in a specific area of the mine, hiring his own men, and collecting by the ton for ore delivered, from which he would pay his men and pocket the difference. There were entrepreneurs who did just that. But Froylan to some extent took after his father. He did not want that much re-sponsibility, or perhaps he felt that his schooling was not enough, and he was happier on ground that was familiar. He was capable in his work and proud of his capabilities. He never complained and seldom needed help.

Brígido

Brígido Márquez was a family man. He had survived the revolution by ac-commodating himself to the inevitable. So long as the mining company needed his help, he was available. When pressures from the revolution be-came too great, he would perhaps join roving bands of revolutionaries for the moment, adding his presence to their activities as long as they centered in the immediate area. When they went far afield he would drift back to his family in the mining town, bringing what provender he had been able to come by, and rejoin the local resisters who rendered a semblance of protection to the town.

His brother Lucas was active with the Villistas and made it a point to check on Brígido when he was in the vicinity. If the family needed food, Lucas would manage to steer some in their direction. If Lucas needed help, Brígido would find a mount and ride with him for a week or two. But as soon as he could he would return to his family, where his real interest lay.

In 1920, Brígido had become the regular *mozo*, or groom, for the mine manager. His domain was the stable, or, more precisely, a makeshift corral inside the hacienda, where he took care of the five horses that belonged to the mine: Pancho, El Alazán, Santiago, El Prietito, and his own mount El Mono. Routinely he dressed in dungarees with a disreputable hat to keep the sun off, which was good enough when he fed or groomed the horses. But if the Señor or any of his family were riding that day, he would dress in his tight-fitting leather trousers and leather vest decked with silver studs and don his twenty-four-inch felt sombrero complete with beaded work and colored tassels — the symbols of his station. He would bring the horses saddled and bridled and ready to mount, help the Señora into the saddle, check the length of the stirrups, and test the girths. When all were mounted, he would get on El Mono and follow the party at a discreet distance, keeping an eye on those ahead to be sure all was well.

As we have said, he was a family man. When a new birth was imminent, to add to the three daughters already present, Brígido was filled with anticipation — until the baby was born. When the Señora heard and congratulated him, he was downcast. "Alas, Señora," said he, "It is another female. She cannot help me with the horses." He would wait for another time, but for now there was one more mouth to feed.

His responsibilities did not end with the hacienda. Wherever the horses went they were in his charge. If the Señora went to a neighboring mine to call on a friend, he took care of the horses when she was there and was at the ready when she prepared to leave. If the Señor and his family went into the hills on a picnic or an overnight camping trip, Brígido rode with them and enjoyed himself as much or more than the others. He always looked on the bright side of things and could see no reason to look for trouble until it actually arrived. If it did he could handle it, so why anticipate?

And when at long last his first son arrived his life was complete. As soon as the boy could walk and wear a hat he was at his father's side helping to carry food and water for the horses and walking them after a strenuous ride.

Without deserting his own, Brígido attached himself to the manager's family, and indeed he was a welcome addition.

Antonio

Antonio and his mule ran a business of their own. Antonio fed the mule well and the mule responded with good service. The mule seldom displayed the stubbornness common to his breed but did his job well — as long as he considered it reasonable.

Their business was the mail run to and from the city and the mine. The route was seven miles each way over the mountain roads; they arrived daily at the mine in the late forenoon and returned in the early afternoon. They delivered more than mail. When fresh milk was available from a ranch on the outskirts of the city, Antonio stopped there and picked up one or two gallon cans, which he slung over the withers of the mule with scant protection from the sun. Or he might bring canned goods ordered by the Señora by phone from the fancy grocer. When the load was light Antonio rode atop the mule, sitting between the saddle bags on the padded cushioning provided for the heavier loads. But when a trunk had to be carried, or a modest piece of furniture, it would be balanced on the top and secured with heavy roping over and under. Then Antonio walked and spoke sympathetic words to the mule along the way, keeping one hand on the load to be sure it kept its balance.

He had probably not yet reached his fortieth year. He lived in the city and never spoke of family. After the mail was delivered at the mine he would sometimes come to the back yard of the manager's house and visit with the cook and second maid, or perhaps share leftovers from the *gerente's* kitchen. Or he would take his *pañuelo* of lunch and eat with others at the hacienda gate. He did not drink when he and the mule were on the job.

But there were times when he arrived at the mine partly loaded. He had perhaps had a bad night in the city and had needed a pony or two to start him on the day. Then the cook or one of his compadres would keep an eye on him to be sure that he could handle the return trip in good order. The next day he would be as good as new.

On occasion Antonio might disappear for several days. The mail would be run by special courier, on foot. In time it would develop that Antonio had taken a "vacation" and traveled to another city where there was a festival or carnival, for a change of scene. It was no doubt great while it lasted but usually wound up to his sorrow. If he was not involved in a knife fight in some cantina over a girl, he was sleeping it off in some doorway and waking with all his money gone. It would be a long walk home.

Then he would come sheepishly to the Señora, who was more sympathetic than the manager, and ask for a loan to tide him over. It was always given, and would be paid back in small weekly installments — more or less regularly on payday.

Antonio and his mule lived more or less happily in their own way.

CHAPTER 13

Life at Cubo

While John and I were in the States at school we were kept in touch with the life at home with frequent and graphically descriptive letters from Mother, and from Dad at times.* Most exciting was the arrival of a baby brother at Cubo in April 1922. Later, unrest regarding presidential succession in 1924 would muddy the waters. Some excerpts will bring the scene to life.

Luella

[January 7, 1922] Yesterday came my 1922 engagement calendar and I was so glad to get it. I seem to need it to keep my accounts with Antonio and also how much various Mexicans owe me. Froylan went on a five-day trip to Dolores with his family just after Christmas and so owes me 5 pesos which he seemed to think he must borrow. Antonio's stepdaughter got married so he had to have a day off and owes me 15 pesos — and the small boy who works in the garden, Aucencio by name, had to borrow 5 pesos for some reason or another and still owes me 2.50. So you see, as each one pays a little something each week on his debt I have to have some place to keep these complicated accounts.

---

*Unless otherwise noted, all letters of Luella and Irving quoted in this chapter were addressed to Robert.

[January 23, 1922] The day all the animals are blessed came this last week and they did something Dad and I never saw before. The priest went up and stood against the wall of the Pantheon and all the animals and owners went up there to get the animals blessed. Such a procession you never saw. Burros all trimmed up with colored tissue paper — fringed and pasted on to them — painted dogs and turkeys, hens, etc., horses, and guinea pigs — and such quantities of birds in cages, very gay with flowers — and cows and goats and sheep. We went along too to see the doings, and there was just a short service and then the priest walked around a little, sprinkling holy water (from a jar carried by a boy in surplice) and the drops of water were supposed to fall on the animals but most of them went harmlessly to the ground, though different people rushed around to get their animals close by so they'd get a drop. About two days before that Angela had put our three canaries in the same cage and the male had stopped singing, so when I got home I asked her, for a joke, why she didn't send the canaries to be blessed and she, most seriously, said she had tried to find Concepcion to take them but couldn't find her, but the padre was going to be at the church mañana to bless more animals and she'd send them over there, and behold she did! most gaily decorated as to cage, and behold further! the canary has been singing ever since!

[March 1, 1922] My old horse, the Alazan, is so lively you'd never know him. He is used so little that when he is ridden he wants to tear across the country and cut up generally and has given me one real scare when he wanted to light out and I wouldn't let him, so he began rearing — then I got off, as soon as Dad could get hold of his bridle. He needs you boys to take some of the life out of him.

[March 11, 1922] I have some news for you. . . . we are going to buy a new baby which we hope will be delivered about the last of April, so when you get home this summer you'll find a small sister or brother here ready to make your acquaintance.
We decided if all the family we have will go away and leave us for most of the year all there is to do is to get some more family who will

stay home for a while longer. Otherwise we'll get already to feel like old married folks, looking forward to grandchildren!

Irving

[April 9, 1922] We telegraphed to grandma on the 7th telling her of the arrival at Cubo of a new brother . . . so you have undoubtedly heard about it by this time. The new boy came tagged with his name which turns out to be Richard. . .

We did not expect him quite so soon, in fact were not looking for him for another week yet, so were without a nurse. But Dr. Geitz got out here in good season, and Mrs. Moore was on hand to act as nurse, and they both did fine. . . . Mother is doing fine, and is in good shape. Our real nurse, Miss Lee from Mexico City, arrived in Guanajuato last evening and we had her come out at once to Cubo, so she is now on the job.

Luella

[April 21, 1922] We are very happy to have you show real enthusiasm about the arrival of small Richard. . . . He was very tiny a week ago when he only weighed 5 1/4 pounds. This morning he was weighed again and has gained a pound in a week, so he is 6 1/4 lbs. today. That is a lot to gain in a week.

That summer John and I made our first acquaintance with brother Richard, which added spice to life, but, alas, he was not ready to join us in our teenage activities and in September we were off again to school. Correspondence from home continues.

Luella

[September 3, 1922] After seeing you off on the train our trip home from Silao to Guanajuato in the hired car was more eventful than the trip down. It rained most of the way as you doubtless know, but we were on the edge of the storm so didn't get any real downpour. Also there were side curtains under the back seat, so we were fairly waterproof except for a few sprinkles — but the roof leaked and in an aguacero [cloudburst] we would have gotten nicely wet. Also the rain came in that hole at the back where the window should have been. So the driver gave Dad his most very greasy hat to stick in the opening. It just fitted and kept out the rain but I kept an eagle eye on the hat to see that nothing jumped out of it. But we got stuck on that long hill—the first two times the driver was able to start his engine again and make a few more rods. The third time the engine refused to crank and there we were at 6 P.M. with the rain descending at its hardest (on our trip) merrily reposing at a slant on that hillside a long way from the top of the hill—also from home, supper, and Dick. The driver had several bright ideas, none of which proved of any value—then Dad suggested a second time that the gas didn't reach the engine. This time the driver investigated and found it was indeed so. Thereupon the three men pushed the car back and horizontally across the road to get the engine on a level. This time it started and we were off again—Dad at the rear pushing and the ayudante on his knees on the floor of the front seat, his head in the gasoline tank, blowing—and me on the back seat trying to guard my various trastesitos [little dishes] and candlestick—also my hat, which I held under my knees as the roof leaked—and so we made the hill, though Dad took a few spells off and rode instead of pushing, in the more level stretches. The poor ayudante had the worst of it and the driver had no mercy on him saying, "Sople! Sople" [Blow, blow] every time he brought his head up to get a breath. We made the office in Guanajuato in two hours but it is a wonder we ever got there for Dad looked into the gas tank when we were stuck and it was well-nigh empty.

[October 6, 1922] Brigido tied Dad's sweater on behind the saddle on our return trip from Guanajuato and when we got to the top of the trail he saw the sweater was gone so he went back hunting for it, but of course didn't find it. So now he says his honor is gone too and he wanted to pay for it—the sweater—so as to get back his honor. Dad not agreeing to that he went home and got drunk and was incapacitated for the rest of the day instead. I don't know whether he is around today or not. He told me one day he was grieved because you hadn't written him! Better send him a postcard.

[October 30, 1922] Last night, Sunday, at 2 A.M. four muchachos feeling pretty good sat down on the steps of the cantina opposite our bedroom and sang to the world at large for about an hour—quite a midnight concert, not at all appreciated by Dad and me, I assure you. Dick never woke up.

[December 6, 1922] I am pretty busy right now. Mr. and Mrs. Fisher, Carlitos, and Buster McBride came out to Cubo Saturday afternoon in the Fordie and stayed till Sunday afternoon. It took five peons and their own mechanic to push them up the hill out of Cubo and then they just barely made it. It would go a few yards, then stop, wait for the water to stop boiling, pour in more water, go another few yards with the aid of said peons (Mrs. Fisher and the children walking) and repeat, on up the hill. Mr. Fisher says next time he is coming on a horse.

By this time Angela's niece, Altagracia, had come up from their home near Mexico City to be with Angela and to serve as Mother's maid.

Luella

[January 9, 1923] First I'll have to tell you the latest excitement. José Velasquez [the Company electrician] wants to marry Altagracia! As far as we can see he has seen her twice, once when he came last Thursday morning to get my electric iron to fix and once when he came to return said iron! Yesterday came the padre to see Angela about it. Today José writes her a letter to say he'll not wait over fifteen days! Such is the excitement that reigns in our household today. Now Angela has sneaked out the upper gate to see the padre to tell him she has to write Alta's brothers and sisters for permission, and Dad and I think they better wait six months and give the thing some serious thought—and Dad says he'll talk to José about it.

(One week later) The love affair progresses and is now an acknowledged engagement. Dad had a talk with José and among other things asked him how he knew Alta anyway. He said you only had to see her to know she was the right sort and he had written her two letters. Then Dad said we liked him and she was a very nice girl (in other words gave them our blessing!) but wanted them to wait a few months and not be in such a hurry. So then José appears Sunday afternoon, all dressed up and really he's a mighty nice-looking fellow, and asked to see Angela. So

he and Angela have a session in the dining room and he tells her he
didn't want to wait but the Señor says they better wait six months so he
guessed they'd have to, and meanwhile he'd like to call on Alta every
Sunday afternoon for about 15 minutes in Angela's presence. How would
you like to woo like that?

[February 28, 1923] Angela and Alta departed Thursday last saying (or
Angela said) they were going to Leon with their Guanajuato amigas and
wanted to be away until Monday. It is now Wednesday evening and no
sign of them, but Antonio reports that their amigas never left Guanajuato so now we feel sure that they went to Mexico City and preferred
lying to telling the truth. That last makes me hot. For the rest I am
rather enjoying the change. I was tired of Angela's cooking and I guess
that is one reason I am glad to fuss over things myself. Also I am having
a beautiful time having no messes sitting around in the kitchen. I hate
these messes Mexicans always seem to have around. . . .

Next morning—well Angela and Alta blew in before I was up this
morning. It seems they planned on Leon but the invitation was for January 15, and they got around to accepting it on February 24 at which time
the amigas decided they no longer wanted to go. So being already in
Guanajuato they must perforce go somewhere and went to Silao, and
there after much indecision bought tickets to Mexico. All this I believe
because Angela went with that small covered basket with a little lunch in
it—that was all her baggage and Alta went empty-handed—no clothes
except those they had on! And so Mexicans go off for a five day vacation!
And so they went to Mexico! to visit their family and were gone a week!
Too bad to spend all that carfare for such a short time and they might
just as well have stayed longer as it turned out.

Irving

[June 9, 1923] Mother of course has written you of the great wedding
a week ago today when Altagracia became Mrs. Jose Velasquez. It was
the biggest wedding that Cubo ever staged and was a surprise to me.
The bride and groom went from Cubo to Guanajuato in an auto, instead
of on burros or horses. It was some wedding all right.

Our new maid (?) who takes Alta's place is about forty and looks it. She tiptoes around the dining room and gets on both our nerves. But I guess we will not be too independent for we could easily get a worse one.

Luella

[September 11, 1923] Well, we had our eclipse as scheduled. Monday the 10th was very cloudy, but as 1:30 approached Dad got himself a piece of smoked glass, and as the sun finally came out for a few minutes just as he looked, and behold it already had a small chunk out of it. Great excitement! Concepcion in the back patio was wringing her hands and trembling with fright, and Angela hustling to go over to sit with Altagracia during the terrifying performance. Felipa was calmly going on making her tortillas so quien sabe whether she was scared or not—and the eclipse getting bigger. Dad soon gathered Mr. Hudson, Mr. Benson, Froylan, Pablo, and Jose around him giving them all a look—"ten cents for a look at the sun" he told us. Soon the gardener's force were off hunting up glass to smoke for themselves, and a little later there was all the hacienda Mexican force on the lower patio, one-legged friend and all, taking turns looking through smoked glass—and me going out to the back patio every little while to give Concepcion and Felipa a look and try to calm Concepcion's fears. It was very interesting to watch and really quite spooky. It was mighty close to total. Finally Concepcion decided the world wasn't coming to an end after all and was able to eat her dinner and go on with her work, having lost about two hours' time!

[January 25, 1924] I have been scrapping with the cook mostly lately, until one day we had a blowup and she asked permission to sacar her cosas [remove her things] and kill her pig and I told her to go to it; whereupon she commenced to tell me all the trouble I'd have getting a cook from Guanajuato, and I told her that had nothing to do with it and finally she said it was "como Usted diga" [as you say]. I said "Not at all. It is for you to decide. If you want to stay and do things as I want them done you may stay—if you don't you'd better go." (She began saying we didn't seem "contentos" with her and I said we weren't at all contentos with her at present.) Fortunately Dad came in and broke up the conversation which was in danger of going around in a circle, and we've never referred to it (Angela or I) since! Angela evidently decided she preferred to stay and the atmosphere is quite friendly and clear again. I am sure thankful she didn't go! For I'd have been most awfully up against it.

Although interspersed from time to time with sporadic eruptions of revolutionary activity in 1923–24 and 1927–28, as we shall see later, the general tenor of life in Cubo and Guanajuato was not greatly affected. Our kaleidoscope continues in letters from home:

Luella

[November 30, 1924] We left the Guanajuato office at 11:15. I was tired and cross and Dick beginning to get hungry and we poked along and finally reached the top of the trail when Brigido said, "There's someone coming after us and beckoning frantically." It was the young boy from the office in town tearing up the hill on a horse and gesticulating at an alarming rate. We felt something really serious must have happened for them to send after us that way so we turned back and went to meet him. When he got up to us he said Mr. Carrouché had phoned to know if we had left and not to let us come out as "estan asaltando el camino" [they are assaulting the road]. Well what could we do but turn back? There was Dad with a two-year-old in his arms and quite helpless (no gun in fact) — we had no way of knowing how many, how well armed, etc. — but I was sore — halfway home, and the most tedious half, and all to do over again. But back we went and landed at the DeVotie's about 12:45, as they were eating. Finally Dad got hold of Carrouché and there was nothing to it! He had called the office to ask if Dad had left as he wanted to talk to him and suggest he take more precaution with the payroll next day as there had been one or two peons held up a week or so ago there by the rieles [iron rails placed to brace the hillside] on the road down to the Presa, and Mr. Gisholt was off to Dr. Romero's wedding, and the Mexican boy who talked with Mr. Carrouché got all het up, dashed to the Pension for a horse and off at full gallop to prevent our being held up. So we ate at the DeVotie's and came on home, having a peaceful ride as usual. Absolutely nothing had happened, and there seems no authentic information as to anything at all ever happening.

[December 14, 1924] I finally learned as definitely as possible about the holdup on the Guanajuato-Cubo road. One Sunday afternoon there at the rieles Williebaldo's son got off his horse, tied it and left it with his blanket over the saddle, and went a little distance — three men came along and said, "Con permiso, ¿vamos a llevar su covica?" [If you please, or "with your permission," we are going to take your blanket?] — "Why? It isn't yours." — "No, but we need it." Whereupon young Williebaldo pulled out a pistol, and the three would-be bandits, being unarmed, departed. Or, as Dad says, not receiving the permission they didn't take it. Brigido told me this tale — seeing nothing humorous about it — when I asked him what he knew of the much-talked-of holdup. So I continue to ride the road without fear.

Irving

[March 16, 1925] Last evening we rode from Gilmore's house [the Power Plant in Guanajuato] to the hacienda at Cubo in one hour and one minute. This is the fastest time I have ever made; the weather was cool and windy and the horses were full of life and insisted on going fast of their own accord.

[April 9, 1925] For the past week our interest has centered in the stabbing of poor Lucas Marquez [Brigido's brother]. He was stabbed to death at Villalpando by a couple of drunks that had it in for him on account of some old disgustos [quarrels]. Lucas was not armed at the time and they took the opportunity to do him in. I doubt whether they would have done it except that they were drunk. We were all much upset over it, because we all had sort of an affection for Lucas. He leaves a wife and five small children. The Company cannot help much, but I shall try to help from time to time. Luckily there are three brothers left to help take care of the family.

Luella

[November 2, 1925] Mr. Sampson [an engineer living at the mine] took his wife for a ride yesterday and on the road to Guanajuato her horse started bucking and threw her off. So then Mr. Sampson took that

horse and with spurs and whip started disciplining him. Then just as he
was getting the horse in hand the bit broke and of course the horse
bolted. He rigged up the chain for a bit and Mrs. Sampson got on and
rode the horse home! I admire her courage. I told Mr. Sampson he'd
never get me on a horse after he'd thrown me and he said, "Oh, you
don't want to do that or the horse will think he has conquered you." I
assured him the horse would have conquered me and was very welcome
to think so.

[November 23, 1925] After a week of cold, raw winds and some rain,
Saturday was lovely — clear and sunny with a nip to the air, that makes
me think of fall in New England and made me want to get into the hills,
so I launched the idea of a picnic in the Cañada on Sunday. Everyone
fell for it, and then Sunday dawned cold and raw, mist low over the
mountains and a piercing wind. However, we went all the same, leaving
at 9 a.m., and that climb up around the mountain towards Capulin was
one cold climb. We all just about froze. After we crossed the Cubo River
things got better till [Sampson's daughter] Daphne's horse bucked her
off and fled over the hills toward Cubo. Brigido and Mr. Sampson went
after the horse, and the rest of us proceeded slowly, Daphne on foot.
She wasn't hurt, and they caught up with us at the Puertecita into the
Cañada. Without further novedad [incident] we arrived at the site of the
"Outside Inn" in the Cañada, and found Carmen and Froylan and the
lunch and a fire going and the same cold wind blowing and no sun and
we continued to freeze. Brigido looked down at his feet as he stood in
the path and saw a small silver disk he used as a watch charm which he
lost when he was there with you and Dad last, and we found other things
left by you boys, so we concluded there has been no one there since. We
got two fires going, cooked bacon, fried potatoes and sausages, and
made coffee, all of which was very good, and the sun came out and the
wind died down and it was very lovely there. We walked upstream and
those trees with the white bark all had yellow leaves, and against the rugged cliffs with some green shrubs they were beautiful.

The city of Guanajuato was fast becoming an important part of life at
Cubo. The hour-long horseback ride to town was by now routine and Irving

and Luella became more active as members of the Guanajuato foreign colony. In town their quarters now were the upstairs rooms of an office maintained in the city by the Cubo Company, which served very nicely for an overnight stay or for a weekend. Many times too Luella would ride into town for an afternoon of bridge with the ladies of Guanajuato and ride back the same day.

Guanajuato seemed to be reviving in the middle 1920s. The Casino was reorganized and a "very fine" French chef brought in to improve the cuisine. Not to be outdone, "J. Rosario Luna, Prop." of the Hotel Luna, on the other side of the Jardín de la Unión from the Casino, sent a printed invitation to a select group of townspeople:

> [October 1, 1925] I have the honor of inviting you to the opening of the New Addition to the Hotel Luna on Saturday, the third of this month, at 7:30 in the evening. Fully convinced of the refinement and good taste of my distinguished clientele, I have spared no expense to make sure that this Addition will have the comfort and elegance so well deserved by the cultured inhabitants of this one-time opulent and legendary City. . . .

The Casino provided a place for Luella to entertain, though it hardly afforded a country club setting. It was built of stone in the Spanish fashion, and one entered through heavy doors to a flagstone courtyard with archways leading to the various club rooms. Upstairs were a ballroom and some smaller rooms suitable for bridge or for a dinner party. Of one occasion Luella writes:

> [November 12, 1926] Last week I gave a luncheon for twelve at the Casino and three tables of bridge afterwards in the upstairs sitting room of the Company office in town. I told the Casino chef, Pancho Drivet, that I was poor and couldn't pay over two pesos a plate and he said "Muy bien" and we had a delicious five-course luncheon and coffee at that price. I would have paid five pesos a plate for it if I hadn't gone at it this way.

On weekends the men would join the ladies at dinner and bridge, and sometimes for variety spend Sunday afternoon at the "cine" in downtown

Guanajuato. These were all-afternoon performances generally running three hours or more with two full-length features drawn from Hollywood's best of the early 1920s. Comic relief was provided by some of the Spanish dubbed in to replace the English captions of the old silent films — Hollywood could have used some better interpreters. Accompanied by a certain amount of hissing and booing, three hours was enough.

In March 1925 the following notice was circulated among the foreigners:

> A number of the foreign colony of Guanajuato have talked of the desirability of forming a golf club, and at their suggestion the present invitation is addressed to you, with the request that you give the matter some thought and attend a meeting to be held at the Casino, Sunday night at 8:00 P.M. . . .

In due time the club was organized and a seven-hole course laid out in rolling hills six miles west of Guanajuato down the river toward Silao, and the course was given the distinguished name of Santa Teresa Country Club. There were no green valleys; rather, the course roamed over the tops of barren hills that had been cleared of rocks and cactus for the fairways. Wooden clubs were endangered by loose gravel or some hidden rock, and a slice or hook could land you in an arroyo thick with cactus. The greens were sand. But these were minor problems to the dedicated sportsmen of Guanajuato, and the facilities were garnished with a small shack, or "club house," which provided shade for the ladies and served as a watering spot where the men could roll dice for the right to buy the drinks.

One year later, as president of the new Golf Club, Irving put up a loving cup as a trophy for their first tournament. He wrote:

> [February 16, 1926] The thing that is occupying most of our attention and causing the greatest worry just now is the golf tournament which is being played off. The first complication was whether or not the ladies should be included in the tournament. When I put up the cup, I had no idea of including the women as it never occurred to me that they would ever think of playing. I never believed in women competing against men. However, when this idea became known to the fair sex it caused a small upheaval, and as the life of the golf club seemed to be threatened we had

a meeting of the board of management and decided to invite every-body—first having been assured on the side that no women would play anyway.

But the women reckoned without their Mrs. Flynn, who insisted on going in for the express purpose of cleaning up on the men, and carrying off the cup. . . . Well the lady is in it with both feet and is out to win regardless, and has been pulling all sorts of illegal stuff, including playing up her ball to the green while her opponent is off hunting a sliced drive, and then miscounting her strokes. The result is that another schism faces us at present. . . .

Así es la vida, and the path of the president of a golf club is not all strewn with roses.

CHAPTER 14

The Cubo Mine

As we have said, the Cubo-Villalpando mine was an old one, dating from Spanish days. Streaks of silver sulfide ran in and out through a vein of quartz that was extensive, both vertically and horizontally, in the Villalpando Mountain, sometimes opening up into large bodies of ore, sometimes thinning out to practically nothing. This vein was an offshoot that ran at an angle from the Mother Lode of Guanajuato; smaller tributary veins were scattered through the nearby mountains. To mine it at a profit required skill and perseverance, sometimes guided by a miner's instinct. There were ups and downs, and spirits moved with ore values.

Irving found the mine in poor condition from the abuse of the revolution and the misguided efforts of the men who had been in charge of reactivating it. To get it back in running order the most urgent task was to rebuild the staff from top to bottom. Word got around the mining community that he had returned, and he exploited the good will of his name to attract back his Mexican miners. Among them was Dionisio Paz, who had been a contractor for the Cubo mine, that is, a person who would take over specific pieces of work and bring in his gang. The contractor would guide his drillers to "point" their holes where they would be the most effective, and the drillers' job included charging and "shooting" their holes to break the rock. Peons would remove the broken ore.

Irving had not been back a month when he received a letter from Paz, then working in Pachuca, asking to be taken back at Cubo. Irving had a warm regard for Paz and wrote him at once to come and bring some men who could work machine drills. Paz had asked Cubo's rate of wages. Irving admitted, "the regular rate of wages here in Guanajuato for machine men would not attract drillers from Pachuca." To make the job competitive, he offered to pay by meter of hole drilled rather than by the day — fifty centavos a meter — and he thought good men could drill eight to ten meters of hole a day. "What I want is some men who want to work and make money by working hard."[1]

There were also good men who had stayed on at Cubo. One such was W. B. López, *almacenista* (warehouseman) of the mill, who wrote Irving upon the new year in 1921 asking for a raise. He had worked a long time, "since this Company started to operate," yet his salary was only twenty-five pesos a week. This was the same salary as the *almacenista* of the mine, although "there is much more movement in this *Almacen*." He added politely: "My Father also, as you know worked for this company a long time and lost his life working for them and my Mother never received any gratification. I do not claim anything, I wish to tell you of our services and I think you will consider them." López sent this in English, but he used Spanish when he requested contributions for the annual festival of the Virgen de Dolores, whose image "is venerated in this Mine"; he signed this letter "*Encargado de la fiesta*" [Director of the Festival].[2]

The Mexican staff was not the only problem; it was also urgent to find men for supervisory positions. As general superintendent Irving had full authority over the company's operations in Mexico; this included the mine and mill at Cubo and the office in Guanajuato. Directly under him were the mine superintendent and the mill superintendent, each of whom was in charge of the shift bosses (also called foremen) in his area, one for each shift. In practice these men were all foreigners, and they used English among themselves. Since foreigners who worked in Mexico had few roots, it was a continuing challenge to have these positions suitably filled.

Shortly after Irving's arrival, Hollis located a new mine superintendent, S. R. Moore, whom he found by writing to an acquaintance in charge of a mine in British Columbia. Hollis offered a position to Moore in June 1920,[3] and by August 1921 Moore had become mine superintendent at Cubo.

Irving gave his superintendent authority, but he kept a close watch on the working of the mine, and provided him with written instructions on how to improve efficiency:

> [August 3, 1921] The *almacenista* would check out and check in all pieces of steel [drills] taken out and returned by each contractor. In this way we would soon find out where the steel was going, and what contractors were careless about returning dull steel.
>
> As there is a big question as to how much tonnage is coming up the North Shaft, I would like the hoist men to keep a tally of the number of skips of ore hoisted each shift. . . . This might tend to make them work more steadily.
>
> I believe it would make for better efficiency if the Moctezuma Drift were given a thorough cleaning up, and all old timber, scraps and other trash removed. . . . Some work by the track crew would do away with all the water standing in the track and make that spot more attractive. . . .
>
> I am putting this into writing partly for my own sake, and because it is very easy to forget to do things that you plan at some particular time, because other things are always coming up to displace them.

The Tajo mill also cried out for a knowledgeable guiding hand. Almost as soon as he arrived, Irving found a good mill superintendent, one who proved so successful that he was lured away in September by the offer of a better position. This time Irving chose someone who knew and liked Cubo. Since his ignominious dismissal in April 1919 by Leslie, Carrouché had been living in Mexico City, but he did not give up hope of returning to Cubo. Word now reached him of the vacancy at Tajo, and he wrote Irving to apply for the opening. They met to discuss arrangements, and Irving followed with a letter offering him the position. It is worth quoting at some length because it reveals his conception of how the mine should be run. Carrouché had asked to be "turned loose" in the mill and receive Irving's moral and financial support. Irving replied:

> [September 29, 1920] This does not correspond exactly with my ideas of the functions of either a Mill Superintendent or a General Superintendent. In case you accept the position you may count on my cordial

support and cooperation on any proposition that you propose in connection with the mill when we are both agreed that it would increase the efficiency of the mill. In the case where we were unable to agree on any point I shall have to insist that my wishes prevail over yours. This is absolutely necessary for the sake of general discipline.

As a matter of fact, after having talked matters over with you personally I feel sure that on all essential points we are practically agreed, and in every point that was brought up during that conference our ideas corresponded very closely.

It is my desire and hope to have someone in charge of our mill experienced enough and with enough initiative to work out the mill problems himself. In other words if I can feel that the mill is going to be run right whether I am around or not it will be a great relief to me and will allow me more time for other parts of the business that need attention. . . .

Regarding shift bosses. It has always heretofore been my policy to do the hiring of all white men on the job. . . . These men will of course be under your orders and their job will be to do what you tell them to. There will be no misunderstanding on that score. In the event that any such man does not fill the bill you and I will get together and see what is to be done. This plan is quite practical and satisfactory because I have had personal experience with it with one of the largest industrial companies in the United States. . . .

Personally I believe that we can run the proposition in entire harmony, and not only that but also make a great success of it, because I feel sure that one of your main ideas in wanting to take the position is to make it a success. I also — after talking with you — have confidence in your ability and was much pleased at your viewpoint.

Carrouché responded by telegram that he was accepting the offer.

Irving had made a good choice. He recognized potential where Leslie had seen only insubordination. In the next years the two men worked together to modernize the mill and introduce new methods.[4] Carrouché and his Mexican wife did not become intimate friends of the Herrs, but they showed great warmth toward the Herr boys, as Bob's reminiscences reveal. Carrouché's wife bore him a son soon after Dick's birth, whom they named Ricardo. They moved from the house across from the mill to the Cubo hacienda, and the two Ricarditos became daily playmates.

Carrouché and Moore had wives and children, lived in houses on the site, and had achieved relatively successful and stable positions as mill and mine superintendent. The account book shows that Carrouché made seven hundred pesos a month in 1921–22, Moore six hundred. They might go from here to a better job, as Carrouché's predecessor had done. By comparison, Irving's Cubo salary for 1920, which we discover from an account at the end of Luella's diary—Irving always played his own income, like his poker cards, close to his chest—was $6900. At $575 or 1150 pesos per month, plus house, servants, and other perks, Hollis had sweetened the pot handsomely to get Irving back to Cubo.

Beneath the superintendents, the shift bosses were more likely to be single men, or at least not accompanied by their wives. H. Jenkin was night shift boss at the mill. Irving had hired him on Carrouché's recommendation at one hundred seventy-five dollars, or three hundred fifty pesos per month. "The Company provides a room, but board at the mess and washing, etc. will be for your account."[5] W. B. Anthony was foreman of the mill. Hollis had interviewed him in Los Angeles for the position of mill superintendent, but when Irving named Carrouché to that job, Hollis recommended Anthony for the lesser position. Anthony was having one hundred fifty dollars sent monthly to his wife, whom he had left in Los Angeles, and according to the account book received one hundred fifty pesos in addition.

He did not, however, work out, for he could not come to terms with the culture new to him. After three years Irving had to dismiss him. His letter to Anthony read:

> [November 8, 1923] Yesterday afternoon Mr. Carrouché informed me of the trouble which occurred shortly before, between yourself and Ignacio Rangel, our Master Mechanic. I heard of this with considerable regret, but in view of this occurrence, and also knowing that you are not as much in sympathy with the type of Mexican labor upon which we must depend as I believe those forming the American Staff on the Company should be, I believe the best interests of the Company require that I ask for your resignation. . . .

It will be best, all around, that you leave at once, and I will arrange to pay you one month's salary dating from the day of your separation.

Outside the chain of command, but higher in esteem than the shift bosses, were trained men who carried out various specialized jobs. Frank Pool had the title of master mechanic and a salary of two hundred fifty pesos. The Englishman Robert Vaughan held the position of mine engineer and surveyor. His salary was five hundred fifty pesos. He left at the end of 1922, apparently the victim of economies at the mine.[6] To replace him Irving offered the job to P. R. Hudson, who had applied from Mexico City, describing himself as familiar with construction work. Irving replied that Cubo was reopening two outlying mines that had been closed for twenty years, Capulín and Cebolletas. "I have not had time to look after the work in Capulin and Cebolletas, and while it by itself is not sufficient to warrant putting a white man on the job, there are other things that will have to be done soon which I cannot look after either." Most important of these was to erect an aerial tram connecting Cebolletas with Capulín. Hudson should come for a two months' trial to see "whether we hit it off well together."

[November 23, 1922] I can start you off with a salary of $200 U.S. per month. This will not be the maximum pay however later on. Your expenses will be for your own account, i.e. board, washing etc. We have a mess at the Tajo Mill where you will have quarters. The mess cost has been running in the neighborhood of sixty pesos a month, per man.

Unlike the men with families, single foreigners had rooms and took meals at the Tajo mill a few hundred yards above the mine hacienda.

The roller-coaster fortunes of the mining business attracted men who could live without putting down emotional ties to people or places, the kind of person who would have been pushing the American frontier forward a couple of generations earlier. Several of the foreign men on the Cubo payroll had had experience in the World War. These men were rolling stones, but they had a sense of camaraderie and stuck together in a pinch, or so a small incident among the Cubo group indicates. Captain L. R. McDonald, who was working at Cubo, was forced by an ailing arm to travel to Mexico City for treatment. From there he wrote Irving in pencil:

[August 18, 1920] I arrived O.K. but could not get into a hospital, I am taking Swedish massage and I am improving wonderfully. He says I should be able to come back in about one month. It necessitated my getting a room, and eating out as everything here is very high. It will cost me 300 pesos for my room, board and treatment.

If I can get this I will work and repay same when I get back, if not it will be necessary for me to come back and work with one hand until I can pay my indebtedness and can save enough to go and have this fixed. . . .

Irving was faced with a dilemma:

[August 20, 1920] After receiving your request the problem to be solved was how to get this money, as I was unable to persuade myself that I had any right to charge this to the Company. It was therefore necessary to take it up with the men, and both Smeddle and Pool were willing to chip in $75. each. I expect to add an equal amount and to make up the remaining fourth from the Company. . . .

We were all very glad to hear that you are in such good shape and that the arm will come back so quickly, and that it was not as feared, that you might have a year or more with it out of business.

Now I feel rather sure that all things considered you will not take it in the wrong spirit if I (an old man of your own age) undertake to caution you. Five years of hell [in the World War?] is enough to rack any man's nerves to the ragged edge, and for a man in your condition to be in Mexico City without any too much to do is in my opinion a bad thing. I want you for your own sake, and for Pool's and Smeddle's sake to make the money we have advanced go just as far as possible and do just as much good as possible. You know what I mean, and I want to say in addition that all of the boys up here including myself think mighty highly of you, and want to see you come out on top. So pull up that belt of yours a notch, just consider that you are on duty, and make it your job right now to get the arm in shape as quickly as possible.

"All of the boys up here" were determined to stick together to bail out one of their own and let him know that they were pulling for him.

The mine responded to Irving's direction by yielding some new ore bodies in the early twenties; one or two of them were quite rich. In December 1921 the Cubo Company showed a nice profit, but three months later when the rich ore was gone they showed a loss for the first time in six months. As Irving wrote to his sons early in 1922, "Most of our good ore has been mined out, and we do not seem to have any luck in opening up any new ore bodies." So work was started in some old diggings at Capulín and on cleaning out an old shaft at Cebolletas, both thin prospects in the hills beyond the Tajo mill. Irving wrote to Robert:*

> [February 10, 1922] It begins to look as though there were quite an old mine at Cebolletas, and I have hopes that we may be able to make a good mine out of it.

Also work was continued on unwatering other portions of the Villalpando mine in hopes of finding some new feeders for the mill.

To bring the ore the half mile or more from Capulín and Cebolletas to the mill, an aerial tramway was built though the mountains which required a 140-foot bridge across the river to carry the tram. This helped to keep the mill running for another year, but as soon as Villalpando could carry the load, the two C's were abandoned. They had been slim pickings.

In 1923 new ore was found. There was a big hole in Villalpando Mountain where ore had been mined out over the years, but work continued to drill and test the vein lower down, and to drive tunnels at either end to see what could be opened up. They were now down to the sixth level, some 1200 feet below the surface, and Irving noted:

> [April 30, 1923] We have got almost twenty meters drifted through now that will average over a kilo in silver assay, and the face of the drift [or tunnel] is still in ore. This is a place where I had always thought there was nothing but borasco waste.

Six months later he was discouraged again:

---

*Unless noted otherwise, all letters of Irving and Luella quoted in this chapter were addressed to Robert.

[October 11, 1923] There is nothing new in the mine. We believe for a day or two that we have struck a new ore body and then that particular drift gets out of ore again almost before it has gotten into it. I started up La Loca 7th East, which is the San Felipe Tunnel level, because I have a hunch that there is an ore body between the present face of it and the Tajo side. I shall let you know if we strike it.

The vicissitudes of mining were not limited to finding ore, but keeping it as well. Irving wrote to Robert:

[January 20, 1922] We have been having a great time in the juzgado [tribunal] over a bunch of ore that Pancho Medina and Lucas held up on the road out of Villalpando. There was a carpeta [brokerage] up in Villalpando who we all knew was buying stolen ore from Cubo. So about three weeks ago the owner of the carpeta started to Guanajuato with eight burro loads of ore, and Pancho and Lucas promptly held him up on the road just as he was leaving Villalpando, despite the fact that he had a license to buy ore. They called me up on the phone, to know what to do, and after consulting with the Jefe [mayor] here, I told them to bring the ore to Cubo so we could have a look at it. This they did, and we found six sacks of very high-grade Cubo ore, stuff that will go about 60 kilos to the ton.

Then I called up the Presidente in Guanajuato and sputtered forcibly about allowing carpeteros to buy stolen ore. So he said to send the ore and the man into the Inspeccion de Policia. The ore finally landed in the juzgado, and the carpetero brought an action against the company for highway robbery. So instead of prosecuting the carpetero we have been defending ourselves for having tried to get our own stuff.

This all happened before January 1, and on the 1st an entirely new bunch of city officials came in, following the election. Also we found that the carpeta was really owned by a man who is a big ore buyer in Guanajuato, and on January 1st this man became head of the City Council. So this did not help us any, as you can guess. The final upshot of the matter was that we made a deal with this man, by which it was arranged that the juzgado should return the ore to Cubo. Cubo would pay the man for what he paid out on the ore, and he agrees that while he is on the City Council there will not be any more licenses issued for carpetas in the district of Cubo and Villalpando. So on the whole we came out not so badly.

By 1926 ore was being mined from the eighth level, and the ninth level was being opened up at 1,700 feet below the surface. Underground work shafts were lengthened and artificial ventilation for the lower levels was on the way. In May 1926, Irving wrote: "If we don't go broke first I intend to have a real U.S.A. mine—it is almost a necessity on account of the depth we are reaching."

Before the year was out the price of silver began to fall. India, which had always hoarded silver, was switching to gold coins. From an average of 70 cents an once in 1925 the price of silver dropped to 60 cents by October 1, 1926, and to 52 cents by October 31. Cubo's cost was 66 cents an ounce, and the average cost for the Guanajuato mines was 63 1/2 cents. Shutdowns were imminent. Meetings with government officials brought some hope of reduced excise taxes. Irving wrote to Robert:

> [November 2, 1926] I do not know yet whether we will continue to run or will shut down. I have figured out ways and means and the only possible way to continue is to cut down salaries and wages—this among other economies we hope to make. I am figuring on a cut of 10 percent in salaries and wages all the way down the line, including myself.
>
> It looks like the Federal government would cut about 1/3 off of our federal tax on silver, and the State government is going to cut its tax on silver in half, and all this helps. Sirena [a Guanajuato company] has posted notices that they are going to shut down and notices are up also for La Luz. I wonder if Cubo will be next.

Luella added:

> [October 18, 1926] The fact of the matter is Dad has no intention in the world of shutting down, short of positive orders from Chicago—and he hasn't heard from Mr. Hollis in three or four weeks. He is hunting up good ore, first on the map and then in the mine, and finding it by golly.

The Cubo mine continued to run.

Problems other than ore reserves and silver prices faced the mines in Mexico during the twenties. Since Carranza's time the labor movement had been gaining strength in Mexico. The Regional Confederation of Mexican Workers, known as CROM, was organized in 1917 by a radical leader, Luis Morones, who was active during the Mexico City strikes of 1916. By 1920, CROM claimed a membership of one hundred thousand, and by 1925–26 this had risen to one million members. Calles, who became president of Mexico in 1924, was said to be allied to Morones, further strengthening the "Sindicato," or labor movement. The Cubo mine began to feel the effects in the early 1920s.

In 1922 the drillers went on strike at Cubo. This was the fault of the American mine superintendent whose Spanish was poor and who could not really understand their problems. The situation was soon corrected, but it opened the door to labor agitators at the mine. Then on November 1, 1924, a new labor law was passed that set minimum wages and, among other things, made it illegal to fire a man without "just cause."

Irving perforce became well versed in labor law and spent much time with the Federal Labor Department in Guanajuato. After one two-hour session he remarked that he felt as if he were in Russia under the Bolsheviks. He had been called before them to answer complaints. It seems there were two or three Communists in the machine shop at the Tajo mill who were agitating to have the master mechanic thrown out. Irving countered with a petition signed by the rest of the mechanics and others asking to have said master mechanic kept on. Also, Irving had fired one of the aforesaid Communists for ample cause, which cause must now be shown. Needless to say, he won on both points. Even the new government officials knew his reputation.

The *Rebeldía*, a labor sheet printed in Guanajuato, found it useful to malign and otherwise attack both Irving and his master mechanic and they "printed some very rotten stuff." Irving at one time spoke about this to the governor. Curiously, within the month two masked men entered the *Rebeldía* printing office at night and did a good job of smashing the equipment. The government knew nothing of this officially, but the two masked men were the chief of police and the colonel in charge of the state troops in Guanajuato.

Early in 1925 one of the largest companies operating in Guanajuato, with a payroll of some fourteen hundred Mexicans, did shut down. Regulations and related expenses under the new labor law, continuing complaints from the authorities and from their workmen, and lower grades of ore created losses with no real prospect of recovery. This company had been working over low-grade ores left behind by the Spaniards and their successors from the earlier excavations on the Mother Lode, such as Rayas and Valenciana. The undertaking did not yield enough to meet the excise taxes and the labor cost brought on by the revolutionary government, and Guanajuato suffered accordingly.

Two years later Irving commented:

[August 25, 1927] Cubo is in the doldrums just now, partly because of bad weather which always gives me the blues, partly because the ore is getting darn scarce in the mine, and partly because of the political and otherwise situation in the country. It does look as though the government were doing its damndest to kill all industry and is raising taxes in consequence on account of the resulting lack of income. I am not feeling especially happy and feel more than ever that Mexico is a good country to get out of as soon as it is possible.

As part of the "just cause" rules in the labor law there was a clause providing that a man who was treated badly could resign and collect damages, usually three months' salary. This came home to roost when Irving fired one of his American employees in 1929. Luella told the story to Robert:

[February 26, 1929] Dale, who has been in charge at the mill since Buchanan left, shot off his mouth (only!) to Dad in the office in town yesterday morning, and has left the employ of the Company. He has never been really loyal to the Company and has been much too thick with Kurtz [who worked for another company that sold ore to Cubo]. He went to town with Kurtz Saturday in a car and told Gisholt [our office manager], that it was for the account of the Company.[7] So Monday morning Gisholt told him "the boss is not conforme with that." Dad happened in at that moment and Dale said, "You'll furnish me transportation to town or you can go to hell." Dad, "You are quitting right now." Then they had it hot and heavy. Finally Dad said, "As to transportation to town you've had it ever since you came to Tajo. All you ever had to do was come down to Cubo and get a horse," but he was too high hat for a horse. He threatened to sue for three months salary, and he and Kurtz have their heads together and are plotting something.

[March 5, 1929] Dale's name came up in the Junta de Conciliacion yesterday and he demanded the three months salary, his lawyer reading four long pages of quejas [complaints] (Dad didn't bother to listen to them) and Dad's lawyer said, "Nothing doing." Next it will go to the Junta de Arbitraje and we'll see how far he gets. He has of course not the ghost of a case, but that doesn't always mean a lot, or anything, down here. But neither has he any standing, nor friends, among the Mexicans, that we know of. By the way, Felipe Torres told Gisholt recently in a casual conversation that Dale showed Kurtz all the assay books last summer — so Dale lied about that.

[March 9, 1929] Dale's case against the Company came up again this week. It lasted from 6 until 10:15 P.M. and was adjourned until Monday. The Company's case is in the hands of a lawyer [Mexican], so neither Dad nor Gisholt went to the Junta but it must have been rich. Kurtz was testifying for Dale and our lawyer got him so mixed up that he didn't know what he was saying at the end. First he was asked a lot of questions — "Do you know Dale was fired?" and a lot of cases cited as reasons why Dale found it impossible to work for this company, and to every one he said yes, he knew it. Then our lawyer began to cross question him — "You say you know so and so — were you present? — where did it take place? — who else was there?" and Kurtz was never present, never knew where it took place nor who else was there. Then "How do you know it is so?" and all he could answer was "Dale told me." Finally the lawyer got him so all he could answer was "I know nothing," until the President of the Junta said, "How is it you can say 'yo constaba' [I certified] to all these questions and now you are saying 'yo ignoraba' [I did not know] to exactly the same questions?" Finally our lawyer said, "This man is not fit to testify; he is an hombre incompleto [unfinished man]." Kurtz says, "Perhaps you don't know who I am. Ask Mr. DeVotie who I am. He says I am the best miner who ever came to Guanajuato. Ask Dr. Hislop. Ask the British Ambassador." Our lawyer: "I do not need to ask Mr. DeVotie who you are. Nor do I need to ask Dr. Hislop who you are, much less the British Ambassador. In a small colony like this we all know each other and the reputation each has. I know all about you, more than you have any idea I know. I know just what your standing is in the foreign society here, in the Mexican society, and with the governmental authorities." They say Kurtz was almost nutty before he got through with him. After court adjourned Dale told the company representative on the Junta that he was sick of the whole thing and wished he could drop it, but his lawyer won't let him. Dale told Gisholt the same thing yesterday. Meanwhile his lawyer — about the shadiest one in Guanajuato — is bleeding him and he, Dale, is running up a hotel bill and the case goes on.

Irving continued:

[April 12, 1929] Kurtz has gone — and it is lonesome as the dickens without an A-1 enemy around. Dale still walks the Plaza. It is now seven weeks since he decided to get three months pay out of me. His affair became quite a political matter, with a bunch of grafters and sin verguenzas in the City government bucking the Governor who is on our side. We won in the Junta Municipal on all counts but Dale appealed again to the Junta Central where he tried to bribe the seventh man, who is the government representative and has the deciding vote, to decide the thing in his favor, but the Governor got in on that just in time.

The whole gist of it is that there is 2,000 pesos involved. Of this total, Dale will have to pay one-half to his lawyer and *others* — the others being those who do the voting. And with 1,000 pesos considerable influence can be purchased.

[April 29, 1929] A few days ago Dale came around and caved absolutely. Wanted to settle on the basis of getting his railroad fare to the States, but was forced to take only his twenty-four days due for the time before he was fired, and he signed all kinds of receipts and actas. So we won out in toto. I hope he goes the way of all sin verguenzas.

Notes

1. The correspondence between the Cubo mine and the Chicago office for the period after Irving's return has not been found in the Cubo archives, but one can get a sense of how he proceeded from a binder labeled "General Correspondence" (ca. 1915–29) (hereafter cited as GC). It contains letters to and from individuals, many of them applications for jobs at the mine or offers of positions there. This letter dated February 26, 1920 is from Irving to Paz.

2. Lopez to Irving, letters of January 5, 1921, and February 28, 1920 (GC).

3. Hollis to J. P. MacFadden, Supt., Sandon, B.C., June 11, 1920 (GC).

4. Projects for improvement of the mill from both men are in the Cubo archive in a binder labeled "Mill Data, Mill Experiments," along with Carrouché's assessments of the working of the mill.

5. Irving to Jenkin, February 19, 1921 (GC).

6. Irving to Vaughan, December 23, 1922 (GC).

7. By 1929 the wagon road from Cubo to Guanajuato had been improved enough to permit automobiles (if the car was sturdy). Irving had a company car, a Chrysler touring sedan, and regularly drove back and forth from Guanajuato to Cubo.

CHAPTER 15

Personae Gratae II

Pancho Medina

A man of authority, Pancho Medina was tall and well built with no excess weight but enough to hold his own in an emergency. A certain amount of Spanish blood mixed with his Indian heritage lent a sharpness to his features and a touch of Castilian pride to his bearing. He was in charge of security, the *jefe de policía* for the mine.

Even in 1920 after the revolution had subsided, there were still roving bands of *sin verguenzas* in the hills, and when some were known to be in the area Pancho would accompany the Señora and the *mozo*, Brígido, on a ride to "town" — the capital city. In 1920, when John and Robert returned to Cubo as teenagers, he was the man assigned to accompany them on excursions outside the hacienda and to teach them how to shoot.

Watchmen at the hacienda gate and at the mine entrance and the shaft head a mile or so up the mountainside were in Pancho's charge, as were the night watchmen who were strategically placed. When there was any sign of trouble these men were armed, and Pancho made the rounds to be sure they knew what to do and when to do it. It was enough. Any marauders who came near the mining town knew better than to test his *policía*.

His private life was his own. Although the manager no doubt knew his circumstances, Pancho never talked about his family affairs nor volunteered information about his past. He was the *jefe de policía*. He knew his job and he did it well. He was courteous and kind, but stood by his privacy. He had the respect of all the mine employees.

On Saturdays the mine payroll was picked up at the bank in the city, seven miles away, and brought under armed guard over the mountain road to the mine. Discredited during the revolution, paper money was no longer acceptable, and the payroll was entirely in silver coins carried in canvas sacks over the back of a mule. The armed guard, with Pancho in charge, wore side arms, and carried Winchester or Mauser rifles. One Saturday early in 1925, as the party rounded a turn in the mountain road, four or five bandits opened fire from an ambush, wounding all of the escort, including Pancho. He fell from his horse, and as he lay wounded in the road he raised his gun and shot two of the thieves, killing them.

Luella's letter to Robert described the episode:

[February 9, 1925] Our men hadn't a chance in the world. It was cold-blooded murder. The bandits had it sized up that they couldn't get the money without putting our men out of business first—and they couldn't either and Dad takes considerable pride in that. Of course it is always your best men that suffer in such a case, as they are the men you put on such a job. Two men from Calderones were further up the road and hid behind a rock and witnessed it. There were six bandits—some down over the side of the road out of sight, the others behind a bend in the road. Our men came on as usual. They saw and heard nothing until they heard the shots, within ten feet of the bandits they were. First shot got Pancho in the stomach and knocked him off his horse, whereupon two jumped on him to finish him and he finished them instead.

Lucas and Williebaldo turned back towards town, Lucas emptying his revolver as he went but being peppered with shots. Their rifles were of course tied to their saddles, no time to get them into action. Brigido got through them and part way up the trail before he was hit. The doctor took the bullet out of Lucas's lung yesterday. Brigido's wound is not serious but the x-ray shows the bullet very near an artery. It is going to be mighty ticklish business getting it out. Fortunately we have in Guanajuato now the most skilled surgeon we have ever had, and fortunately

Sunday morning Mass at the church with his family, a Sunday noon parade around the bandstand at the Jardín to the strains of grand opera played with verve by local talent, during which he exchanged casual or more-than-casual glances at the well-dressed señoritas circling the other way.

When at length a baseball game was organized at Cubo with equipment provided by the mining company, Ricardo was among the leaders who arranged teams for competition. Play was on an open field atop a hill just outside of town, and the teams, sometimes with only five or six men on a side, included anyone among the workers who wished to participate. Ricardo was enthusiastic and took great pleasure in performing at the plate or in forcing an out, not too different from an American boy of his age.

Atenedoro Tinajero

Atenedoro Tinajero was an educated man. He presided over the mine office, kept the accounts, and guarded the walk-in safe that housed documents, account books, petty cash, and, on weekends, the weekly payroll. The payroll was all hard cash, as has been noted, and on Saturdays Atenedoro would allow the Gerente's teenage sons to help count and stack coins in wooden trays to be carried to the pay window for the paymaster.

It was Atenedoro who did his best to keep track of the Cubo Company's resources during the critical years of 1915 and 1916 after foreign representatives had been ordered out of the Guanajuato district because of the turmoil created by rebel activities, as we have seen from his correspondence with Irving in 1916. With limited authority he stayed on at Cubo in critical times and tried to account for the ores being taken from the mine with or without the knowledge of the owners. And he tried to help the people of Cubo when corn was scarce or unavailable.

In his letters to Irving he had urged that an American be sent back to take charge, as he had been unable to get effective help from the local people. There was no feeling here of foreign exploitation, but rather of the need for responsible parties to resolve a dangerous situation.

Tinajero represented a large segment of Mexican society that regarded foreign ownership and management as beneficial to the community.

CHAPTER 16

Reminiscences IV

The other world was now becoming a serious business. I was at Harvard and quite ready to be free of the growing irritations of a closely supervised preparatory school routine. Harvard was a man's world. You chose your courses within the limits of required work; you were assigned a room and you paid for your board; and you signed up for some sport, because this too was a requirement. Whether or not you went to classes, slept in your room, or ate in the dining hall, or whether or not you took your daily "exercise," was strictly up to you. No one cared. But attendance at classes was monitored. If at the end of a midsemester marking period your grades were below subsistence level, and if this matched a poor attendance record, you were invited to the dean's office to discuss the matter. If at midyear this condition persisted you suddenly found that you were no longer enrolled in the college. One of my freshmen roommates had this enlightening experience.

My major in college was History, Government, and Economics, with American history as a field of concentration. I had given serious thought to mining engineering because I liked what I had seen of Dad's activities, but he warned me off.

"It's OK," he said, "if you don't expect to have a family. But living in odd parts of the world where the mines happen to be isn't the best way to raise a family." Apparently he and Mother had had their doubts at times, but we children never knew it. For us it had been great. He went on to say that if you were in the mining field the best answer was to be a consulting engineer.

"Then why weren't you a consulting engineer?" I asked.

"Because," he said, "I'm too honest. When a man has invested money in a loser, he doesn't like to be told he was a fool. If you tell him his mine is worthless he will write you off for having given him bad advice and go to another consultant who is willing to string him along for a few thousand dollars more with 'possibilities' here and 'possibilities' there until he decides for himself that there are better opportunities elsewhere. I couldn't do that."

Before we knew it, it was June again. The enchanted highway through the cornfields and over the prairies would begin to beckon. Soon we were once more on the Golden State Limited leaving Chicago and the East far behind. Lying in the upper berth, I could hear far ahead the deep, resonant notes of the whistle as we approached a crossing, insistent, long, drawn-out, like some winged cello calling for its mate. Underneath the wheels rode smoothly on the track beating out the tempo set by the powerful locomotive with never a variation, poketa-pok, poketa-pok, poketa-pok. We would be doing a steady seventy miles an hour over the plains. It put me to sleep.

At home Angela had been cooking for two and when we arrived she doubled the quantities because now there were four. We ate everything that was prepared and as she watched the empty serving dishes come back to the kitchen she gradually added more. Each year we practically starved for at least a week until at last Angela would come to the Señora and say: "It is not possible! We require three times the food that we did for the two of you." Mother would point out that we liked her cooking, but I am sure that the altitude and the mountain air as well as freedom from the pressures of school all helped to increase our appetites.

In Guanajuato during the summers things were livelier as we grew older. There was the time Mother and Dad rode into town to meet us and because the train came in late in the afternoon we were all to be overnight guests of the Chippendales. Cocktails were served before dinner and John and I kept pace with the others. At dinner I remember that it was quite an achievement to find my mouth with the fork, but I succeeded, and after dinner Mr. Chippendale passed the cigars. I had tried one or two before without getting sick so I took one when it was offered. Whereupon Mrs. Chippendale turned to Mother and asked, "Do you allow your children to smoke cigars?"

Mother replied, "Mrs. Chippendale, there comes a time when all we can do is sit back and see what we have brought up."

About this time Carrouché's daughter, Josephine, was coming of age and interested in boys. In addition to her father's astuteness she had a sense of intrigue, perhaps acquired from her mother. They lived at the mill, not far from the Cubo mine but a long way from town, and I suspect that her nose was out of joint because the American schoolboys paid her little or no attention. One Saturday I was having dinner at the Hotel Luna with Aunt Polly, who was visiting from the States, when the waiter came up to me and said that the Señor Mendoza would like to speak to me outside. Mendoza [name altered] was the name of a high government official and he had two sons, the older a very upright young man and the other somewhat less so. It turned out to be the younger son. As I was still fresh from school, my Spanish was not at its best, but I caught the gist of his rather vehement remarks. The Señorita Carrouché lived not far from our house at the mine, no? And as we were newly arrived from the north we would of course not know, but he wished to inform me that the Señorita was his girl, and I would please remember this. I assured him that I had no desire to cut in on his territory and that he need have no concern. Somewhat puzzled, I rejoined Aunt Polly.

Frank DeVotie, our American friend in town, knew the Mendoza boys well and he had the hot dope. It seems that Josephine had been talking to her hot-blooded boyfriend on the phone, telling him how popular she was with the American boys, myself in particular, and what good times we were having out at the mine. It is barely possible she thought that this would increase his regard for her, but at least it would stir things up. Frank did what he could. He explained to the older brother that he had been out at the mine with us and when Josephine "walked in the front door, we went out the back," and please get this across to his brother. But this would not stop the girl from talking, and he warned that I should be on the alert because the younger brother was even now gunning for me. I went about my business, but for a while I did not ride alone and I carried my gun where it could be readily seen until things quieted down, because this young man had been in shooting scrapes before.

There was a rule of living here that possibly dates back to the early days of the Spanish conquest when Cortés set the example. One must live up to one's station. Cortés conquered the Mexican Indians partly by assuming a status superior to theirs and never displaying any weakness that would undermine this posture. Later the Spaniards denied Indians the right to wear Spanish clothes or to own horses or firearms, enforcing a superiority that they had always claimed. In the 1920s even after the Mexican Revolution this attitude was retained to some degree by the upper classes, and foreigners did the same to help maintain their status in these surroundings. It was expected of us not to withdraw from any challenge and to conduct ourselves honorably. Partly for this reason we always dressed well, followed the Spanish example of courtesy to others, and felt a responsibility to maintain control of our emotions and our equilibrium. After my experience at the Chippendales I was conscious of the latter whenever drinks were served.

One summer my college roommate, Barrie Foster, came to visit us in Mexico for a few weeks, and together we reconnoitered the area. Not far from the hacienda was La Rosa Mountain with a sheer face that rose five hundred feet in a vertical cliff overlooking the surrounding hills. At the back it tapered off with a more gradual ascent, but even on that side at the top there was a vertical rise of about eight feet that could be scaled through rock chimneys. Its top was a flat table of rock about the size of two football fields placed end to end. On this table (and nowhere else in the vicinity) there occurred specimens of geodes — a geode is defined as "a nodule of stone having a cavity lined with crystals or mineral matter." I had been up there before and found some of these, but they were not easy to find because they looked for all the world like any other rounded stone until you broke them open and disclosed the beautiful colored crystals that lined the inside, although on close examination the outside surface could be identified. Our thought was to climb La Rosa Mountain from the back in the early morning to see the sun rise from the top, and incidentally to find some geodes.

This meant getting up at four A.M. sun time. Mexico at that time was experimenting with daylight saving time, much to the confusion of everyone, including the railroads, who by now had given up running by timetables because of the confusion, and simply took off when they always had, hoping to arrive at the "usual" time. We had no alarm clock and asked the night watchman at the mine office to wake us at four A.M. He wasn't confused. "Sí, Señor," he said, "natural time or artificial time?"

We started on our climb as the light was beginning to break and could see that the top of La Rosa was blanketed with a cloud. We hoped that it would lift and went on our way. It didn't lift. High on the shoulder we struck the mist and having come this far decided to go on to the top anyway. We found a rock chimney and made our way to the table top where visibility was about six feet. There would be no sunrise for us, but at least we could look for geodes and we wandered up and down with our eyes glued to the ground. It was a fruitless search and at length we came back to the rocky edge to begin our descent. I located a chimney and started down first, Barrie one step above me. A few feet lower, as I reached with one foot for the next step down, an odd feeling came over me and I realized that there was no step. We were on the 500-foot sheer face. I brought my foot back and said, "Barrie, we're on the wrong side. Go back up." At the top we headed directly for the opposite side of the table top and had no trouble getting down.

On weekends in town the two of us sometimes had dinner by ourselves and on one occasion at the Hotel Luna on the Jardín de la Unión we decided to have a bottle of wine with our meal, and ordered port. No problem. We were served a full bottle of port wine with the meal and no questions were asked. As a matter of fact we enjoyed it very much and it started off a great evening. Another time we ate at the Mexican-American Casino, a town club sponsored by the local businessmen, and once again ordered port wine with our meal. But the casino had a French chef of long standing and high reputation. No wine appeared. Food yes, but no wine. Finally I asked the young boy who was waiting on us what had happened to the wine.

"*Un momento*, Señor," and he disappeared for some time. At length the chef himself appeared, accompanied by the waiter carrying a tray with two bottles and two small glasses.

The chef said, "You ordered port wine?"

"Yes."

"But, Señor, port is a sweet wine. Here, taste it." He poured some in one of the small glasses and handed it to me to taste. I said yes, it was very good.

"Ah, but you do not drink sweet wine with your meal. You must drink a dry wine, like this," as he poured from the other bottle. "See? That is dry."

I said, "Yes, *muy seco*," and so it was settled. We had a bottle of claret, and I have since learned to like it, with the meal, that is.

We rode in the mountains of the Continental Divide, explored old mines and ranches long since abandoned by the Spaniards, and saw the sights of Guanajuato. The mines in this area had originally been discovered by the

Indians, and had been worked by the Spaniards as early as the sixteenth century. These centered on a very rich deposit of silver in a quartz vein of large proportions, called the Mother Lode, and here the Spaniards opened up the Rayas and Valenciana mines, famous for their massive workings and vertical shafts built soon after. We went down the Rayas shaft.

The Rayas shaft is truly remarkable. It is drilled vertically through solid igneous rock to a depth of one thousand feet, where it meets the vein that runs through the rock on an inclined plane. The shaft is thirty feet in diameter from top to bottom. The Spaniards used Indian slave labor, and black powder for an explosive. The top of the shaft is finished in masonry in the shape of an octagon down to perhaps one hundred fifty feet below ground level. The purpose of this was to provide eight sides for hoists; a pulley was used to drop an iron bucket down each of the eight sides and bring up ore, water, tools, and men, in that order. At the surface, on the outer periphery of the shaft, were eight walled enclosures that housed the hoist drums, mounted vertically, so that mules could be driven around the enclosure to activate the hoist.

Below ground, at the bottom of the shaft, there was more masonry, Spanish castles under ground. Here, where the vein had been mined out, there were masonry walls to discourage cave-ins, stone stairways to give access to the unmined areas, and well-worn roadways leading through caverns and tunnels that had been the walkways for Indians who carried baskets of silver ore on their backs to the bottom of the shaft where it would be hoisted to the surface. One can imagine that it was a beehive of activity with dozens of men at the rock-breaking faces and streams of humanity winding their way back and forth to the loading point at the shaft. Others would be breaking and fitting waste rock to form the masonry walls and stairways, and the whole would be supervised by strategically stationed Spanish mine bosses armed with muskets and no doubt equipped as well with rawhide whips. Heavy smoke from burning torches fixed in the rock walls would take its toll of the air that filtered through the tunnels from the shaft and other openings.

Because the Indians were volatile and always restless, the Spaniards, we have been told, had a rule that the peons could not talk to one another. No verbal communication was permitted except to the bosses. But they were allowed to whistle. From this the Indians evolved a whistling code, used sparingly, we may assume, to avoid detection. Sounding like bird calls, they were in reality Indian words formed by the notes of the call much as you might whistle "Come up and see me sometime" if you could not say the words. To communicate over distances in the hills, the Mexicans sometimes still use the whistle language, which carries far. As children in Mexico we used it ourselves.

In the river valley below the shaft head and running out from Guanajuato were the great haciendas at Marfil where the ore was processed. After the lower grades were sorted out, the ore was transported by mule or burro to a hacienda where it was ground fine with millstones and spread out on a broad flagstone patio to dry in the sun. Later, salt and chemicals were added to start the extraction, then quicksilver, and the whole mass was mixed for days by the feet of many mules driven in teams back and forth across the patio. In time the mules' hooves disintegrated with the action of the mercury, but there were plenty of mules. At length the pulp was washed away, leaving the mercury with the silver, which was separated and used again. The remains of some of the sixteenth- and seventeenth-century patios can still be seen in the Guanajuato River valley.

Another visit we made was to the Panteón, or cemetery, on a hill that overlooked the city from the north. Here, to those who can afford it, burial space is rented either in the ground or in vaults that line the walls of the large enclosure. Rental is for a specified number of years, or in perpetuity for the very rich, but if rented only for a specified term the grave will be opened at the end of the term and the bones removed to make room for another paying customer. Deep underground are a series of tunnels that some say are reminiscent of the catacombs of Rome, and here the bones that have been removed are sorted and neatly stacked in piles. In one tunnel will be the femurs, in another the skulls, in another the pelvises. One could wish that firewood might be stored as compactly. For appropriate financial recognition to the attendant, they are opened to public view. With the high altitude and relative dryness, the climate is such that occasionally one of the bodies removed from a vault will be mummified, all the skin and hair still intact. These of course add to the gruesome display for visitors to see and increase the amount of the tip that would normally be expected, so the shrunken bodies of the mummies have been stood up against the wall of one of the tunnels in their frozen attitudes, certainly an appropriate reception line for a graveyard. They were naked when we saw them, but they have since been draped with sheets to conform to the proprieties, which has spoiled the effect.

After a week spent in Mexico City seeing the sights, including the floating gardens of Xochimilco, the Paseo de la Reforma with its sidewalk cafés, Chapultepec Park, the Cathedral, the sunken National Theater, the Alameda with its well-kept gardens, the Thieves Market, and Sanborns, all much as they are today, we headed north again. Just south of the border the train stopped long enough for passengers to wet their whistles before reentering Volstead's liquorless land. Barrie, being adventurous, bought a pint of good whiskey and slid it in his hip pocket in order to escape detection by the U.S. customs authorities. No sooner had we settled down again in our Pullman seats than one of the armed Mexican border guards who had just come aboard invited him into the men's washroom and proceeded to search him. Upon finding the whiskey, which he had most assuredly seen Barrie buy and put in his pocket, the guard assumed a righteous air and appropriated the bottle, explaining that it was not permitted to take it across the border. No doubt the border guards kept themselves well supplied by beating the U.S. Customs to the punch, with or without legal authority.

CHAPTER 17

Continuing Revolution

Throughout the twenties sporadic revolutionary activity added spice to life in Mexico. Venustiano Carranza had been elected president in 1917 for a four-year term under the new constitution, which stipulated that he could not succeed himself. In 1921, therefore, he would be out of a job, but by choosing his successor he could at least arrange to live in comfortable circumstances. He had only to present his choice as the sole candidate in the coming election. Three of his generals (De la Huerta, Obregón, and Calles) took exception to this procedure. Obregón marched against him and, as we have noted, on May 21, 1920, Carranza was killed. In September, Alvaro Obregón was elected president. Pancho Villa had withdrawn; and, to be sure that he was out of the way, the government provided him with a fine estate in northern Mexico where he lived happily until his assassination in 1923. Things were relatively quiet for a year or two.

There was talk of revolution in 1922, but, said Luella in a March 1 letter to Robert, "As long as it continues to be mere talk it doesn't worry us and we aren't looking for real trouble." When a few railroad trestles were burned out on the railroads in the north, Pancho Villa proclaimed that he would get out and fight anyone who tried to start something, and no one did.

The question of presidential succession came up again in 1923, in anticipation of elections in 1924. Whether to preserve the stronger government that

he represented or whether to safeguard his own future, Obregón also decided
to pick his successor, and chose General Plutarco Elías Calles. These two
might well have had an understanding that they would trade places every four
years if things went well. This left De la Huerta out in the cold. Of this period in politics Irving wrote:*

> [September 30, 1923] The principal excitement in Guanajuato this
> week has been the inauguration of the new governor, Mr. Colunga.
> It was arranged that president Obregon was to come up from Mexico
> City for the ceremonies, and in order to make the fiestas as complete as
> possible the present government, of Madrazo, collected all the money he
> could. The mining companies were asked to come across with 2,500 pe-
> sos, which we did. We thought this was too much, but as we were all
> very keen about Colunga we were willing to do it. At the last moment
> Madrazo asked us to put up 1,000 pesos more because he was still short
> and had been able to collect only 150 pesos from all the merchants com-
> bined in Guanajuato. I thought this a holdup and still feel the same, that
> the Gringo companies are being worked for a bunch of suckers, which
> we are. It seems that Madrazo also obtained 15,000 pesos from the State
> funds.
> At the last moment Obregon found that he could not come because
> he had a cold. So all the splurge for nothing. Of course it was not a cold
> that kept him away. It was high politics going on in the City. And now
> we learn that Colunga is immediately going back to Mexico City to be
> Secretary of Gobernacion in Obregon's cabinet — so we will not have
> Colunga for governor after all, at least until after Obregon's term ex-
> pires about a year from now.
> There is something doing in politics. De la Huerta has resigned from
> the cabinet on account of bad health, which means that he is going to
> run for President against Calles, and I believe there is going to be some-
> thing doing.
>
> [November 8, 1923] In Mexico the only thing of interest now is the
> presidential election campaign. It is on in full sway and though the elec-

---

*All the letters of Irving and Luella quoted in this chapter were addressed to
Robert.

tions do not come until next July the air is full of politics and in Mexico City this includes daily shootings on the streets and in the Chamber of Deputies, between Callistas and De la Huertistas. It does not look any too encouraging.

In December 1923, De la Huerta and his followers took to arms and started what was known as the "De la Huerta Revolution" aimed at Obregón and his presidential candidate, General Calles. Fighting developed along the railroad lines, traffic was frequently interrupted, mail was uncertain, and foreigners avoided travel whenever possible. From Guanajuato, Irving wrote:

[December 14, 1923] All the automobiles have disappeared from Guanajuato. People have either lost their keys or the cars are broken or else sold. This is the result of the revolution. . . . We are not feeling particularly happy, but we never do under the present circumstances. We will make the best of it and hope for an early settlement of the present troubles.

Luella was more graphic:

[December 10, 1923] Well, here we are again — revolution and cut off from all the world, no trains, no mail, no express, no nothing! The question is how much of a revolution we are in for and how long are we liable to be without mail, etc. . . . Dad was over at the Palacio and heard the news — De la Huerta insurrection and the army division in Veracruz with him. . . . Obregon issued a proclamation full of virtue and patriotism about upholding the constitution and the honor of the country, etc., etc., etc., — just as if he wasn't president right now by virtue of an exact similar revolution! An amazing people — and most annoying! The point is that the retiring President insists on naming his successor and then he puts all the force of the government at his disposal for conducting his campaign, which is paid for out of the national trea-sury! In this instance Obregon was putting forward Calles. Carranza put forward Bonillas. Neither was a popular candidate and neither could have been elected in an honestly conducted revolution. Calles is decidedly unpopular with a big majority . . . so the popular candidate finally said "To hell," or something equally emphatic and started a revolution.

Luella

[December 24, 1923] I am sure much parcel post is held up in Guadalajara, as all parcel post for Guanajuato goes first to the customs there and the rebels still hold that city. This holdup in parcel post packages is about the only way we notice the revolution now. The talk is that Obregon, Calles, and De la Huerta are trying to get together peacefully. Let us hope they do.

[December 31, 1923 – Regarding plans to go north] Truth to tell there is no chance to plan the future for us in this stupid land of revolution. Quien sabe what will happen next. No one can find out just how matters stand – you can't believe the Mexican newspapers, which are filled with government victories – and the rumors that fly about are fully as unreliable. The rebels don't seem to gain much, and the Federals make little headway against them. It is a mighty unhealthy situation and one that if prolonged is sure to breed bandits and general lawlessness, and upset business and put the country back years – and this revolution is absolutely without excuse. There were excuses, plenty of them, for the series that started in 1910, and it took until Obregon's revolution in 1920 to get rid of the series. Now the country has had three years of relative peace and increasing prosperity, and this particular bunch in power – Obregon and Calles and De la Huerta – ought to know enough to cut out turning the country upside down, just because the latter two each wants to be the next president. Mexico at peace has enough disadvantages. Mexico in revolution is – to me mentally – hell! There, now you know how I feel.

Irving

[January 26, 1924] The revolution is the main theme of interest down here, and even this does not afford much interest because we can find out so little of what is going on. I suppose the truth is that very little is going on, whereas not being in the know, we have an idea that a great deal is doing, only we do not know about it.

A few days ago a small bunch of rebels got into Silao. There they got hold of an engine, got up steam and then sent it down the railroad line toward Irapuato, about the time that the north bound El Paso train was due to leave Irapuato for Silao. They sent the engine down the line wild, with the idea of wrecking the northbound train. As a matter of fact the engine went dead and stopped about twelve kilometers from Silao, and the northbound train was able to stop, so there was no wreck. But the rebels had the right intentions just the same. This sort of thing is not warfare, as the northbound train was simply a passenger train.

Luella

[February 8, 1924] There seems to be hope right now of the revolutionary situation clearing up in the course of the next few months. The Federals are apparently winning, but there are now a good many roving bands and railroad travel is quite uncertain.

[February 15, 1924] The principal news with us is that we almost lost one of our horses, the Prietito, last Saturday. In fact he was gone for forty hours. Mr. Hudson started to town on him Saturday afternoon and when he got to the corrals he was approached by four soldiers — mounted — two from one side and two from the other, the leader wearing a mask below his eyes, and with rifles pointed at Mr. Hudson. He was told to halt and turn over his horse. He asked on whose say-so and they said Estrada, which is the name of the rebel general in Guadalajara, so of course Mr. Hudson thought some of the rebel force had penetrated to our little neck of the woods. But it seems Estrada is also the name of the Captain of the State troops in Guanajuato, and these were nothing more than State troops sent out to guard (?) the road out this way. They were in Cubo early that afternoon (I saw them) and had tried to get our local jefe to give them an order on the hacienda for horses, saddles, etc., which he refused to do. Anyhow Mr. Hudson asked where was their authority to take the horse and they patted their rifles and said, "here is our authority," so he had to dismount and they turned over to him one of their good-for-nothing nags and they (one of them, who used to be a watchman here in the hacienda, by the way) mounted Prietito and rode off. Mr. Hudson rode to the cocinas ["kitchens," the name for a section of the road to Guanajuato] and then left the nag with Antonio who was just behind him, and walked into town and entered his complaint at the troop headquarters and called Dad. He was assured the horse would be returned as soon as it got to town, but by some oversight — not knowing what horse it was! — it went out again Sunday afternoon early and didn't come in again till late Monday morning and finally landed at Cubo again by hired porter Monday afternoon, with a sore back and pretty well tired out. So much for Prietito's adventures. The soldier in charge who took the horse was put in jail, so we are all hoping that is the end of such doings. I went in to town Tuesday of this week for luncheon and bridge and made the round trip sin novedad.

De la Huerta's bid for fame was doomed to failure. Both Obregón and Calles were stronger men and had the forces of the government behind them. Also in his three years as president, Obregón had done much to reestablish the authority of the government, as shown by the adventures of Prietito. In 1924 Calles was "elected" president.

AFTER TWO MORE years of peace and quiet, things began to pop again. This time it was the Church. The revolutionary Constitution of 1917 had set up restrictions on the power and the properties of the Church, which President Calles now proceeded to enforce. The Calles government decreed that all priests must be native Mexicans, that Church sacraments would be forbidden, and that religious vows would be banned. Monasteries and convents would be disbanded. "Calles' Law" was posted on the doors of all the churches. But the Catholic Church was a worthy foe. First it rejected the constitution and ignored the rules and regulations. The government replied by ordering nationalization of Church property and began to close church schools. The Church then claimed it could not function or conduct services, thus leaving the question for the people to decide. For several years no church bells rang in Mexico.

As in most poor countries the people were dependent on the padre, or some spiritual guide, to ease their conscience. Confession and absolution saved the soul. How could they steal or knife an enemy tomorrow if they had not confessed and paid their penance for last week's mischief? And there were many who were devoted Christians and wanted to say their prayers in church. Unrest among the people grew and in 1926 there began a long series of minor and major revolutions in various parts of the country led by "Cristeros" who supported the Church.

The state of Guanajuato became one of the centers of revolt. There were frequent reports of rebels in the mountains between Guanajuato and Dolores Hidalgo and they visited ranches and haciendas asking people to help the cause. In some ways life at Cubo was reminiscent of the earlier days of 1914, when residents waited for roving bands to descend on the town and hid saddles and bridles lest they be commandeered. But there was a difference. These men wore metal badges inscribed "Cristo Rey." They were well behaved and by and large the people were behind them.

Luella

[December 4, 1926, from Cubo] As to a revolution we have all been rather expecting one to break one day, in particular if the United States should withdraw recognition over the land and oil laws,* which seemed imminent, and everyone felt sure things would start popping on all sides. Yesterday's Mexico City paper, the Excelsior, said Mexico had at last acceded to all the U.S. demands. Today's paper says that is all a mistake. So quien sabe. But at last we have an ambassador down here [Dwight Morrow] who means exactly what he says and has persuaded the Washington government to back him up, which is the only way to treat these people. But personally we would prefer to be north of the border while it happens. The Calles government is on a very shaky platform — it will take very little to topple it. The will to oppose him is everywhere and many are the preparations being made.

[January 4, 1927] We may need protection most any day or night now. Brigido is hiding saddles and bridles this morning and taking one of the horses to Guanajuato so we'll have only three horses and perhaps be able to keep one or two of those if we are visited for arms and horses. A revolutionary band [Cristeros] visited a hacienda between here and

---

*Laws enacted to implement provisions of the Constitution of 1917 that assigned to the Mexican nation subsoil rights to minerals, including oil. The United States vigorously objected and on October 30, 1926, warned Mexico not to deprive Americans of their property rights. The laws were modified and the dispute resolved in 1927 (for the time being) with the help of U.S. Ambassador Dwight Morrow.

Dolores yesterday asking for both—very well behaved but needed arms and horses, which they got. This is authentic, not a rumor. The air of the State of Guanajuato is full of revolution—a stamp office raided for funds in a small town—haciendas raided for arms and horses—and that sort of thing all over. Most any day now our mail may be cut off. We do not think it will be for long and are full of sympathy, but dread the process, never knowing what may develop. There is always an element of danger about it and we don't enjoy danger, nor the thought of it.

On the following Sunday the men played golf as usual at the new golf club six miles outside of Guanajuato.

Luella

[January 28, 1927, from Cubo] A bunch of State cavalry arrived in Cubo about 11:15 last night; clattering by our bedroom window they sounded like one hundred at least, probably there were about twenty. What they did here I haven't heard. They were silent—not even walking their horses back and forth to cool them off—and we went off to sleep, to be aroused by their leaving for Guanajuato again, probably around two or three A.M. We hear from various sources that there is a bunch of up to eight hundred rebels in the campo [countryside] between here and Dolores, well armed and mounted and very well behaved. Virgilio ran into some of them last weekend when he went over to his mine beyond Santa Rosa. They advised him against going farther as there were Federal troops over that way and they were a bad bunch! But he went on and encountered no Federals.

[February 6, 1927] Here we are "in the heart of the campaign" as it were! One hundred men and horses ("El Gobierno") camped on the lower patio. Nothing really very exciting but for a little while we had that uncertain feeling that accompanies this sort of thing in Mexico always. On the whole it has to date, at least, been entertaining, and a break in the monotony of life.

[February 12, 1927] Since then Cubo has been quiet. The Government troops have been chasing over the hills after the rebels. The Excelsior reports a Federal victory in the Cubo "Battle"—and the rebels are on the point of being wiped off the map. Which shows about how much to believe of what the papers report. The same bunch of Federal troops that was here, reinforced by others, visited a mine the other side of Guanajuato and took sixteen boxes of dynamite and a small electric machine for using same — and all Dad can think of is they are planning to blow up railroad tracks. On the way over there they went into ranch houses and broke all their dishes and stole all money, clothes, blankets, etc. Disgusting business.

The new golf club, six miles out of town, was of course exposed, but it lay to the west in open ground and the rebels preferred the mountains of the divide that were east of town and afforded some protection. Also there was nothing at the club except when the members came to play, when they themselves would be the booty. Still they would not back off from their appointed rounds.

Irving

[February 21, 1927] On Friday some troops were rushed up from Silao and went out to Santa Rosa [the golf club] after the revolutionists. It seems the latter laid in wait for them in a sort of canyon just beyond Santa Rosa, and as the Federals filed through opened fire and killed a General, a Mayor or Major, and several soldiers. They also captured a machine gun. This has thrown Guanajuato into tense excitement. The Gringos also got a message that our Juan, our Santa Rosa caretaker, had been approached on two different days by a small group of mounted men who asked him how many Gringos came down there to play golf, and when they came, and who they were, etc. This was last Friday, so yesterday morning we were all a bit nervous and wondered whether there was some plot on foot to kidnap us or simply to rob us. At any rate everyone went down as usual, that is the men folks — no women except Mrs. DeVotie. Juan denied the whole story and we had a peaceful morning and nothing doing. We think now that perhaps some of the local ranch hands wish to cultivate the land where the links are, and decided to scare off the Gringos. So much for that. But you can see that with all the happenings there is bound to be more or less excitement in the air. The joke of it is that everyone is really like the Irish. I mean the natives of course. They are all agin the government and have a secret sympathy for the rebels. So the rebels get tipped off on all that the government is doing, and I suppose that vice versa the government gets a lot of bad tips.

Shortly after this, in March 1927, the federal government sent five thousand troops to quell the rebels in the State of Guanajuato, with headquarters at Dolores Hidalgo across the mountains from El Cubo. Things were quiet for a while on the surface, although they still bubbled underneath.

CHAPTER 18

¡Viva Cristo Rey!

Overlooking Guanajuato from the north, some twelve or fifteen miles away, stands a peak that might have been the cone of some volcano. Visible from all directions, it is said to be the geographical center of Mexico. Earlier a road had been cut that wound around the peak to reach the summit. In Mexico this calls for a monument to mark the spot, and what better monument for Guanajuatenses than a statue of Christ that would also serve as a mark of faith? Accordingly a massive statue was erected on Cubilete Mountain big enough to be seen from far away, and it became fashionable to drive out to Cubilete to picnic and see the view. Also it became a rallying point for the Cristeros. With the churches closed, Mexicans from various parts of the country made pilgrimages to Cubilete to worship there.

At last, in 1928, as the revolution grew hotter, the federal government decided to remove this symbol of opposition. Luella wrote:*

> [February 22, 1928] Perhaps you know that the Federal army recently dismantled the statue of Christ on top of Cubilete, shot the caretaker, and destroyed the road up the mountain. Mexicans from

---

*Unless otherwise noted, all letters of Luella and Irving quoted in this chapter were addressed to Robert.

all over have been making monthly pilgrimages up the mountain and the Federal government got sore. They ordered first one general, then a second, to destroy the statue and both refused and advised against it — knowing local conditions — but a third general from some other part of Mexico was sent to do the dirty work. The result is considerable local resentment and unrest, and Saturday morning last at 8:30 a bunch of fifty from out Santa Rosa way fell on Guanajuato and for a little while there was much excitement. They were after the man at the head of the Commission that decided it should be done — at least so the story goes, and it sounds reasonable. They didn't get him and after shooting into the cuartel [barracks] at San Pedro and at any official seen elsewhere and taking any horses in sight — including our Alazán, which Carillo rode right into their midst, as he was en route to the office to come out with the payroll — opening the doors of Granaditas and letting out all the prisoners and burning the archives, they left town again along about 10 A.M.

Meanwhile at Cubo we got reports from time to time over the phone from Gisholt and were all advised not to leave Cubo. Mrs. Moore was having a dinner and bridge party of sixteen that evening and I hated to miss it, but Dad said nothing doing, so I called her up and said we couldn't go. She seemed rather surprised as by that time it was all over — being about noon. I told Dad at luncheon that I'd wager we could go to town and never see a soul. . . . Then at 2:30 Dad came up to say Reynoso was going to town and we could go too if we wanted to, and you can bet I did. Fortunately Mrs. Moore hadn't yet succeeded in getting substitutes for us and we went to the party.

Sunday passed uneventfully but Monday morning we were greeted with conflicting rumors as to a bunch of one hundred forty-five men that went through Cubo at 3 A.M. headed for Guanajuato and we wasted the whole morning sitting around the Guanajuato office calling up Cubo and Tajo and hearing that all was "muy pacifico," "no hay nada," etc., but I couldn't get Dad to budge. I got sore finally as Dad had been filled up with rumors and dire predictions but there seemed no foundation for any of them and I didn't believe any of it. Finally we came out in the afternoon and those one hundred forty-five men are still a mystery — the deputy delegado counted them though a crack in the door of the

Jefatura — if you believe they ever existed, which almost no one in Cubo does. So you see this corner of Mexico is back to normal again.

The unrest will doubtless continue for a while but the so-called rebels are friends of all the countryside and merely have it in for those in authority, in which most of us sympathize with them.

Luella

[March 27, 1928] We had another visitation Friday evening last. Mr. Buchanan [now mill superintendent] was here for dinner and a poker game was scheduled for the evening. Dad was called to the phone during dinner, to be told rebels were in the vicinity of Villalpando, but we seldom pay any attention to those tales. About 8 o'clock we were playing poker in the sala when Silvestre, the watchman, came and said, "Quiere hablar con el Señor [He wishes to speak with señor]," and Dad went. We sat for a while thinking Dad was at the phone, but as time passed I began to wonder so went in the dining room and looked out the window, to see the street full of armed and mounted men. I went back and reported and Carrouché [now mine superintendent] and Buchanan departed to see what was doing. Not a shot nor a grito — in fact all was silence. Finally Buchanan came back and I asked if he'd seen Dad and he said no and then I got a bit uneasy and wondered where Dad was anyway — had they taken him off somewhere, etc., etc., etc.? But of course it was all right or you'd have heard long since. When Dad left the sala he went down the steps to the office to be greeted, without warning on the part of the watchman, by six armed and mounted men in front of the office, and they said, "Will you come down to the gate and see the General?" and Dad says he thought "And will I return?" But when armed men invite you to do something you most always do it, let me warn you. At the gate he was met by the Colonel, son of the General, and he asked for a loan. So Dad suggested he come up to the office and talk things over. The escort of six accompanied them but Dad asked if they couldn't talk by themselves, so the Colonel told the six to stay outside. He was a nice young chap, son of Delfino Hidalgo, a well-known rebel chieftain. He says they have been all over Zacatecas and Jalisco, that there are a lot of rebels in Jalisco and that they will keep on till they win — that the present government is a government of tyrants.

Hidalgo is brother-in-law to Pedro Barrón [a storekeeper in Cubo] and for that reason they have left Cubo alone, not wanting to get Don Pedro in trouble. He also said that it was no part of their program to interfere with nor harm foreign companies. He said, "We know just when your payroll comes out and just how much of an escort it has and we could take it any time we wanted to, but we don't want to. That isn't what we are out for." They all had on aluminum discs with "Viva Cristo Rey." Dad asked how much of a loan he had in mind. He said "two hundred pesos"—a big relief to Dad. He sent for Enrique and asked, "How much money is there in the safe?" Enrique was scared stiff but he knocked off a few hundred pesos and said "five hundred." But our rebel friend was content with his two hundred for which he insisted on giving a receipt, though Dad told him he much preferred not to have a receipt. It was a relief not to be asked for a horse. . . .

They stuck around town till midnight, after which some of them went up to the mill at Tajo and took Manuel Lopez the almacenista and carried him off to shoot him, blaming him for the arrest of one of the rebels who visited us in February 1927. Manuel was put on a horse behind a rebel, with his hands tied behind his back. On the trail to Villalpando he managed to fall off his horse and down the hillside, breaking a leg and injuring an ankle. They shot and threw rocks after him but he crawled on his hands and knees and got to the mill and is now in the hospital in Guanajuato.

There were at least one hundred in the bunch. They went over Santa Rosa way where the next morning they ran smack into a bunch of over four hundred Federals who were scouting the country. There was a fight and some rebels were killed and they lost some horses, after which they were "dispersed"—doubtless to reunite a little farther along. The Federals also got some cans of sardines, guaraches [sandals], etc., which had been donated a few hours previously by Cubo merchants.

After graduating from college in June 1928, I went back to Cubo for my last summer vacation before going to work in the United States. There was little excitement those three months. Though the family now had an automobile provided by the company to keep up with the times in Guanajuato, the road over the mountains to Cubo was doubtful at best, and pretty bad in the rainy season (summer), so with us horses still prevailed. Because of the Cristeros we avoided riding into the hills but went back and forth from Cubo to Guanajuato *sin novedad*. Nor was there any trouble on the railroads. President Calles had maintained a fair degree of order, even arranging to have his predecessor, Obregón, reelected as his successor during that summer. (Though Obregón was assassinated shortly after, Calles retained control through an appointee, Emilio Portes Gil, who served as provisional president.)

While things were quiet Irving and Luella shared in some of the political activity in Guanajuato. As Luella told it:

[September 20, 1928] Last Saturday evening, September 15, Dad and I went to the Palace at about 8:50 P.M. to attend the opening of Congress, a thing neither Dad nor I had ever done. There was a little over an hour listening to Governor Arroyo Che's address and I was interested in seeing how much of it I could get, and in the things he reported on. Then we were asked to stay on (the peons who had gathered in good number were allowed to depart) — and cognac, sandwiches, cheese, olives, and sliced sausage were served, all good. And just before 11 o'clock I (along with other ladies) got a front row seat in the balcony next to the one from which the Governor was to give the Grito — and on the stroke of eleven Arroyo Che came out onto the balcony bearing a Mexican flag and made his little speech, ending with "Viva Mexico!," in which the peons who were packed solid in the street below joined — and the band, lined up on the street in front of the Palace, played the National Anthem — and skyrockets were shot off and finally a set piece of fireworks in front of the Parroquia church was lighted. It was all very impressive and interesting and I was glad to have finally heard the famous Grito, given all over Mexico at 11 P.M. on the night of September 15.*

But the fires of revolution still burned. As time wore on, the rebels, harassed by government troops, became less orderly and gradually more

---

*The famous "grito" given all over Mexico on the night of September 15 is a reenactment of the *grito de Dolores* (shout of Dolores) given by Padre Miguel Hidalgo in the town of Dolores (now Dolores Hidalgo) on the morning of September 16, 1810, calling for revolution against Spanish rule.

desperate. By December 1928 things were pretty hot around Guanajuato, and one José Padrón was said to be leading a band of rebels now turned outlaws who were camped in the mountains back of Cubo and Villalpando, probably in the Cañada which had once been our picnic ground. They were no longer "friendly" rebels but out-and-out bandits. Luella wrote:

> [December 6, 1928] We had another rebel scare the night before last, and I was ready to pick up and leave Mexico. Nothing happened but there are bands in the hills and I would like to live the rest of my life where I could sleep all night and not have one ear out for rebels.

> [December 14, 1928] Dad is in San Antonio, and Dick and Carrouché and I are holding down Cubo. Carrouché went to town the 12th, a holiday, and Dick and I were here when a rebel scare developed. Eighteen rebels went through Peregrina and were seen by Perez Vasquez taking the trail to Villalpando. So I sent Brigido to town with three of the horses and arranged with Enrique to hide out 1,500 of the 1,800 pesos in the safe and then — "What happened? Nothing!" to quote Al Smith. The rebels deployed — is that the word? — and went around Villalpando Mountain towards San Isidro.

In January 1929, Padrón's men raided the Tajo mill, took the superintendent's horse, all the arms and ammunition, and what money they could find. The following week they raided a mine on the other side of town near La Luz and kidnapped two young Americans who were shift bosses in the mill, asking a ransom of one thousand pesos apiece. This was a new way to get money, provided it worked, and eager to show that their hearts were in the right place the kidnappers even asked that a blanket be sent out to them "as one of the American boys was cold!" The trial run was a success, they got their money, and decided that there must be more where that came from.

Soon came a report that seemed authentic that Cubo was next on the list and Irving would be kidnapped. As we were seven miles from town and fairly close to bandit hideouts this would have been easy and logical, so Irving got in touch with the governor in Guanajuato. He suggested that Irving remain in Cubo as "bait in a trap," and sent out a number of soldiers disguised as peons to spring the trap. What happened? Nothing.

Irving commented:

[February 7, 1929] I am asking to have the soldiers remain for some time and it looks as though they would. I would be very rich pickings for those fellows if they could get away with me. It would probably be a matter of ten thousand pesos to get set loose. Things are none too good around here and it does not make one sleep any too easy.

Two days after this was written, on February 9, Luella and Irving gave a party at the Casino in town to celebrate their twenty-fifth wedding anniversary, which "went off very successfully."

Things got worse, as Luella described:

[February 26, 1929] There is more or less a reign of terror in the foreign colony in Guanajuato. . . .

When we think of Underwood sleeping peacefully at eleven P.M. only last Wednesday to wake up with a pistol in his side and to be confronted with his watchman held between two bandits, to be told to get up and dress while they waited, and to be shot down in cold blood at three the next afternoon — it is enough to frighten us all, so long as Jose Padron is at liberty. So Dick and Felipa and I are going to town this afternoon and are staying there the rest of this week. Dad wants us to move into town, he'll rent a house or he'll send us to the States, but I'm not ready for that — so I'm going in for four days and after that quien sabe.

This event becomes clear in a letter Luella wrote to her sister Edith:

[March 12, 1929] This whole foreign colony has been much worried about those of us living outside of the city ever since January 15 when two young men were kidnapped and carried off for ransom. Three fourths of the amount was paid and the two men were safely back thirty hours later, having rather enjoyed the experience. We none of us felt easy after that, this bunch had had their taste of easy money and that was bad. But we went about our business and leisures more or less as usual until the evening of February 20 when the next two were taken, older men this time (36 and 58) and living on the very outskirts of Guanajuato, and in every way it was a very bold performance and scared us all. Then two days later we learned they had been killed when a bunch of troops came unexpectedly on the band and it was a case of let the Americans be captured, or else kill them — and it was decidedly the Mexican of it to choose the latter. We all felt the men were safe if we could keep the troops off until at least some of the ransom was paid, but the governor couldn't be made to see it that way. He didn't much care if the Americans were killed nor did the general in command of the state troops and they both more or less frankly said so. What they wanted was to make a gesture *at once* of going after the band. Well, they made their gesture, the Americans were killed, and the leader of this local kidnapping band is still at large.

[Richard adds: I have a very clear recollection of the funeral of the two Americans. Felipa, the maid who took care of me, and I went down to the Jardín de la Unión and stood across from the Teatro Juárez among the crowd lining the streets. The procession passed in front of us, led by flower-decked vehicles, no doubt the hearses, and they were followed by cars and cars and cars. Mother and Dad and every other foreigner must have been in the procession, along with many Mexicans, and of course the crowds on the streets were mostly common people of Guanajuato. It was the most inspiring event I recall from my childhood in Guanajuato, rivalled perhaps only by the Mardi Gras parades of bands and floats, but those were very different in spirit.]

Both state and federal troops persisted in the hunt for José Padrón, and there were other pitched battles in the hills. A regular garrison of ten state troops remained at Cubo for protection, and Luella noted:

[March 30, 1929] We ride back and forth to Cubo with four soldiers "armed to the teeth," patrolling the road on horseback and they stay in the hacienda — rather entertaining when we aren't worried.

In March and April a guard of five soldiers was sent down to the golf club on weekends so the foreigners could play.

Luella

[June 22, 1929] In town last Tuesday Dad ran into Major Aranjo of the Guanajuato State troops, he being the man who has hunted Jose Padron for the past four months and had several fights with him and killed a few of his men. So Dad chatted with him a few minutes and he said there were no gente del cerro [men of the hills, i.e., outlaws] out our way except perhaps two or three scattered around. While he was saying it ten of Padron's men were at the Tajo mill hunting all over the place for Buchanan [the mill manager] and Jesus Tinajero, as we learned next morning at 8:30 when Buchanan called Dad from Cubo. Ten men went into Tajo at 9 P.M., leaving their horses and a few men at Capulin, and others posted on every egress from Tajo so no one could leave the camp. First they tore out the phone in the mill and smashed it and the Power Company phone. Then they went down through the mill, led by Pancho Baez, head watchman, with a pistol at his back. They told him to find Tinajero — he said he didn't know where he was — he was in the little room off the machine shop eating his supper, as all the workmen knew. One of the men got to Tinajero and without saying a word "me dió la seña [he gave me the sign]." The sign that gente del cerro are at hand is two curved lines across the front of the chest (sign of the double belts of cartridges), and Jesus disappeared. They went down through the mill, Pancho leading a fuerza [with the gun on him], and then asked where "ese gringo" was and Pancho said "in his house" — "Lead us to him" — so they went up the river and up the hill to Buchanan's house. Meanwhile the night watchman at his house saw them coming and gave two short quick raps on the door, then rushed down to the kitchen door and told the servants to warn el Señor. At the raps Mr. and Mrs. Buchanan got up and put on some clothes and Buchanan disappeared out a back window of his bedroom — on the side of the arroyo where, like Winnie-the-Pooh, he had "an escape" — just as they came in the front door. His watchman said he wasn't home and Mrs. Buchanan likewise, but they searched the house from top to bottom, opened trunks, took his six-shooter and machete, found the bed open and one put his hand on the sheet and said, 'But it is still warm!' . . . They chewed the rag for close to three hours, Mrs. Buchanan along with them. They demanded one thousand pesos, and finally came down to five hundred. Then Mrs. Buchanan told them to go off and they'd send out the five hundred next day. They went, taking Buchanan's watchman to show him where to bring the money. Of course if the five hundred pesos were not forthcoming they'd be back next night and kill them all.

Dad got in touch with the Governor and at seven next evening a destacamento [detachment] of ten State troops came out to Tajo and are staying there. The following morning at six A.M. Aranjo and his men went through Cubo, out after them. The next afternoon Aranjo sent a dead soldier in to Cubo to be sent on into town, and this morning we learn they had quite a fight yesterday and he killed four of their men and captured five, and eighteen horses, and is at Santa Rosa with them waiting for troops from town to come out and take the prisoners and horses in. But, as always so far, Padron escaped.

Order was gradually restored throughout Mexico by government forces and late in June 1929 an agreement was reached between Church and state. The churches would reopen early in July. On July 6, Major Aranjo telegraphed the governor from San Felipe, thirty miles north of Guanajuato, that he had captured José Padrón — dead.

Irving

[July 6, 1929] On the fourth of July when we were coming home from the golf links, we got into Guanajuato amidst a very lively clangor of bells. All the churches were pealing forth their campanas, and it was because the churches were being opened again. The noise sure sounded good. The streets were full of people rushing to the churches to have mass or something or other.

Luella

[July 9, 1929] There seems to be a good deal of mystery about just how Jose Padron was captured and killed. Various stories are rampant and all are absolutely unlike in all points. What we believe is that he was betrayed by one of his followers — though tales of a big battle and many killed on both sides are reported — but no dead soldiers have been brought in, a good sign that isn't true.

CHAPTER 19

Depression and Departure

On the evening of February 9, 1929, as noted above, Luella and Irving gave a party at the Casino to celebrate their twenty-fifth wedding anniversary. It was a gala occasion and included their many friends in the Guanajuato foreign colony. As Luella told it:*

> [February 14, 1929] Pancho [the Casino chef] served the best dinner I ever ate there. I left it up to him to make it different and he did, also very attractive and delicious. The music was good for Guanajuato and we played bridge till after 10:30. Four families of our guests clubbed together and gave us a perfectly beautiful hand-made silver bowl, in the so-called Guanajuato design — quite large. We are crazy about it both for itself and because it is such a lovely memento of Mexico. . . .

It was a quarter of a century since Irving had taken his young bride from the Winship household in Somerville, Massachusetts, on that week-long train trip that ended with a horseback ride across the barren Guanajuato hills. Mexico had been their married life, save for a few years here and there when inhospitable working conditions or Mexico's civil war had driven them elsewhere. Their three sons knew Cubo and Guanajuato as their home; they were as at ease in

---

*All of the letters of Luella and Irving quoted in this chapter were addressed to Robert.

Spanish as in English. Yet Luella and Irving kept their sons aware that they were Americans; the family always spoke English and read American newspapers and magazines.

The Cubo mine had been a constant in their lives: the hacienda, the village, the personae gratae. But the background had changed; the twenties were a different age from the days of Porfirio Díaz. The revolution had intervened. In many ways it had made activities more difficult for Americans and other foreigners who worked in the country.

The Mexicans who knew Irving and Luella maintained their respect and affection for them. The couple never had to worry about disloyalty among their close employees. On Irving's side, despite his frustration with the ever changing Mexican regulations and officials, he recognized the justice of the revolutionary objectives. About the beginning of 1926, he sat down to respond to the request from his Harvard yearbook editor to write in three pages "an intimate account of what [he had] done these twenty-five years" since graduation. One can visualize him, most likely sitting at the table in the living room in the L-shaped house of the hacienda, with his pipe in his mouth, his constant companion and solace, summing up in his own mind the meaning of these years:

> Looking back over the twenty-five years that have elapsed since our Class took their field, I find it somewhat difficult to lay my finger on anything I have accomplished that seems worthy of putting into print. . . . I have written no books, — and I have failed to keep copies of the few Mining and Engineering Journals, which contain articles of mine, written during periods of bad luck when I was out of a job. I was not a participant in the World War. I belong to no learned societies. I have held no public offices, and I have received no honorary degrees. . . .
>
> I am still in Mexico, occupying precisely the same quarters that were mine more than twenty years ago. I hope to occupy them a number of years more, — this to depend upon how much farther down our ore-bodies extend, and upon whether foreign companies will continue to be allowed to exist in Mexico. At present the political atmosphere is not favorable. . . .
>
> For the past fifteen years the feelings of us foreigners here can be likened to a barometer, — first up, then down. But we are still here, and in the final analysis we expect to remain. Perhaps, too, in a very humble way we

are setting an example in sobriety, steadiness, and law-abidingness, that is unconsciously helping to stabilize this quick-blooded people, inexperienced in self-government, plunging from one mistake to another, and yet at heart working forward toward an ideal worthy of the respect and admiration of us all.*

Two years later, in March 1928, Irving wrote a fuller but equally positive evaluation of the Mexican Revolution in response to inquiries from Robert, who at the time was studying Mexican history at college:

[March 1, 1928] Subsequent events pretty clearly show that quite independently of any action of President Wilson the Mexican Revolution would have succeeded. It was far more powerful and more deep-seated than any of us realized at the time and would have succeeded regardless of any action taken by the United States. So Wilson's meddling served no real purpose except to engender dislike and suspicion of U.S. motives by all Latin American countries, to place American lives in danger in Mexico, and to boost the idea that the United States is imperialistic.

I believe the Revolution has been a good thing for Mexico. It has modernized it and is bringing it forward from medieval times to present-day times. In doing so a great deal of damage has been done also, inevitably. Also considerable picturesqueness has disappeared. But where there used to be two classes — upper and lower — there is developing a large middle class. Some of this existed before the Revolution. But it has grown very rapidly since the Revolution. Mechanics, tradespeople, chauffeurs, railroad workers, etc. Working conditions are unquestionably *greatly* improved, due to labor unions and labor laws which are purely an outgrowth of the Revolution.

I believe the automobile has done almost as much as the Revolution for Mexico. Among other things it is resulting in *road building* and this is a great modernizing and civilizing influence. Also it has opened up a lot of industrial opportunity, such as garages, agencies, and the like.

---

*Harvard College Class of 1901: Twenty-fifth Anniversary Report, 306–7.

The changes that were taking place would inevitably end the hospitality that American companies in Mexico had inherited from the Porfiriato. The article in the Constitution of 1917 that returned subsoil rights to the nation was a threat waiting to be implemented by some leader willing to take the risk, though how to do so was not obvious. A more immediate impact would come from abroad. Mexico was tied into the world economy, especially through its export sectors, such as mining and petroleum.

The stock market collapse in 1929 and the beginning of the Great Depression were to mark the end of the Mexican adventure of the Herrs. As the business climate in Mexico continued to present problems under the revolutionary government with difficulties in labor relations, taxes on gross profits regardless of net, and other harassments, the price of silver again began to slide and finally delivered the coup de grâce to Guanajuato mining. By this time John and Robert had finished school and college and were working in the eastern United States. No more summer vacations in Mexico. In August 1929, after living through all the rebel excitement that had ended with the death of José Padrón, Irving, Luella, and Dick finally abandoned their home in Cubo and moved to a rented house in Guanajuato. But all was not sadness in the new environment. As Luella told it:

> [September 4, 1929] We pulled up stakes and moved into town last Saturday, and shut and locked our Cubo quarters. I have left enough furniture so we can go there, in a camping out sort of way, whenever we want to and be perfectly comfortable. Angela has gone to live with Altagracia and we've put her on half pay and she is to come and keep house for Dad, or all of us, in Cubo whenever we want to go there.
>
> We are really quite enthusiastic about our move – the first time we've lived in a house with a bathtub and running water (among other things) in all these years we lived in Mexico. . . . The piano is still in Cubo. Dad asked a cargador on the Jardin yesterday afternoon about getting a bunch together to bring it to town and inside of two minutes six cargadors had gathered and all six had been in the bunch that took it out to Cubo nine or more years ago, and started telling him all the details of that transaction.
>
> [September 13, 1929] I'm all for this living in Guanajuato. It really is a lot of fun, and I get a kick out of such a simple thing as going down

town in a tram car about five P.M., going to meet Dad at the office and having him chauff me around to do a few errands. It is such a change from never moving out of the hacienda for days at a stretch.

[February 7, 1931] We've been having some really good movies recently. But last Monday we went for the first time to one of those in which Mexicans substitute, off stage, in talking for the American actors. It was awful. In the first place we couldn't understand a word — doubt if we could have understood much even if they had talked in English — so knew nothing of the plot. Then it became unsynchronized and the girls' mouths were moving and no sounds coming out. Then the scene changed and two men drew guns on each other on the screen and the girls went on talking — amid howls and hissing and stampings on the part of the Mexican audience. Then Dad and I decided we'd had enough and got out.

[January 22, 1932] Last night we took Dick to a typical Mexican show in a tent on the cobblestones in front of the cine. Titeres [puppets] and a clown and a couple of other vaudeville sort of stunts. Really very good, all of them. We and young Charlie Ramsden were the only foreigners in the audience and I got quite a kick out of it — and Dick had a big time.

With the mining business it was another story. The Guanajuato mines were losing money. Aside from labor costs, one of the heavy burdens was a federal tax on gross production without regard to expenses, or net if any. Regulations also prevented cutting wages or reducing the workforce without authority from the government, which might take weeks or months. Shutting down likewise required government permission. Without it the employer was liable for termination pay of three months' wages to all employees, and ran the risk of forfeiting the property to the government to be run for the benefit of the employees. Silver was now close to thirty cents, but no one was ready to say it would stay at these low prices and that the mines should be abandoned. Running a mine became a salvage operation.

Nineteen-thirty was a year of trying to save the mines and keep the business alive in Guanajuato until times were better. Though doomed to failure, it was a noble effort. In February three mine managers (including Irving

Herr) and the governor of Guanajuato met with the authorities in Mexico City to ask for cuts in production taxes, freight rates, duties, etc., and for relaxation of the rules on wages. Little happened, and in May the managers were again in Mexico City to attend a conference of all the silver mining companies in Mexico to see what, if anything, could be done to solve their difficulties. The government then announced through the press that no more concessions would be granted to the mining companies. No one knew that they had granted any. The Cubo Company applied for authority to cut salaries and wages and continued to operate, melting its product down into silver bars to be held for better prices.

But the handwriting was on the wall. In December 1930, the Herr family took a long vacation through the south and central parts of Mexico. On December 18, Irving says: "We decided it was time that we saw Puebla and Cuernavaca and other points south and east before we suddenly were forced to leave Mexico on account of there being no more mine to run."

On New Year's Eve, they gave a party. Luella wrote:

> [January 8, 1931] We had twelve here for dinner on New Years Eve and at eleven o'clock we all adjourned to the Governor's house to a dance and midnight supper — arriving just in time for the supper and to drink in the New Year with His Excellency. This invitation came after my party was all planned and invited, so I suggested that we could come if we brought our guests — a personal delegation of four came to invite us — and they seemed quite pleased at the suggestion and it really made a very nice ending to my party and a nice way to greet the New Year. The Griffens and Quinns and the artists who are at the DeVotie's got in on it, which they wouldn't have done otherwise.

One more stone remained unturned, and Irving made ready for his last great effort in Mexico — to close the mine down without throwing it on the junk heap. In January 1931, another of the large Guanajuato mining companies had decided to close, and in February, with silver at twenty-seven cents, Cubo filed a petition with the government to cease regular operations. No shutdown notices could be posted until permission was received or the property would be open to confiscation.

Ten weeks later, in May, Irving was in Mexico City. He wrote to Robert:

[May 28, 1931] The trouble I have had trying to close down Cubo has made me so sore. . . . What keeps me here in Mexico City is the Junta Central, which is trying our case all over again after having approved our shutdown petition. It moves slow as death. We are still in Conciliation meetings. Next comes Arbitraje.

It has made me lose all interest in Cubo, or in trying to put it on its feet again. I feel that from now on Mexico is going to be run for the Mexicans and principally the laboring class, and that even if we found some new ore in the mines and could start up again, the Government would probably find some way to do us out of it. And as time goes on things get worse down here.

In June, and without authority from the owners in Chicago, Irving offered to turn the mine over to the workmen, a poker play. It was eight anxious days before the offer was turned down, to his great relief. Apparently the junta was not yet ready to throw the management out and assume operating responsibilities. Finally in August a decree came through from Mexico City that stated that the company's request was justified; the decree authorized the shutdown and provided indemnity of thirty-six days' pay to the workmen. Irving said to Robert:

[August 17, 1931] So in principle we won out, and in money it cost us about 2,500 pesos more than we would have had to pay anyway. The State Government here is very sore over the result as they expected to get about 50,000 to 100,000 pesos for the men — possibly some for themselves. But it was a nasty affair from start to finish, and I am very unpopular here with the State Government.

Things had changed since New Year's Eve at the governor's house.

Cubo was virtually at a standstill, but Irving remained for several months, directing some exploratory work and making up his mind to leave Mexico. After thirty years this would not be easy. He wrote again to Robert:

[October 4, 1931] We have had an entire change of government in the State of Guanajuato since a week ago Friday, and I have breathed a sigh of relief. Old Colonel Avila has been removed from the Cuartel de San Pedro [state troop headquarters] and sent to León to take charge of the police force there. This is a bad loss for Guanajuato as he did a fine job here. In the past few months I felt he was about the only friend I had in Government circles since my break with the State Government. But he has been friendly and I am pretty sure he felt just about the same with regard to Arroyo Ch[e] as I did. He kept on making improvements at the cuartel. He now has a number of mottos in ornamental lettering on the walls around the patio. They remind me of Bible quotations in a Sunday school. The idea is to get ideas on good conduct into the heads of the soldiers. He had a wonderful clock made by a Mexican mechanic in a shop just across from the cuartel. This is an eight-day clock and strikes the hours and quarters, and was made by the mechanic without any plans or blueprints, just out of his head. Then Avila built a clock tower over the main entrance of the cuartel and had the clock dedicated by the retiring Governor. The cuartel was all lighted with large flood-lights and had his own band and the State band and it was quite a fiesta. I received no invitation but took Lue and went and when the Colonel saw Lue he beamed all over. He is a good old scout and wished to be remembered very particularly to you. You must have made quite an impression on him that day we talked to him in his office.

In 1932 the move was made. John had started his own business in Cincinnati, and, looking ahead, Irving had put up some of the starting capital. Now he moved in as a partner in the enterprise and he and Luella left their home in Mexico for good. Irving's thoughts were these:

[June 13, 1932] In a way I hate to leave Guanajuato. I like our home and like living here. But I do not like working in Mexico any more. There is too much Government interfering with one's business. I feel as though our Company, instead of being a business concern, were simply a sort of institution for the purpose of supplying work to a lot of down-and-out Mexican workmen. That is the way the Government makes you feel.

For instance — We have been doing a little development work and a week ago we laid off one of the barreteros [drillers] for some days because he was caught carrying out high-grade ore at the gate. He was supposed to have a castigo [punishment] of loss of work for say a week or two. But soon after this a bunch of nine or more high-graders entered the mine in the madrugada [early hours] of Sunday morning and were seen by some buscones who were going off their night shift. Among the high-graders was this fellow we had laid off. So Pascual told the fellow he would not get his job back. Thereupon he comes into town here to the Junta Federal del Trabajo and makes a kick to the Federal Inspector. The Inspector calls me up and admits that the fellow says he was caught carrying a piece of ore out of the mine, but that he did not enter the mine with any high-graders. So will I please, as a moral obligation, please put the man back to work. The moral obligation I take it is another way of saying that a man needs work so what's the difference if he stole ore from the Company. Now if I put that man back to work it is simply a breakdown of our discipline, and will mean that any other barretero will know that if he gets caught carrying out his puña de metal [handful of ore], all he has to do is go to the Federal Inspector and I will have to put him back to work. The labor law is not so bad, except that the workmen get all the consideration. If it were administered as it is written I would have little kick. But the actual working of it is that the workmen can lie and tell any kind of story before the Inspectors, while the Companies have to prove everything.

This sort of thing prevents working a property with the feeling that you are the boss, and every step that you take you wonder whether it will end up in some case in the Junta. It is not so pleasant, and after doing business several years on that basis, I am about ready to call it a day. The only trouble is that from what I see in the United States papers, I fear that up there things are still worse. So I guess wherever we go life will not be a bed of roses.

However, business in the United States was more satisfying than Irving had indicated. It was the middle of the Great Depression when he arrived in Cincinnati to take part in John's business—the Cincinnati Steel Products Company—but the company survived the lean years under John's capable management and grew to support their families for many years, through war and postwar times. The Herrs joined the University Club of Cincinnati, and at the age of seventy Irving took up painting with some success and considerable satisfaction. We never heard any regrets about leaving the mining business, but in the house, choice Mexican silver and glassware, pots, paintings, and tables shared pride of place with Herr and Winship heirlooms.

For Luella the move to Cincinnati was a new lease on life. She became active in church life and in political campaigns, joined the Cincinnati Women's Club, and made many friends. She was happy to be back in her own environment.

Irving died in Cincinnati in 1959, Luella in 1966.

Reprise

Years later in 1960 I visited Mexico again, this time on
a family vacation with my wife and our two children,
who were old enough to take care of themselves. We
drove down in order to get the full impact of the scenery and the changes that had taken place in the thirty
years since I had last seen it. In many ways it was much
the same, but in other ways the change had been very
great. The ribbon of highway that extended south
from the border was well built and well maintained,
and reached across the northern desert and down
through the mountains of the great plateau — a far cry
from the dirt roads and wagon trails of the 1920s. Gas
stations along the way offered little spots of enterprise
and activity where formerly there had been only a few
adobe huts surrounded by meager planting with perhaps a few goats. Our first stop was Monterrey, which I
remembered as a dusty, dirty spread of calcined houses
bordering narrow streets, where the train would stop
for the "eating station," a doubtful restaurant at which
we would eat gingerly and drink only bottled beer. Now,
as we approached the city we drove down a broad thor-
oughfare lined with modern business houses bearing
names like International Business Machines, Cía.
Goodyear, S.A., Buick-Oldsmobile, and many more.
In town there were good hotels, restaurants where one
could eat and drink as one wished, and automobiles
coursing through the narrow streets. But the real
change was in the people. Gone was the traditional

Mexican sitting on a doorstep wrapped in his serape with his sombrero tilted down over his eyes, waiting for *mañana*. The people were well dressed like any city folk. And they were busy, hurrying to an appointment or back to the office after lunch. *Mañana* was here and there was much to be done.

In August Monterrey was hot, and rather than stay the night we pushed on over the fifty miles of highway that took us up five thousand feet to Saltillo, gateway to the Sierra Madre mountains. Here once more was the feeling of exhilaration from the higher altitude. The air was fresh and the temperature cool again. In Saltillo we stayed at the Hotel Arizpe Sainz, and found ourselves back in old Mexico. First-floor and balcony rooms opened out on a beautiful garden in the central patio with a fountain in the center, and service was in the best Spanish tradition.

The change in Guanajuato was subtle but was there nevertheless. We saw the same buildings, the same narrow streets, the same people walking in them. Old Don Francisco still presided over his specialty store of imported fancy groceries, the Canastillo de Flores, overlooking the Plaza Mayor. Yet there was a feeling of better times that was difficult to pin down. Gradually it dawned on me. The buildings were in good repair, many of them newly painted. Cobblestones in the streets had given way to smoother pavements on the main thoroughfares. The Teatro Juárez had been renovated both inside and out and the interior was once again a resplendent opera house of the 1890s done in red and gold. Gone was the peon dress of white cotton pajama pants and white cotton shirt topped by a serape, and in its place were Sears Roebuck-style pants and jackets, and fancy shirts. Even the straw sombrero had been replaced with up-to-date hats or none at all. The standard of living had been noticeably improved. Traveling schools and bookmobiles had reached into the countryside and were bringing the country people the beginnings of education.

Our trip to the Cubo mine was reassuring. The old wagon road looked just as it always had; a fifty-pound cobble was missing here and there to challenge the unwary and very little had been done to smooth the rough places in the more level stretches where we used to run our horses. But this time we tried it in our car. Horses would have been better and certainly safer. The mine was still operating, the only one in Guanajuato that was still working, and we were told that the miners now commuted by bus from the city over the mountains to the mine instead of living in the surrounding hills. If the buses could make it, so could we, but the maintenance on those buses must have been exorbitant. At the mine the only important change was that the water was now piped down from the spring on the mountain, purified and stored in one of the old cyanide vats to serve the whole town at company expense, as was required by law. In the little marketplace outside the upper gate of the hacienda we found José Velásquez, and his wife Altagracia (once Mother's maid) in their variety store. They were both delighted to see us and served us soda pop.

We walked up to the mill and found that the man in charge was one who worked for Dad after Carrouché left, and who remembered us well. He showed us some beryllium that he had found in the silver ore that he thought might be developed as a by-product of the mine. At the top of the shaft on the hill were some old-timers on the ore cars who had been there all these years and greeted us like old friends. Things had not been as good since Dad had left, they said. It was good to find that there really were not too many changes after all.

But Mexico was moving into a new social order. In the old days it had been the firm dictatorship of Porfirio Díaz, Spanish authority gradually being taken over by foreign capital, and the Church still a dominant factor politically and economically. Now, after years of revolution, it was a new order, a government of the people that served the people and gradually sifted down the benefits of industrial development in the form of better standards of living and schools for the lower classes. Although the one-party system might be classed by some as a benevolent dictatorship, it is probably as close to a democracy as the general level of education will permit. It is a tribute to private enterprise that the government has chosen this course rather than nationalization of industry as in socialist countries, relying instead on a requirement that foreign companies must share ownership with Mexican nationals and bring Mexicans into all levels of local management. Thus free enterprise imported from abroad gradually becomes a Mexican enterprise. As we approach the twenty-first century it would seem that the revolutionary years were in fact a real contribution to modern Mexico.

Epilogue
April 22, 1937

Today outside the wall of the Cubo mine hacienda, a
monument stands dedicated to seven martyrs "massacred by the employers' intransigence on April 22, 1937."
It consists of a line of seven busts on short brick pillars,
facing out from the white wall behind them. On the
wall is a plaque explaining that the Mexican miners'
union, the Sindicato Industrial de Trabajadores Mineros, Metalúrgicos y Similares de la República Mexi-
cana, dedicated the monument to the memory of all,
brilliant martyrs and anonymous helpers alike, who
struggled to organize the miners of Mexico. The
plaque carries the date April 22, 1960, but the monument was not yet in place when Robert visited El
Cubo in August 1960. It commemorates a tragic event
that made the Cubo mine notorious throughout the
country.

On April 22, 1937, the miners' union held a meeting in the pueblo of El Cubo to mark the elevation of
the local body from the rank of a "Fracción" of the
Sección of Peregrina to a Sección of its own, Number 142. Membership in the Cubo branch had risen to
the threshold that justified this change. About eight
o'clock that evening the union organizers from Guanajuato who had attended the meeting were returning to
the city in their automobile when a group of armed
horsemen stopped the car, forced the men to get out,
and shot them, leaving their bodies by the road, where
a local passerby found them and notified the authorities. The *Excelsior* of Mexico City carried the news
on April 24 under a front-page banner headline: "Six
Miners' Leaders Assassinated in Guanajuato." It gave

their names and reported that thirty soldiers had gone out in pursuit of the *bandoleros* (highwaymen) who had killed them. Local people who saw the bandoleros said they were ten men, well armed. "While in some circles the assassinations are blamed on inter-union conflicts, others believe they are the result of the political agitation that continues in that State." The new governor of the state, Luis I. Rodríguez, had only that day issued a call for all Guanajuatenses, especially those who had taken up arms, to restore peace and live in cordial brotherhood.

The attack occurred on a Thursday evening. That Saturday hundreds of miners marched in Guanajuato to ask the authorities for justice.[1] The murderers were never caught, but the event became famous in Mexican labor history. Reports at the time gave the names of six men killed, and a memorial tablet on a post beside the road where they died has six names. The Cubo monument has seven busts and names, a new one having mysteriously slipped in. Union records indicate that it was "by omission" that his name did not appear in the newspaper or the roadside tablet. Apparently it took months, if not years, to get the right body count. Whether six or seven died that evening, their death has become memorable. Every year on April 22 the miners of the Guanajuato region hold a parade in the city. Moreover the national miners' union, responsible for the monument at El Cubo, requires labor contracts to stipulate an annual day of mourning on April 22, when work is stopped. Thus sadly the little-known mine of El Cubo achieved national prominence.

Unfortunately, the story did not end with this tragedy. The person who replaced Irving as superintendent of the Cubo mine was Max Quinn, who was already on the staff before Irving left. He took up residence in the Cubo hacienda with his wife, Beatrice. A letter from Beatrice to Luella, undated but evidently before 1937, described conditions:

> This band [of outlaws] has been bothering [El Cubo] since the 5th of May last year. I think I told you of two three-hour battles between them and soldiers stationed in the church, with hundreds of bullets dropping in the patio, and dozens going through the tin roof but not on through [into the rooms]. The soldiers would follow them a bit the next day but never seemed to catch up. Many, many times we knew for days at a time

that they were at Nayal [a mine several miles downstream from El
Cubo], but always were unconcerned . . . because they never went near
the mill superintendent who has no protection. When they raided
Peregrina, they did not go near the house of the foreigners; they knew
when we go and come from town, so we were positive that they had no
interest in us.

Nevertheless, one afternoon three armed men entered the mine hacienda
and ordered Quinn, Williebaldo, and another Mexican to leave with them.
The bandits stayed in the pueblo, getting drunk and demanding two thousand pesos from the merchants, which they did not obtain. Williebaldo and
the other Mexican managed to slip away, but the gang left Cubo taking
Quinn with them. Soldiers arrived from Guanajuato, terrifying Beatrice
that they would cause the kidnappers to harm Quinn. She arranged with
Mr. DeVotie to have money for a ransom, but no demand for it ever came.
Sleepless from anxiety, on the afternoon of the third day, a Sunday, she received a call from her husband in Guanajuato, where he had walked on his
own, and she drove in to pick him up. He had spent two parching days and
cold nights in the hills with one or two men guarding him, but was little the
worse for wear. Afraid to send one of their men to demand ransom, the bandits eventually freed Quinn when he signed *vales* (IOUs).

> Max left the money where he agreed to leave it and it was never called
> for, so about six weeks later he tried to get in contact with them and finally
> delivered it—has receipts. The Coneja has been killed, they say, and the
> new leaders are from other parts so they never bother Cubo these days.

According to those who remember those years, several Americans connected to the mines in Guanajuato were kidnapped for ransom in the 1930s
by a group of bandits who claimed to be Cristeros. Quinn was just one of
them.

On December 9, 1937, some seven months after the assassinations of the
labor leaders, Max Quinn was in the mine alone. As he stepped off the ladder
of the shaft onto the second level, someone drove a sampling pick, a tool with
a long thin point, into his head, killing him instantly. The murderer or murderers, to make the deed appear an accident, then pushed his body down

the shaft, where it fell three levels, causing several fractures. The *Excelsior* reported that "it is assumed that criminal hands were involved in his death, but the details are not known. Some people report that Mr. Queen [*sic*] had an argument with some non-union workers [*trabajadores libres*], and one suspects that they may have had a part in his death. The authorities of [Guanajuato] are investigating the case, which has caused consternation in all social circles, where Mr. Queen was well known and highly esteemed."[2] The U.S. State Department asked the American consul in San Luis Potosí to investigate the case.[3] He got nowhere, for the governor of Guanajuato proclaimed that Quinn had died an accidental death and closed the case.

Jean DeVotie Dean, the childhood friend of John and Bob, recalls that her father had warned Quinn not to go into the mine alone. After his death, the foreign community, according to her recollection, pointed its finger at highgraders, whom Quinn had been attempting to stop from robbing the mine. His murder is still strong in the collective memory of the Cubo mine community, and its account is different. Residents are confident that it was an act of vengeance for the April 22 assassinations. Although no assassins were ever identified, the miners held Quinn responsible for organizing the attack and dealt with him in a form of people's justice. To an outsider trying to reconstruct events largely from oral accounts, however, it is hard to comprehend how, if Quinn had indeed organized the assassination, he could have been unconcerned about his personal safety.

If ghosts of past tragedies await the inquisitive visitor, the mine itself now offers an auspicious scene. As the result of a Mexican law of 1971 requiring corporations to have at least 51 percent Mexican ownership, in 1972 the heirs of the Potter Palmer Estate sold the mine to a group that met the requirement. Since then it has flourished under the new ownership and management, and rich deposits have been discovered. The mine has now more than twice the levels it had in the 1930s, and the Tajo mill has been expanded and modernized. Heavy trucks bring the ore to it from the mine. In the 1990s the mine is one of the most prosperous in Guanajuato.

El Cubo, however, is a much smaller town than it was in Irving's day, with empty, ruined houses. The miners' union obtained from the company free transportation for the workmen from Guanajuato. Better schooling and other amenities are available in the city, and most miners live there and are transported to and from work by bus. Nevertheless, there is still a community in Cubo, which still has its church and its small set of shops. Complying with an article of the Constitution of 1917, the company funds a primary school in a new building on the road into the village. The company has gone further and established at its own expense a "Telesecundario" school, providing high school-level courses by television in a building above the pueblo beside the road where cars, buses, and trucks travel to and from Guanajuato.

On my first return to Cubo in 1979, I found José Velásquez, the one-time company electrician, still in his grocery store, his hair white but his blue eyes as handsome as ever. "¡Usted es Ricardito!" he uttered in disbelief and joy. Altagracia had died, and he had a new wife and a five-year-old son, who enjoyed showing off our two young daughters to his friends. To a person now in his eighth decade whose first years were spent inside the walls of the mine hacienda, the place is obviously different, and yet much remains from the days I remember to effect profound nostalgia.

Richard Herr

Notes

1. *Excelsior*, April 25, 1937.
2. Ibid., December 10, 1937.
3. Ibid., December 14, 1937 (English-language page).

Index

Latin American Silhouettes
Studies in History and Culture

William H. Beezley and
Judith Ewell
Editors

Volumes Published

Silvia Marina Arrom and Servando Ortoll, eds., *Riots in the Cities: Popular Politics and the Urban Poor in Latin America, 1765–1910* (1996). Cloth ISBN 0-8420-2580-4 Paper ISBN 0-8420-2581-2

Roderic Ai Camp, ed., *Polling for Democracy: Public Opinion and Political Liberalization in Mexico* (1996). ISBN 0-8420-2583-9

Brian Loveman and Thomas M. Davies, Jr., eds., *The Politics of Antipolitics: The Military in Latin America*, 3d ed., revised and updated (1996). Cloth ISBN 0-8420-2609-6 Paper ISBN 0-8420-2611-8

Joseph S. Tulchin, Andrés Serbín, and Rafael Hernández, eds., *Cuba and the Caribbean: Regional Issues and Trends in the Post-Cold War Era* (1997). ISBN 0-8420-2652-5

Thomas W. Walker, ed., *Nicaragua without Illusions: Regime Transition and Structural Adjustment in the 1990s* (1997). Cloth ISBN 0-8420-2578-2 Paper ISBN 0-8420-2579-0

Dianne Walta Hart, *Undocumented in L.A.: An Immigrant's Story* (1997). Cloth ISBN 0-8420-2648-7 Paper ISBN 0-8420-2649-5

Jaime E. Rodríguez O. and Kathryn Vincent, eds., *Myths, Misdeeds, and Misunderstandings: The Roots of Conflict in U.S.-Mexican Relations* (1997). ISBN 0-8420-2662-2

Jaime E. Rodríguez O. and Kathryn Vincent, eds., *Common Border, Uncommon Paths: Race, Culture, and National Identity in U.S.-Mexican Relations* (1997). ISBN 0-8420-2673-8

William H. Beezley and Judith Ewell, eds., *The Human Tradition in Modern Latin America* (1997). Cloth ISBN 0-8420-2612-6 Paper ISBN 0-8420-2613-4

Donald F. Stevens, ed., *Based on a True Story: Latin American History at the Movies* (1997). Cloth ISBN 0-8420-2582-0 Paper ISBN 0-8420-2781-5

Jaime E. Rodríguez O., ed., *The Origins of Mexican National Politics, 1808–1847* (1997). Paper ISBN 0-8420-2723-8

Che Guevara, *Guerrilla Warfare*, with revised and updated introduction and case studies by Brian Loveman and Thomas M. Davies, Jr., 3d ed. (1997). Cloth ISBN 0-8420-2677-0 Paper ISBN 0-8420-2678-9

Adrian A. Bantjes, *As If Jesus Walked on Earth: Cardenismo, Sonora, and the Mexican Revolution* (1998). ISBN 0-8420-2653-3

Henry A. Dietz and Gil Shidlo, eds., *Urban Elections in Democratic Latin America* (1998). Cloth ISBN 0-8420-2627-4 Paper ISBN 0-8420-2628-2

A. Kim Clark, *The Redemptive Work: Railway and Nation in Ecuador, 1895–1930* (1998). ISBN 0-8420-2674-6

Joseph S. Tulchin, ed., with Allison M. Garland, *Argentina: The Challenges of Modernization* (1998). ISBN 0-8420-2721-1

Louis A. Pérez, Jr., ed., *Impressions of Cuba in the Nineteenth Century: The Travel Diary of Joseph J. Dimock* (1998). Cloth ISBN 0-8420-2657-6 Paper ISBN 0-8420-2658-4

June E. Hahner, ed., *Women through Women's Eyes: Latin American Women in Nineteenth-Century Travel Accounts* (1998). Cloth ISBN 0-8420-2633-9 Paper ISBN 0-8420-2634-7

James P. Brennan, ed., *Peronism and Argentina* (1998). ISBN 0-8420-2706-8

John Mason Hart, ed., *Border Crossings: Mexican and Mexican-American Workers* (1998). Cloth ISBN 0-8420-2716-5 Paper ISBN 0-8420-2717-3

Brian Loveman, *For* la Patria: *Politics and the Armed Forces in Latin America* (1999). Cloth ISBN 0-8420-2772-6 Paper ISBN 0-8420-2773-4

Guy P. C. Thomson, with David G. LaFrance, *Patriotism, Politics, and Popular Liberalism in Nineteenth-Century Mexico: Juan Francisco Lucas and the Puebla Sierra* (1999). ISBN 0-8420-2683-5

Robert Woodmansee Herr, in collaboration with Richard Herr, *An American Family in the Mexican Revolution* (1999). ISBN 0-8420-2724-6

Juan Pedro Viqueira Albán, trans. Sonya Lipsett-Rivera and Sergio Rivera Ayala, *Propriety and Permissiveness in Bourbon Mexico* (1999). Cloth ISBN 0-8420-2466-2 Paper ISBN 0-8420-2467-0

David E. Lorey, *The U.S.-Mexican Border in the Twentieth Century* (1999). Cloth ISBN 0-8420-2755-6

Paper ISBN 0-8420-2756-4

Joanne Hershfield and David R. Maciel, eds., *Mexico's Cinema: A Century of Films and Filmmakers* (1999). Cloth ISBN 0-8420-2681-9 Paper ISBN 0-8420-2682-7

Stephen R. Niblo, *Mexico in the 1940s: Modernity, Politics, and Corruption* (1999). ISBN 0-8420-2794-7

Peter V. N. Henderson, *In the Absence of Don Porfirio: Francisco León de la Barra and the Mexican Revolution* (2000). ISBN 0-8420-2774-2

Mark T. Gilderhus, *The Second Century: U.S.-Latin American Relations since 1889* (2000). Cloth ISBN 0-8420-2413-1 Paper ISBN 0-8420-2414-X

Catherine Moses, *Real Life in Castro's Cuba* (2000). Cloth ISBN 0-8420-2836-6 Paper ISBN 0-8420-2837-4

K. Lynn Stoner, ed./comp., with Luis Hipólito Serrano Pérez, *Cuban and Cuban-American Women: An Annotated Bibliography* (2000). ISBN 0-8420-2643-6

Thomas D. Schoonover, *The French in Central America: Culture and Commerce, 1820–1930* (2000). ISBN 0-8420-2792-0